D1522053

VIETNAM GUIDE

CRITICAL ACCLAIM FOR
OPEN ROAD TRAVEL GUIDES!

*Whether you're going abroad or planning a trip in the United States, take Open Road along on your journey. Our books have been praised by **Travel & Leisure, The Los Angeles Times, Newsday, Booklist, US News & World Report, Endless Vacation, American Bookseller, Coast to Coast**, and many other magazines and newspapers!*

Don't just see the world – experience it with Open Road!

ABOUT THE AUTHOR

Judy Moore is a travel writer and freelance author. She is the co-author of *Teach Central Europe*, an educational directory for those interested in teaching in Central and Eastern Europe. In addition to *Vietnam Guide*, she is also at work on another Open Road publication, *Texas Guide*, due out Fall 1997. Judy lives in Austin, Texas.

ACKNOWLEDGMENTS

The list of everyone who contributed support and insight could fill this whole book. The following is my short list of those to whom I owe inestimable gratitude. *In the US*: Stephanie Hinton (for her cunning edits), David Kahn, Mike Rosenfelt, Felicity Wood (my biking expert), Paul Boni (for his expertise about Asia), and Annette Enriquez. *In Vietnam*: Quan Van Thach, Erin Keown, Ronald Movrich, Steve Studebaker, Wilson Fieldhouse, Giles and Patty Hamby, Veronique Dumont, Jon Bedloe, Lorraine Coyne, Wendy Woods, Ms. Ngo Thi Lieu, Ms. Le Thi Thi Truc, and Rita Goh.

HIT THE OPEN ROAD - WITH OPEN ROAD PUBLISHING!

Open Road Publishing now has guide books to exciting, fun destinations on four continents. As veteran travelers, our goal is to bring you the best travel guides available anywhere!

No small task, but here's what we offer:

• All Open Road travel guides are written by authors with a distinct, opinionated point of view - not some sterile committee or team of writers. Our authors are experts in the areas covered and are polished writers.

• Our guides are geared to people who want great vacations, great value, and great tips for both standard tourist sights *and* fun, unique alternatives.

• We're strong on the basics, but we also provide terrific choices for those looking to get off the beaten path and *experience* the country or city - not just *see* it or pass through it.

• We give you the best, but we also tell you about the worst and what to avoid. Nobody should waste their time and money on their hard-earned vacation because of bad or inadequate travel advice.

• Our guides assume nothing. We tell you everything you need to know to have the trip of a lifetime - presented in a fun, literate, no-nonsense style.

• And, above all, we welcome your input, ideas, and suggestions to help us put out the best travel guides possible.

VIETNAM GUIDE

YOUR PASSPORT TO GREAT TRAVEL!

JUDY MOORE

OPEN ROAD PUBLISHING

This book is dedicated to my family: Trudy, Jesse, and Tess.

1st Edition

Front and back cover photos by Judy Moore. Maps by Rob Perry.

TABLE OF CONTENTS

1. INTRODUCTION   11

2. EXCITING VIETNAM! - OVERVIEW   12

3. SUGGESTED ITINERARIES   16
Hanoi & Halong Bay   16
The Northern Highlands   16
Ho Chi Minh City & Environs   18
The Mekong Delta   18
The Central Highlands & The Coast   20

4. LAND & PEOPLE   22
Land   22
People   26

5. A SHORT HISTORY   33

6. PLANNING YOUR TRIP   42
Before You Go   42
    When to Go   42
    What to Pack   43
    Customs   44
    Hotels   45
    Immunizations   47
    Passports & Visas   49
    Travel Advisories   50
Getting to Vietnam   51
    By Air   51
    By Car   51

CONTENTS

By Cruise Ship   51
By Train   52
Study Tours & Learning Vietnamese 52
Travel Agents & Specialists   52
Tour Packages to Vietnam   52
Travel Professionals in Vietnam   54
Getting Around Vietnam   55
By Air   55
By Bus   56
By Cafe Tour & Open Ticket Bus   56
By Car   57
By Motorbike   58
By Train   58
Getting Around Cities   60
By Bicycle   60
By Cyclo   60
By Foot   60
By Taxi   61

7. BASIC INFORMATION   62

Airline Offices in Vietnam   62
Business Hours & Holidays   63
Cost of Living & Travel   64
Electricity   64
Embassies & Consulates in Vietnam   65
Etiquette   66
Festivals   67
Getting Married   68
Health Concerns   68
Hospitals   70
Magazines – English Language   70
Money & Banking   71
Names   72
Newspapers – English Language   72
Post Office   72
Radio   72
Shopping   73
Staying Out of Trouble   73
Stolen Passports   74
Telegrams & Faxes   74
Telephones   75
Television   76

CONTENTS

Time   76
Tipping   76
Water   76
Weights & Measures   87

8. SPORTS & RECREATION   78
Bicycle Trips   78
Golf   79
Running   80
Sailing   80
Scuba Diving & Snorkeling   81
Social Groups   81
Spectator Sports   82
Swimming   82
Tennis   83
Trekking   83
Working Out   84

9. FOOD & DRINK   86
Food   86
Drink   88

10. BEST PLACES TO STAY   90
Modern Hotels   90
    Ho Chi Minh City   90
    Dalat   90
    Hanoi   91
    Phan Thiet   91
    Nha Trang   92
Colonial Accommodations   92
    Dalat   92
    Hue   93
    Nha Trang   93
    Sapa   93
The Untouched Islands   94
    Con Dao Islands   94
    Phu Quoc Island   94
    Phu Quy Island   95

CONTENTS

11. HO CHI MINH CITY   96
Arrivals & Departures   96
Orientation   97
Getting Around Town   98
Where to Stay   100
Where to Eat   107
Seeing the Sights   113
Nightlife & Entertainment   120
Sports & Recreation   122
Shopping   124
Day Trips & Excursions   127
Practical Information   128

12. MEKONG DELTA & THE SOUTHERN COAST   130
Mekong Delta   130
    Mytho – Tien Giang Province   131
    Chau Doc – An Giang Province   133
    Long Xuyen – An Giang Province   134
    Cantho – Hau Giang Province   134
    Rach Gia – Kien Giang Province   137
    Phu Quoc Islands – Kien Giang Province   138
    Bac Lieu – Minh Hai Province   139
The Southern Coast   140
    Vung Tau   140
    Phan Thiet   146
    Phan Rang   149
    Ca Na Beach   151
    Thuy Dong Beach   152
    Con Dao Islands   152
    Phu Quy Island   153

13. DALAT & THE CENTRAL HIGHLANDS   154
Dalat   154
Central Highland Cities   165
    Buon Ma Thuot   165
    Pleiku   168
    Kontum   170

14. CENTRAL COAST   173
Nha Trang   173
Qui Nhon   180
Hoi An   184

CONTENTS

My Son   191
Danang   194
Hue   203

15. HANOI & NORTHERN VIETNAM   219
Hanoi   219
   Arrivals & Departures   220
   Orientation   221
   Getting Around Town   222
   Where to Stay   222
   Where to Eat   227
   Seeing the Sights   229
   Nightlife & Entertainment   236
   Sports & Recreation   236
   Shopping   237
Haiphong   241
Halong Bay   244
Lao Cai   247
Sapa Town   247

16. CAMBODIA   253
Arrivals & Departures   254
Getting Around Cambodia   255
Phnom Penh   255
Siem Reap & Angkor Wat   263

INDEX   269

MAPS
Vietnam & Neighbors   13
Vietnam   17
Provinces of Vietnam   25
Ho Chi Minh City   114-115
Dalat   161
My Son   192
Hue   205
Hue's Imperial Tombs   214
Hanoi   230-231
Phnom Penh   259
Angkor Wat   267

CONTENTS

SIDEBARS

Ho Chi Minh Trail   23
Vietnam's Best Beaches   24
The Wedding Market   28
Cham Architecture   34
Visiting Cham Sites   35-36
Historical Vietnamese Dynasties   38
Recommended Immunizations   47
The Open Ticket Bus Routes   56
Highway 14   58
The Six Classes on Vietnamese Trains   59
Observed Public Holidays   64
Dollar-Dong Exchange Rate   71
Telephone City Codes   75
More Information, Please!   77
Noodle Specialties   86
The Beers of Vietnam   89
Ho Chi Minh City Taxi Service   97
Religious Services   120
Art Galleries in Ho Chi Minh City   124
Saigon's Souvenir Shops   126
Key Saigon Phone Numbers   129
Provinces of The Mekong Delta   131
Beaches in Vung Tau   145
Arrange Your Own Gong Concert   172
My Lai   183
The Tay Son Rebellion   182
Door-Eyes   189
Hoi An's Temples   190
The Demilitarized Zone   201
Ho Chi Minh in Hue   204
Guest Houses in Hue   210
One Day in Hue   215
Taxi Service in Hanoi   221
Hanoi's Art Galleries   237
Do Son Resort   243
Stay With A Village Family   251
Basic Information for Cambodia   254
Take Care in Cambodia   255

1. INTRODUCTION

Vietnam is more than a trip — it is an experience, overflowing with history and teeming with transition. Graceful people, potent emotion, and lush scenery fill the senses. Now is the time to visit Vietnam, while it is awash with change, yet still largely untouched by the modern world. Vietnam Guide provides a blueprint that will lead you to hidden treasures and unexpected surprises!

Vietnam's finest pleasures are found in the simplest things. Skin diving on a deserted coral reef in the South China Sea, drinking a potent demitasse of sweet coffee under the umbrella of a street-side cafe, wandering through the ruins of an ancient people – these are among the many pleasures of a trip to Vietnam. Making the time to absorb daily life, and still taking in the sights of monumental importance is a challenge. Understanding the country's intricate history and mix of cultures will add immeasurably to your experience.

The Vietnamese people are a synthesis of delicacy and strength. Warm friendly smiles and cheering "hellos" of children greet foreigners. In the south, the Khmer (Cambodian) influences distinguish the food and lifestyle of the region, while the north has close ties to Chinese customs. From the southern fishing villages brimming with brightly painted wooden boats to the north's terraced rice paddies ploughed by oxen, I'll help you experience all the varied and fascinating strains of Vietnamese culture. I've also included an excursion chapter to Cambodia's capital city of Phnom Penh and the awe-inspiring ruins complex of Angkor Wat – the site of one of Asia's greatest ancient civilizations.

With this book as your essential guide, you too will discover the vibrancy and wonders of today's Vietnam. I know you'll have the trip of a lifetime!

2. EXCITING VIETNAM! - OVERVIEW

Vietnam is striking in its diversity and natural beauty. From the tall cool mountain highlands in the north through the rugged coastline and fertile south, the countryside is thick with vegetation. Each part of the country is distinct. Coastal wetlands, monsoon forests, and rocky cliffs are enticing. The cities offer their own diversions — excellent restaurants, historical districts with European flair, and lively nightlife.

Even more beautiful than the country are the Vietnamese people themselves. They emerge from economic difficulty and war eager to greet foreigners so anxious to explore Vietnam. Each region has its own traditions and variations in lifestyle. Rural village life continues today as it has for centuries, while the urban centers race into the twenty-first century.

The major cities, rich with the history of many cultures, are blossoming as they open to economic reform. Cham, Khmer, and French have all called these lands home at one time, and each has seasoned Vietnam.

HO CHI MINH CITY & THE SOUTH

Ho Chi Minh City, with its crowded streets and friendly people, rushes headlong into change. At once the astounding rate of transition is apparent: motorbikes swarm in the street, every day more cars enter the congested intersections, and French buildings are overtaken by new skyscrapers edging their way onto the city skyline.

In the midst of rebirth, Ho Chi Minh City has so far been able to retain its timeless grace and appeal, particularly evident in the wide boulevards that cross the historical center and lead to beautiful French buildings.

Most travelers begin their journeys in Ho Chi Minh City (HCMC), formerly Saigon and the capital of South Vietnam.

South of Ho Chi Minh City, the **Mekong Delta** is the country's most productive farmland. The land is an accumulation of fertile deposits that

wash down from the north during monsoons. A rich variety of wetland life calls the Mekong home, from large protected areas reserved for seabirds in the south to dense jungle along the riverbanks in the northern part of the Delta.

The Mekong River is home to millions of people who rely on the water for all aspects of their lives. The river is a highway for transportation, a source of food, and the backyard for stilted houses that line the riverbanks. The people of the Mekong Delta will greet you with welcoming smiles.

THE COAST

The Vietnamese coastline snakes north through the South China Sea. The country is rich with fresh seafood and the central coast provides a bounty of crab, shrimp, squid and fish. Fishing villages, with their blue-trimmed boats and early-morning lifestyle, line the waterfront.

The cities in the central coast blossom with history. The ancient seaport of **Hoi An** reveals itself like a poem, slowly becoming more complex and beautiful. The quiet old quarter immerses you in the diverse cultures which have so greatly influenced Vietnam. Chinese houses and Japanese temples line the small streets, transporting you centuries back in time. Painted fishing boats dock along the waterfront.

The city of **Nha Trang** is becoming known as the center of scuba diving in Vietnam. Here the crystal blue water of the South China Sea supports vast coral reefs and a plethora of sea-life. The warm, breezy weather beckons travelers year-round.

Further north, the city of **Hue** is a delicate mix of Vietnam's imperial past and the exciting present. The city maintains its reputation for being perhaps the most tied to tradition of any region in Vietnam. Romantic dragon boats float down the Perfume River, carrying visitors to pagodas and park-like tomb complexes of the Nguyen kings. Thirteen Nguyen dynasties ruled in the short span of 143 years (from 1802 to 1945). The mausoleums and temples stand as a lasting tribute to the monarchs and their families.

The mammoth walls of Hue's moated citadel protected the royal families and the mandarins of the court for decades. Only modern bombs could shake the ground of the Forbidden Purple City.

Hue will flood you with the elegant past, but also induce you in the present. As a center of tourism, the city is geared for foreigners. Hotels, restaurants and tourist offices happily cater to visitors. The food of Hue is succulent. Regional wine making, a legacy of the Nguyen kingdom, still thrives. If you are lucky enough to be in Vietnam during holidays celebrations, come to Hue. For the Tet (New Year) celebration, Hue becomes awash in traditional decoration and people wearing bright silk ao dais.

The northern coast is markedly different from the rest of the country. **Halong Bay** is peppered with thousands of stone islets that crop out of the water: the story book landscape is unique in the world. Here the 200 kilometer (125 mile) coastline is lined with 3,000 small islands.

THE HIGHLANDS

The mountains that dip south from China extend to the central region of Vietnam. The tall plateaus of the **Central Highlands** span 55,000 square kilometers (34,000 miles) and are home to a number of different minority peoples who live in communal longhouses. These tribes are known for their woodcarvings that figure into religious ritual.

Plantations stretch throughout the Central Highlands, with many of their rubber, coffee and tea trees having lived for generations. At the southern end of the Central Highlands is the city of **Dalat**.

Dalat, surrounded by lakes and cascading waterfalls, is a scrumptious mix of natural beauty flavored with kitsch. For years Vietnamese honeymooners have chosen this small French colonial resort city for their vacations. The cool, crisp air makes the climate unlike the rest of the country. The landscape of sloping mountains is reminiscent of Europe, which is what attracted the French to the area at the turn of the century. And the influence of the French remains in the colonial buildings and food of Dalat.

Elegant hotels and charming old villas offer comfortable accommodation for travelers. The diversions of the area can keep you occupied, or simply enjoy peaceful walks along quiet countryside. This southernmost city in the Central Highlands boasts Vietnam's finest golf resort. Golfers from novice to pro will enjoy the rolling bent grass fairways and picturesque landscape.

The **Northern Highlands** are rugged mountain chains that also dip down from mainland China. Cold winters characterize the area. For centuries these areas were considered inaccessible to anyone other than the tribal people that lived along the mountain sides. The minority villagers wear elaborate embroidered tunics and head dresses and have their own unique traditions and lifestyles. Only in the 20th century did the land of the tribal chieftains become part of the larger Vietnam.

If you are fortunate enough to travel this far north, you will find these minority groups friendly and as curious about foreigners, as the foreigners are about them.

HANOI

The main city of the north, **Hanoi**, is a serene and cultured place. Vietnam's capital is rich with history and for over 1,000 years this area has been a cultural center. Hanoi's many poetic lakes and cool winter climate make the city a favorite of many visitors. You can stroll past gracious old French-style buildings along boulevards characterized by tall shade trees.

The Confucian scholarly tradition is evident in Hanoi's landmarks, such as the ancient Temple of Literature, which pays tribute to Confucian scholars. The museums in the city hold excellent collections that chronicle the country's history.

The city is in an exciting period of change, but unlike Ho Chi Minh City, which races toward development at a breakneck pace, Hanoi is easing into the future. An example of the transition is the new office building which stands where the Hanoi Hilton (Hoa Lo), the largest POW jail in the North during the Vietnam War, once stood.

3. SUGGESTED ITINERARIES

These are a few suggestions of schedules for touring Vietnam. The country is so diverse, your best bet is to mix and match according to your interests and how much time you have. Many travelers choose to fly between major cities to save time.

HANOI & HALONG BAY – *5 days*
Day 1
Arrive in Hanoi and tour the city's old quarter by foot or by cyclo.

Day 2
Visit the monuments of Hanoi including the Ho Chi Minh Mausoleum, the One Pillar Pagoda and the Temple of Literature.

Day 3
Leave for Haiphong, either by train or car. If by train, take an afternoon boat to Bai Chai; by car continue after lunch in Haiphong.

Day 4
Hire a boat in Bai Chai to tour Cat Ba Island and Halong Bay.

Day 5
If traveling by train, return to Haiphong in the evening; take the train to Hanoi the next morning. By car, tour the bay in the morning and return to Hanoi in the afternoon.

THE NORTHERN HIGHLANDS – *6 days*
Day 1
Spend the day touring Hanoi. Take the night train to Lao Cai.

Day 2
Arrive Lao Cai in the early morning. Take the bus to Sapa. Walk around the town in the evening.

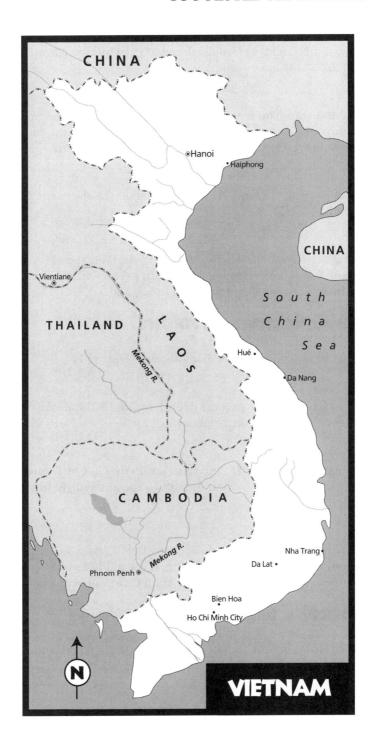

Day 3

Spend the day trekking through the highland minority villages. Either return to Sapa to sleep, or camp out.

Day 4

More trekking. You could easily extend your trip to a full week of walking through the highlands. Should you want to climb the country's highest mountain, Fanxipan, allot four days and three nights.

Day 5

Spend Saturday in Sapa to visit the market. In the evening walk thorough the Love Market.

Day 6

Hire a car to go to Bac Ha for the Sunday Market. Spend the day in Bac Ha with the minority people, then return to Lao Cai. Either take the night train to Hanoi or spend the night in Lao Cai.

HO CHI MINH CITY & ENVIRONS – *4 days*
Day 1

Arrive and spend the day walking through District 1.

Day 2

Hire a cyclo to visit the pagodas in the morning. In the afternoon visit the Binh Tay Market and the neighboring area.

Day 3

Travel by car (or one day mini-van tour) to the Cu Chi Tunnels and the Cao Dai Temple in Tay Ninh. Return to spend the night in Ho Chi Minh City.

Day 4

By car, drive to Mytho to see the Mekong Delta. Take a boat trip along the Mekong River to visit the floating markets and houses. Stop at the snake farm on the way back to Ho Chi Minh City in the evening.

THE MEKONG DELTA – *8 days*
Day 1

Depart Ho Chi Minh City for Cantho. Spend the night in Cantho; take a boat around the Cantho harbor in the evening.

Day 2

Spend the day on the Mekong River, touring islands and floating communities by boat.

Day 3

Continue to Chau Doc. Visit the Temple of Lady Chau Xe and the Sam Mountain. Return to Cantho for the night.

Day 4

Travel to Rach Gia. Spend the day touring the town and museum.

Day 5

Spend the first half of the day touring the archaeological Funan excavations of Oc-Eo culture. Either spend the night in Rach Gia or return to Cantho.

Mekong Delta - Option 1

Day 6

Travel from Cantho to Bac Lieu, with a stop in Soc Trang to see the Khmer town.

Day 7

Visit the bird sanctuaries and nature preserves in the area. Spend the night in Bac Lieu.

Day 8

Return to Ho Chi Minh City via Cantho.

Mekong Delta - Option 2

Day 6

Travel by plane to Phu Quoc Island. Settle in and relax on the deserted beach.

Day 7

Tour the Island and enjoy the solitude.

Day 8

Return by plane to Ho Chi Minh City.

THE CENTRAL HIGHLANDS & THE COAST – *20 days*

This itinerary requires traveling by car. If traveling by bus, allot one extra day and night for travel.

Day 1

From Ho Chi Minh City travel to Dalat.

Day 2

Visit the waterfalls and natural areas.

Day 3

Travel to Phan Rang, with stops at Cham temples along the way. Spend the night in Phan Rang.

Day 4

Travel up the coast to Nha Trang. Feast on seafood in the evening. and spend the night in Nha Trang.

Day 5

Take a boat trip to the nearby islands. Spend a second night in Nha Trang.

Day 6

Travel to Buon Ma Thout in the Central Highlands.

Day 7

Tour the minority villages around Dak Lak Province.

Day 8

Travel to Pleiku; spend the night in Pleiku.

Day 9

Continue on to Kontum; spend the night in Kontum.

Day 10

Tour the minority villages surrounding Kontum. Spend the second night in Kontum.

Day 11

Travel from Kontum to Qui Nhon, stopping to view Cham temples. Spend the night in Qui Nhon.

Day 12

Continue onto Hoi An. Spend the afternoon in the old quarter of Hoi An.

Day 13

Tour the ancient Japanese and Chinese temples and houses of Hoi An. Spend the afternoon at the beach.

Day 14

Visit the monumental Cham site, My Son. Spend the third night in Hoi An.

Day 15

Travel to Danang. Visit the Cham Museum in Danang during the afternoon.

Day 16

Spend the day at China Beach and Marble Mountain. Spend the second night in Danang, or at My Khe Beach.

Day 17

Continue on to Hue, making a stop at famous Pass of the Clouds. Spend the night in Hue.

Day 18

Hire a motor bike and tour the Tombs of the Kings and the Citadel.

Day 19

Spend the day touring the Demilitarized Zone (DMZ). Spend the night in Hue.

Day 20

Fly to Hanoi or return to Ho Chi Minh City. You can spend the day sight-seeing and take the overnight train to Hanoi.

4. LAND & PEOPLE

LAND

Vietnam lies on the eastern edge of the **Indochina Peninsula**, bordered by China on the north, Laos and Cambodia on the west. With dense rain forests, dry forests and rugged savannas, the amazing landscape is a pleasure to behold. The richness of the land is its most striking feature, over half of which is covered by forests.

Fertile rice paddies are cultivated throughout the country, from the thick, submerged bright green fields in the south, to terraced, dry farming in the high elevations of the north. Vietnam's 72 million people reside in densely populated urban and agricultural lowlands and sparsely populated mountain areas.

Vietnam encompasses 127,246 square miles (329,556 square kilometers). From north to south the country measures roughly 850 miles (1,370 kilometers), with over 1,860 miles (3,000 kilometers) of coastline. The width of the country ranges from 560 kilometers (350 miles) to less then 48 kilometers (30 miles). The country claims 100 islands.

Vietnam's mountain chains form natural boarders with Laos and Cambodia, covering over 75 percent of the country's total land mass. Each of Vietnam's four mountain ranges has distinct characteristics. The tallest peak in the country, located in the northwest range, is **Fanxipan** at 10,312 feet (3,143 meters) above sea level. The northeast range meets the sea at **Halong Bay**, forming grottoes and spectacular stone cliffs. The **Truong Son Range** runs from near Hanoi south to Laos. It is the site of the legendary **Ho Chi Minh Trail**, and has two mountain passes accessible by highway. Rubber trees and coffee and tea plantations are found throughout the mountainous areas.

HO CHI MINH TRAIL

*During the war against the United States, the North Vietnamese carved a supply route through the rugged mountainous terrain of central Vietnam. Eventually the road became known as the **Ho Chi Minh Trail.***

Frequent bombing attacks meant the Ho Chi Minh Trail was used under cover of night. Often people transported weapons and supplies on make-shift bicycles or on their backs. The rugged terrain and intense heat made conditions seemingly unbearable.

In 1964, the North Vietnamese government officially began to send soldiers south along the Trail to confront political unrest and the foreign military presence. As the conflict erupted into war, the Ho Chi Minh Trail served as the lifeline for the Viet Cong fighters in South Vietnam. After the war, the Ho Chi Minh Trail was developed into the Truong Son Highway. On tours of the DMZ you will see part of the Ho Chi Minh Trail.

Lakes & Rivers

The large deltas of the **Red River** (Song Huong) in the north and the **Mekong River** in the south are fertile, with rich soil and good climates. These regions produce the country's main crop, rice. The country boasts rich mineral deposits of oil, natural gas, coal, iron and gold. Fishing is a main industry along the coast.

Although the Mekong River is the best known, the Red River is the largest in the county. It flows from the mountains of China to Halong Bay, with the **Duong River** branching off in the north. The Red River is a source of fish and seafood, and nearly half of the Red River Delta is cultivated.

In the south, the Mekong River drains down from Tibet into the **Mekong Delta**. This delta, an accumulation of fertile deposits, covers the area from Phnom Penh, Cambodia to southern Vietnam. The rich soils are continually replaced, adding land mass year-by-year. This is the heart of Vietnamese agriculture, with two full rice seasons per year and a variety of crops ranging from green vegetables to tropical fruit.

The Mekong River divides into nine branches, all of which support communities. About 15 million people live in the Mekong Delta, many spend most of their lives directly on the water, in boats or "floating" houses (which are supported by stilts). Village life on the Mekong supports a unique system of dependence upon the water, which provides everything from their occupation (agriculture) to recreation.

Visitors to the Mekong travel by boat through the small river branches. Stilted houses line the banks and people bathe and swim along the riverbank. Children ride bicycles to and from school along tropical paths. The lush environment nurtures a tranquil lifestyle; many visitors say the people in the Mekong are the friendliest in the world.

VIETNAM'S BEST BEACHES

The most beautiful beaches along Vietnam's central coast luckily are not the ones which draw the most crowds. Swaying palm trees, rolling sand dunes and deserted waters can be yours if you go a few kilometers off the usual path.

__Thuy Duong Beach__–Just twenty kilometers north of Vung Tau you can escape the weekend crowds and relax on white sand. Of course, the beachfront restaurant at Thuy Duong serves good, fresh seafood. The closest town, Long Hai, lies about 5 kilometers from the coast. Even on a holiday when Vung Tau is booked-up, you should have no problem getting a room at the __Long Hai Hotel__, Tel. (84 64) 868010, or the __Palace Hotel__, both in Long Hai Town.

__Mui Ne Beach (Coco Beach)__–At its busiest, Phan Thiet is a sleepy town. But if you really want seclusion and privacy, venture to Mui Ne. This part of the coast, a few kilometers north of Phan Thiet, is known for tall, red sand dunes and a deserted coastline. The "Coco" in the name of this beach stands for coconut. And its a fitting title, because the coconuts are falling off the trees here. As you stroll down the seemingly endless pristine beach, stop to slice a coconut open and enjoy the fresh juice. The only place to stay on Mui Ne Beach is the __Hai Duong Resort__, Tel. (84 62) 823591.

The country has three main regions: the north, central and south. The north shares similarities to Hunan, China. It is an area of rolling mountains and a dramatic coastline. Hanoi lies on a highly cultivated central plain, near sea-level. The Red River delta keeps the plain fertile.

The mountainous north, known as **Bac Bo** to Vietnamese and Tonkin to French, encompasses the Red River Delta and Hoang Lien Mountains. In the far north the mountains of China's Hunan region dip into Vietnam. These mountains yield minerals and coal, which is widely used as an energy source. The steep terrain is cultivated in terraced fields. Dry rice is grown here and there is only one growing season, compared with two in the fertile Mekong. Many of the roads are so steep they are nearly impassable, and some areas so remote that they remain unexplored. At Halong Bay the mountains meet the sea in a spectacular array of thousands of small rock islands marked by cliffs and grottoes.

Even in the most remote areas of the country, modern concerns encroach on the natural beauty. Among the problems facing the people of the Northern Highlands are soil erosion (from slash-and-burn land clearing and terraced agriculture); pollution of the land and air; and the

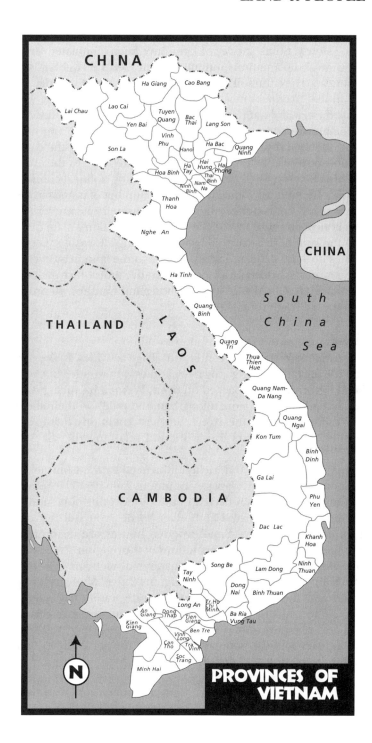

PROVINCES OF
VIETNAM

growing threat of the loss of tradition. The diverse animal population is dwindling slowly. Some species of tiger have been eliminated already.

The pine and plantation mountains of the **Central Highlands** rise to a long plateau. Here the soil is bright orange basalt and very dry. This is the region that produces most of the country's coffee and tea. The hot climate is the natural habitat of the tiger, elephant and buffalo. Today these animals are scarce, and protection measures are being taken to safeguard their survival. The **Central Lowlands** run along the coast and have a monsoon forest climate. Fishing is the lifeblood of the area. The **South China Sea** is oil-rich, andremains a burning political conflict with the People's Republic of China, who claim a number of islands in the sea.

The south is characterized by the 40,000 square kilometer (25,000 mile) Mekong Delta, which produces most of the nation's main rice crop. Much of the land here is covered by water during all seasons. Fertile top soil washes into the delta and actually adds to the land mass every year.

The country is divided into 44 administrative units which include four cities (Hanoi, Ho Chi Minh City, Haiphong and Cantho), 40 provinces, and one special trade zone (Vung Tau).

PEOPLE

Social life for Vietnamese centers on village activities. In the country-side you still see farmers irrigating rice paddies with wooden buckets, and small children riding bare-backed on oxen. Women balancing *don ganh* (baskets hung like scales from a long bamboo pole) on their shoulders walk rhythmically down the street. Ancient traditions thrive in each community. And neighbors live, work and relax together like a large family.

Vietnam is a diverse land, richly influenced by the Chinese, Indian and Khmer peoples, with a tapestry of unique cultures. The complexity of the country's history is reflected in the variety of its populations.

In the south, along the Cambodian border you will find Islamic mosques in Khmer towns. Small wooden houses are decorated with crescent moons and stars, representations of the religion. Protestant and Catholic missionaries brought Christianity to Vietnam. The Central Highlands are the area where these religions thrive. Many tribes people are Protestant, the churches here incorporate traditional beliefs with Christian. The Chinese Confucian influence remains strongest in the north.

Today, over half the population is under the age of thirty, and the population is growing very rapidly.

Ethnic Groups

Some 54 ethnic groups make up the population of Vietnam. A full 88 percent are **Viet**, or ethnic Vietnamese, who live mainly on the river deltas and coastal lowlands. Ethnic Vietnamese trace their heritage to Chinese who settled northern Vietnam centuries ago. Practically everyone speaks Vietnamese, with the exception of some remote highland tribes. Most young people speak English, and many older speak French.

The Vietnamese people entered the lands from China sometime around the first century AD. They brought rice farming to the region, and the Vietnamese language still bears some similarity to Chinese. For centuries Viet people used Chinese script. However, many customs, such as dress, are purely Vietnamese.

Many women wear colorful *ao dais*, the traditional Vietnamese costume of long, tailored shirts with loose pants. Men, especially in Hue, still wear ao dais for formal occasions. Women may adorn themselves with silk headdresses, and men wear scarves wrapped like a small turban. Historically, common people had to wear simple shirts and pants in brown, black or white. Members of the court were permitted to wear colored clothes, the only people allowed to do so.

Minority Groups

There are fewer than six million minority people. The smallest minority group is the **O-du** of Nghe An province. They have a population of fewer than 100. The largest group, the **Tai**, numbers over one million. For the most part the minority people live in the mountainous regions which cover two-thirds of the land.

The minority people maintain their cultures and traditional lifestyles which have survived centuries. The Vietnamese constitution grants the right to use native languages in legal proceedings and education.

The various tribes historically exist autonomously. There is little intermarriage and each tribe respects the other's boundaries. Some highland tribes inhabit specific altitudes and rarely travel to higher or lower areas.

At the time of the first Vietnamese independence (during the Han Dynasty) many of the tribes were part of feudal systems or united under regional chieftains. The strategic importance of the highlanders has long been recognized by the Vietnamese leaders who established war-time alliances with the tribes. But not until World War II, during the wars with the Japanese and later the French, did the political alliances between Vietnam and the highland peoples become solidified.

The diversity of the ethnic minorities is shown in the variety of languages they speak. The largest language groups are from Austro-

THE WEDDING MARKET

In the Northern Highlands, the unique courting ritual of love markets are held by a number of minority groups. Young people seeking courtship come by foot or by horse, some travel for days to reach the market. During daylight hours a large market for household goods and supplies is held. Then under cover of night the love market begins.

As dusk falls ancient songs are sung. Should a couple fancy each other, they exchange verses; boys begin the song. The boy then may tease the girl by trying to snatch a scarf or bracelet. If she enjoys the flirtation, she plays along.

Married people sometimes go to the market alone to engage in a fleeting romance, (with the spouse's permission, of course). In the town of Khau Vai, Ha Giang Province, the annual love market is a rite of spring held on the 27th day of the third lunar month. A weekly "Love Market" takes place once a week in the town of Sapa.

Asiatic, Malayo-Polynesian, and Sino-Tibetan families. Many minority people learn Vietnamese.

Most minority societies are patriarchal. The family unit is of primary importance, especially to women who often must depend on a husband or male relative for complete support. In many minority societies women may not inherit or hold wealth. Monogamy is practiced in some societies, while others permit partners outside of marriage.

The largest group, the **Tai**, are related to Thai people and use a language and script of the Thai family. They may have migrated to Vietnam at the same time as the Viet people. Tai tribes distinguish themselves by the color of the clothes they wear: Black Tai, Red Tai and White Tai.

Another significant minority group is the **Hmong**, who live in the mountains bordering China. They speak a Meo-Dao dialect, which has some similarities with Vietnamese. The Hmong use a Latin-based script developed in the 1960s. Once known as Meo people; they now consider the name derogatory. Like the Tai, the Hmong are divided into subgroups which are distinguished by the color of dress: Black Hmong, White Hmong and Green Hmong.

Black Hmong women wear many sets of large engraved hoop earrings. The Black Hmong men wear black shirts and trouser; women dress in black shirts and skirts. They wrap small turban-like scarves as headdresses.

The **Red Hmong** wear long embroidered jackets which hang low in back. They wear short, colorful skirts and wrap their legs in embroidered cloth. The women wear a large red headdress, some adorned with coins, others with tassels. In Sapa the Hmong women come to town daily to sell crafts to tourists.

Other Northern Highlands minority groups include the **Muong**, which number fewer than 100,000 and the **Dao** which have a population of 470,000.

Central Highland tribes are different than those in the north. The typical communal long-house stands on tall stilts; a wood pole is used as stairs and often has a fertility symbol carved near the top. Some villages use a long-house with a tall, thatched roof for religious ceremonies.

Many people in the Central Highlands wear sarongs and no shirts. They use small baskets carried on their backs to carry supplies and small children. They are skilled weavers.

The **Ba Na**, who live in the northern plateau of the Central Highlands are masters of hunting with bows and arrows and still use this method. Buffalo hunts are often part of elaborate ritual celebrations. A brutal funeral tradition is carried out by Ba Na men, who use burning spears to slash their chests as a show of mourning.

The **Ede** are a tribe of the Central Highlands. Ede families live in long communal houses, with as many as eight generations under one roof. The **Buon Don**, who live near Buon Ma Thout in Dak Lak province, are famous for their elephant hunting. Elephants are used in ceremonies, and once were hunted, and domesticated for transportation and use in battle.

Cham & Khmer

The **Cham** people dominated southern Vietnam for over a millennium and remain a significant ethnic minority in Vietnam today, numbering less than 100,000. The ancient kingdom of Champa covered much of modern Vietnam, from the Mekong Delta to north of Hai Van Pass. The South China Sea and the mountain chains which run parallel, formed its natural borders. Fishing and agriculture were the economic mainstays. Trade was a highly developed enterprise and brought the Cham into contact with foreign powers, including India and China.

The ancient Cham left a legacy of beautiful temples which preserve their culture, yet their origins remain a mystery. The Cham may be descents of Malaysians or Indonesians since their language is Malayo-Polynesian.

The **Khmer** people of Vietnam are descendants of the ancient Khmer civilization which thrived in Angkor Wat, Cambodia over 500 years ago, and today 90% of Cambodia is Khmer. The Mekong is the cradle of Khmer civilization, and today the vast majority of Vietnam's 700,000 Khmer live in the Mekong Delta and adhere to Theravada Buddhism.

Chinese

The overseas Chinese are descendants of seventeenth and eighteenth century Chinese immigrants. Most live in urban areas and work in commerce and coal-mining. During the French colonial period, separate administrations were established for the overseas Chinese." The Socialist government attempted to assimilate the "overseas Chinese" and nationalize commerce in the south, resulting in a wave of immigration in 1978.

The greatest concentration of overseas Chinese is in Ho Chi Minh City's Chinatown, Cholon.

Overseas Vietnamese

Vietnamese emigrants to other countries are known as "overseas Vietnamese" (*Viet Kieu*) in Vietnam. One of the largest Vietnamese populations in the world is in Los Angeles, California. With the opening of Vietnam, many Viet Kieu are returning for visits or to live in Vietnam. Over 300,000 Viet Kieu came into Vietnam in 1995. They often find themselves the subjects of resentment and discrimination.

Language

Vietnamese is spoken throughout the country by the vast majority of the population, and is taught universally. It is part of the Austro-Asiatic language family, specifically in the Viet-Muong branch of the Mon-Khmer subfamily. Vietnamese bears similarities to Chinese and Thai, although speaking these languages will not be of much use.

Vietnamese is an extremely difficult language to learn, especially for Westerners. It is tonal which means fluctuations in your voice can radically change the meaning of a word. There are six different forms of addressing people, which denote age, respect and relationship.

Fluent speakers distinguish accents of northerners and southerners, and some words are used differently. For example the word "street" is "duong" in the south and "pho" in the north. Even in areas where regional tongues are spoken, Vietnamese is usually understood. English is widely spoken, especially in cities where many students study English. French is less common.

Chinese has exerted the strongest influence on the Vietnamese language. Not only did many concepts and ways of expression originate in Chinese, but until the seventeenth century a derivation of Chinese pictograms were the script. The Vietnamese form of Chinese writing, called *chu nom* was used widely from the thirteenth to the fifteenth century.

In the seventeenth century, Jesuit missionaries introduced a specialized Latin script using Roman letters with accent marks to denote tonal variations. Alexander d'Rhodes is credited with developing this Latin script while constructing the first Vietnamese dictionary for Europeans. This script, called quoc ngu, is used today. The Latin letters make reading signs easy, but unfamiliar accents make pronunciation difficult.

Tapestry Of Religions

Vietnam is home to diverse religions, each of which coexist and survive despite a history of religious persecution.

Over 70 percent of Vietnamese adhere to **Buddhist** tradition. Vietnamese Buddhism has its roots in the Mahayana tradition. The teachings emphasize that compassion and wisdom exist in a peaceful universe. **Hoa Hoa** is a radical form of Buddhism which removed the temple and its rituals from worship. Hoa Hoa began the south in 1939.

Cao Dai, was founded in 1926 by Ngo Van Chieu. The Cao Dai faith is an intellectual form of spiritualism which aims to unite a variety of beliefs, including pieces of Christianity, Buddhism, Confucianism, Islam and European literature. Among the practices of the Cao Dai are vegetarianism and four daily prayers. The Cao Dai believe in a supreme being which is represented as a single eye with light radiating from it, and is shown in religious art. The largest Cao Dai temple is in the town of Tay Ninh, near Ho Chi Minh City.

Christianity is a major part of the religious tapestry. The nation's 3 million Catholics live in the south, along Highway 1 where you will see Catholic churches in nearly every town. European missionaries brought Catholicism to Vietnam during the seventeenth century and the French built Catholic churches in the colonial cities. The belief spread throughout the country. Under fear of communist persecution, Catholics fled the north in 1954 and resettled primarily in the Central Highlands. Protestantism is practiced mainly by the tribes people the Central Highlands. Roughly 400,000 Protestants live in Vietnam.

Confucianism probably entered the country during the first period of Chinese domination in the third century BC. Confucian teachings emphasize the study of literature and individual's responsibility to society. It is a philosophy that prizes regulation and order highly. The Confucian influence is strongest in the north.

Taoism began in China and may be thought of as a mystical opposite of Confucianism. The belief embodies numerous forms of spiritualism including astrology and animism. At the supreme position of the Taoist pantheon is the Jade Emperor. Taoism is based on the teachings of Lao Tzu, who lived in the sixth century BC. Many aspects of the mysticism of Taoism, such as astrology and certain superstitions are factors in the daily life of most Vietnamese.

The ancient Cham took elements from the many culture with which it came in contact. India maintained ties with the Cham, and **Hinduism** became an integral part of Cham life. Cham temples, altars and sculpture portray Hindu gods, primarily Shiva. Hinduism is still practiced by the Cham people. There is one Hindu temple in the country, in Ho Chi Minh City.

Islam has perhaps only 50,000 followers. The local variant of Islam, Bani, is practiced by Cham people. In the Mekong Delta, Islamic symbols decorate houses.

Vietnam's religious minorities have maintained their beliefs and identities despite political pressure to assimilate. Minority tribes in the Northern Highlands still practice ancestor worship and forms of animism, and in the south-central highlands fetishism is common.

5. A SHORT HISTORY

PREHISTORY

Vietnam is one of a handful of Asian countries that can trace its origins to the dawn of civilization. Archaeological sites allow glimpses of the era before recorded history. At the country's oldest site, **Pho Binh Cave** in Bac Thai Province, archaeologists found stone tools from the Neolithic period and engravings on the walls. The walls of **Dong Noi Cave** in Ha Son Binh Province are adorned with ancient pictographs.

ANCIENT KINGDOMS

The ancient kingdoms of Vietnam contributed to the modern tapestry of Vietnamese culture. By the second century BC, the Khmer people of Cambodia inhabited the Mekong Delta. Their empire, Funan, was ruled from the famous cities in the area of Angkor Wat in Cambodia. For centuries the Khmer co-existed with the Cham, the people living in the area that is now present-day Vietnam. After the fourth century AD, Khmer power declined, at the same time the Cham empire reached its strongest era.

Despite the elegance of their tradition, the Cham were a fierce, warlike people. Civil wars, Chinese campaigns, and foreign raids were common elements of the Cham tradition. As powerful seamen, they engaged in piracy. The Cham empire is marked by such exotic images as elephants decorated for battle and tributes of rhinos and tigers sent to pacify distant empires.

Some of the earliest accounts of the Cham stem from Chinese records of the third century, BC. During the **Han Dynasty**, the Chinese began to push their sphere of control toward Cham lands, known as Champa. By the second century AD the Cham people kept the Chinese authority in the region at bay, with successful border raids and uprisings.

At this time Indian colonists entered the region, bringing Hinduism and Sanskrit writing to the Cham. Shiva is in the Cham pantheon. Mahayana Buddhism and later Islam also became integral aspects of

Cham culture. Cham monarchs were often deified, such as the queen-goddess **Po Nagar**.

CHAM ARCHITECTURE

The people of ancient Champa left their unique temples as a lasting legacy.

The tall, red, brick sanctuaries are called towers and many stand over 20 meters high. These buildings are used for religious purposes only. Characteristically, Cham towers stand on a hill and have an eastward orientation. A temple site may have more than one tower building.

A tower usually has two doors, one front and one rear, and two false doors. The towers have tall roofs which are terraced, or become smaller toward the top in layers. Often small towers are built onto the roof layers. Some temples have flared decoration on the roof corners. Other temples have roofs with straight angles.

The main tower usually sits on the highest plateau, with smaller buildings on lower elevations. Some sites have stelae (stone tablet) towers, and gate towers.

Traces of the religions that influenced the Cham religion are found in the sculpture and reliefs. Hinduism and Buddhism figure prominently in the decoration of the towers. Shiva, Vishnu and lotus flowers are common motifs.

The Cham maintained well defined cultural and military borders between the Khmer people to the west and the Viet people on the north. For over 1,000 years Cham kings kept strong ties to India, and some traveled by sea to the Indian continent. Ruling families had dynastic names that pay homage to Indian culture, such as **Gangaraja**, **Panduranga**, and **Bhrgu**.

In the north, sandwiched between the Chinese and Cham kingdoms, the Viet people showed increasing strength. With the disintegration of the Chinese **Tang Dynasty** in the early tenth century AD, the Viet people seized independence. Suddenly the Cham faced yet another enemy eager to encroach upon their territory. To further complicate matters, the Khmer kingdom began casting hungry eyes on, and marching troops toward Champa. Ongoing battles raged between the Viet kingdom and Siam (Thailand).

By the late thirteenth century the warring factions exhausted themselves, and were forced to turn attention to the Mongol Khans, whose empire soaked up lands from Bulgaria to Korea. On more than one occasion the Cham king brought war upon his country by refusing to pay tribute to the great Khan.

Weakened by the battles against Khmer, Mongol and Viet peoples, the Cham people began to lose the defined borders of the empire and to integrate with the Viet. By the mid-fourteenth century the Cham empire weakened and decentralized. Although it lasted until the eighteenth century, it was no longer a solid political entity.

Of the fabled walled cities and military watchtowers, all that remains are scattered Cham "towers," which are actually religious temples. Time wore down the red-brick buildings, and the wars of the twentieth century destroyed a great deal. The most famous of Cham sites are **My Son** and **Po Nagar** (for more information on My Son, see Chapter 12, *Central Coast*, section on Hoi An; for more on Po Nagar, see sidebar below).

VISITING CHAM SITES

Near Phan Thiet

Isolated **Pho Hai** *is the country's oldest Cham site. It is believed the towers were constructed during the ninth century AD; they are still used for rituals. The site consists of two main towers, both in disrepair. Strong Cham and Khmer influences are evident. Although detail has worn off these ruins, the glory of ancient Champa makes a strong statement in the architecture.*

The coastal setting and lack of tourists adds to the atmosphere. To reach Pho Hai, take Highway 1 north from Phan Thiet. About 2 kilometers from the city turn onto the small, paved road which runs east. Follow this road about 5 kilometers.

Near Phan Rang

Near the small town of Phan Rang, on the southern coast, the three towers of **Po Klun Gari** *show the beauty of the Cham empire. Nine years of restoration on the group ended in 1990. The walls and doorways are reinforced, and parts of the walls have been patched. Elements on these towers are in far better condition than others you may see.*

Stairs lead through the free-standing arch at the base of the temple to the central tower, the sanctuary for offerings, and the gate tower. Well-preserved flame ornaments decorate the corners of the roof tiers.

The site is known for friezes, many of which have been destroyed. Some survive on the outer walls of the towers. Engraved lotus flowers and dancing Shivas can be seen on the main tower. This is one of the few places that Cham new year ceremonies are still held.

Ba Toc, *also called* **Hoa Lai**, *is in poor condition. An interesting controversy surrounds the temple. Some believe this temple was built by a Khmer king during the reign of the Cham King Po Klun Gari. Others maintain that the buildings are even older, dating from the first millennium. The towers have fine examples of relief carvings. They are some of the*

CHAM SITES, CONTINUED

most accessible since they stand just off the highway, and not perched atop a hill like all other Cham towers.

*The temples of **Po Rome** stand on a hill overlooking Hau Sanh town. These are towers date from after sixteenth century, which marks the end of such construction. The main temple is dedicated to the worship of the Cham King Po Rome. During the rainy season (from August to October) the roads are impassable.*

Near Nha Trang

Po Nagar *temple, dedicated to the queen-goddess Po Nagar, is undergoing reconstruction and preservation. The original temple was built in the eighth century, but was destroyed. The main temple is a sanctuary which is still used to pay homage to Po Nagar. The wardrobe along the back wall holds the gowns and headdresses that adorn the statue on the altar. The outfits are changed every month. The faithful who have success and wealth donate the outfits as a way of giving thanks. To reach Po Nagar, take highway 1 north. Just after you cross Xom Bong Bridge, about 2 kilometers from the city center, you will see the temple on the western hill.*

Near Qui Nhon

*One group of Cham towers is in the middle of a neighborhood close to downtown Qui Nhon. The Two Towers, or **Thap Doi** date from the 1200s, and have been partially reconstructed. The Two Towers have heavy lines and thick archways, distinctively different from other towers. The architecture looks more solid than other towers, in part because layers and decoration are absent from the roof. The neighborhood children who play at the towers will find you as interesting as you find the towers.*

*The name **Bahn It** means "wedding cake." The four towers are also known as the Silver Towers. This group is an extremely well-preserved site in a lovely location overlooking a pagoda and two rivers. To reach Bahn It, take Highway 1 north from Qui Nhon, and turn at the sign to Tuy Phouc. The road that leads to the site is just south of the towers. You can park at Nguyen Thieu Pagoda which is down the dirt road. The tranquil setting is the home of a monastery.*

THE VIET PEOPLE

The Vietnamese people trace their culture to waves of immigration from China that occurred in the first millennium BC. The Yuan River Valley became the home of Sino people who would later be known as the Lac Viet, ancestors of the modern Vietnamese. They brought irrigation and wet rice farming and masterfully-created pottery and metalwork. Their culture spread through the central and northern areas of modern day Vietnam. The united lands soon emerged as the Dai Co Viet.

Legends say the first ruler of Vietnamese lands was **King Hung**. The Hung Vuong Period, a Bronze Age feudal society administered by the Hung Dynasty, lasted for nearly 1,000 years. This is the first national period for Vietnam. The development of the society is shown in the extraordinary metal work that remains. Famous bronze drums attest to the exemplary skill of Vietnamese artisans of 3,000 years ago. As the national character emerged, so did the traditions that span centuries.

The Chinese Han Dynasty annexed lands of northern Vietnam in the second century BC and maintained control for over 1,000 years. During this time the foundations of Confucian society became integrated into the Vietnamese way of life. Chinese language and philosophy was taught and appreciated.

As Chinese customs spread, the Vietnamese people struggled to regain autonomy. There were numerous revolts in this period. The most famous uprising took place in the year 43 AD when the **Trung Sisters**, Trung Trac and Trung Nhi, led the Vietnamese people against the Chinese. They met with great success at first, but in the end the Chinese squelched the revolution, and the Trung sisters drowned tragically. They are still revered as national heroes.

In 939 AD, **Ngo Quyen** led the Viet people to independence. At the famous battle of Bach Dang River, Ngo Quyen won victory over the Chinese navy. During this period the capital city of Hoa Lu was founded in north Vietnam. However, true independence was short lived and after the death of Ngo Quyen, Vietnam soon submitted itself as a vassal state of China.

From a muddle of battles among hostile factions emerged the leader who solidified the empire, the first Emperor Ly. Under the **Ly Dynasty** of the eleventh and twelfth centuries, material culture flourished and the capital was moved to Thang Long (modern Hanoi). Viet soldiers pushed south into the territories of a weakened Cham empire. Buddhism took root.

In 1281, the **Tran Dynasty**, known for its great warriors, was in power when the Mongol empire of Kubla Khan requested passage through Viet lands to wage campaigns against Champa. The Viet and Cham peoples united against their new foe. When the Viet nation refused the Khan's request of passage, Mongol forces descended upon Viet and Cham lands. Both were forced into paying tribute to Kubla Khan, yet both resisted. The Tran Dynasty remained in control of its lands until the late fourteenth century.

HISTORICAL VIETNAMESE DYNASTIES

111 BC-43 AD – First period of Chinese Domination
44 AD to 543 AD – Second period of Chinese Domination
544 AD to 602 – The first Ly Dynasty
603 to 938 – Third period of Chinese domination
939 to 967 – Ngo Dynasty
968 to 980 – Dinh Dynasty (Dai Co Viet Kingdom)
980 to 1009 – Le Dynasty
1010 to 1214 – second Ly Dynasty (Dai Viet Kingdom 1054 to 1164)
1225-1399 – Tran Dynasty
1400 to 1407 – Ho Dynasty
1407 to 1427 – Fourth period of Chinese (Ming) domination
1428 to 1789 – Le Dynasty (founded by Le Loi)
1788 to 1802 – Tay Son Rulers
1789 to 1939 – Nguyen Dynasty

From 1407 to 1427, the Chinese **Ming Dynasty** successfully invaded Viet lands and forced the rulers into submission to China. Under Ming rule, the Vietnamese were forced to use Chinese dress, language, and customs.

In 1418, a man known as **Le Loi** (born Nguyen Trai, a man of humble beginnings), began a campaign to expel the Chinese. After years of desperate fighting, independence came in 1427 with China's acceptance of Vietnam as a separate power. Le Loi reestablished the **Ly Dynasty** and moved the capital from Hanoi to Hue, where it flourished. Trade with Europe began in the early 1600's, when Portuguese and Dutch traders came to Hoi An (Faifo) and Pho Hien. At this time Christian missionaries planted the seeds of Catholicism. The Latin-based script used in today's Vietnamese writing was developed.

A period of territorial expansion southward left the Ly empire weak, and clans arose, threatening stability. The Trinh in the north and the Nguyen in the south became locked in a brutal power struggle. The Nguyens sought allegiance with the French and Dutch.

From the midst of an ineffective government came a grassroots rebellion. Three brothers known by the name of their home village, **Tay Son**, instigated civil unrest against the Vietnamese Nguyen leader in 1771. Within seven years the Tay Son controlled south Vietnam, including Saigon. Through the following two turbulent decades, the Tay Son pushed north, eventually taking Hue, Hanoi, and fending off the Chinese. **Nguyen Hue,** one of the Tay Son brothers, took the Vietnamese crown in 1789 and established the last Vietnamese dynasty. This dynasty was prone to internal conflict and was overthrown after a few years by the former ruler, Nguyen Anh, who later took the name **Gia Long** and ruled from 1802-1820.

Attracted by the fertile land and abundant resources, the French increased trade and missionary activity in Viet lands. In the late nineteenth century, following a military attack on Danang, the French installed a colonial government that controlled the county from 1883 to 1939. The French contributed to the development of agriculture, including draining the Mekong Delta, increasing rice production, and introducing new crops.

They also developed coal mining in the north and improved the country's infrastructure with the building a modern rail system. Vietnam produced raw materials and trade was of primary importance; however, manufacturing was overlooked.

COMMUNIST VIETNAM

In the early 1900's, communism began to gain popularity. **Ho Chi Minh** (whose name means Bearer of Light), united Marxist and humanitarian philosophy in his teachings. In 1929, he formed the Indochina Communist Party. He lived many years in exile, ill with tuberculosis. The Vietnamese Communist Party was officially founded in 1930.

While in China, Ho Chi Minh founded the **Viet Minh**. This group served to unify the struggle for an independent Vietnam under communism. After the Japanese entered the country in 1940 and helped throw out the French, the Viet Minh expelled them.

On September 2, 1945, the Democratic Republic of Vietnam declared itself a nation after the Japanese surrendered to the United States. Soon after World War II ended, communist Viet Minh guerrillas again rose up against the French. When the French refused to recognize Vietnam as a sovereign state, war erupted once more and lasted for a number of years. In 1954, the Vietnamese victory over French forces at Dien Bien Phu led to the Geneva Agreement that officially split the nation in two: communist North Vietnam, supported by the USSR and the People's Republic of China, and the Western-backed South Vietnam. The 1954 Geneva Agreement also established the **demilitarized zone** (DMZ), a neutral area surrounding the dividing line between the two countries along the 17th parallel.

Finally, in undisputed control of the new North Vietnam, the Viet Minh continued to fight for complete reunification of the nation under communism. In the late 1950's, the guerrilla force known as the **Viet Cong** began to organize in the South with the support of the North's government.

Free elections, scheduled to be held in 1956 under the Geneva Agreement, were not held after the South's president, Ngo Dinh Diem, refused to cooperate. Long solicited by the French, the United States entered the conflict. The number of American advisors steadily increased in the early 1960's, but escalated dramatically after President Lyndon Johnson's Rolling Thunder bombing campaign in early 1965. Officially, Americans were involved only in a "police action," yet they participated in some of the war's bloodiest fighting. By 1967, there were 389,000 Americans troops stationed in Vietnam, and the US was heavily committed to driving the Viet Cong out of South Vietnam.

In January 1968, the North launched the **Tet Offensive**, and Viet Minh troops attacked major cities in South Vietnam. The ground which the North took was eventually regained by the South. But many look upon this event as a decisive show of the North's strength. More importantly, perhaps, than the military implications of Tet were the domestic consequences: the offensive shocked the American people perhaps more than any other single event in the war, and the antiwar movement – already strong – gained tremendous momentum after Tet.

In 1970, President Richard Nixon publicly unveiled the American bombing and invasion of Cambodia. Nixon's goal was to cut off the Viet Cong's supply routes from the North, but the campaign produced few tangible results. This ironically coincided with the gradual withdrawal of American troops from Vietnam, as Secretary of State Henry Kissinger had earlier begun secret negotiations with the North Vietnamese. The **Paris Agreement**, signed on January 27, 1973, ended direct participation by the United States in the Vietnam War, although aid still came to the South's government. The fighting waged on as the North advanced southward, city by city.

On April 30, 1975, Saigon fell. This is now known as the Liberation of Saigon. The Vietnamese government struggled to form an independent socialist state, but in the long run could not reach economic stability free of Soviet assistance. The United Nations accepted Vietnam as a member nation in 1977.

Besides the obvious destruction of war, other internal restructuring resulted. Over one million refugees fled the country during the war. After the war, many rural populations shifted as about four million people were moved to "new economic zones" for the purposes of agricultural development. Entire villages were placed on land suited for farming, and guidelines intending to increase productivity were instituted.

Political problems lingered after the South Vietnamese government disbanded. Diplomatic antagonism from China intensified when the Vietnamese invaded Cambodia in 1979. Vietnam installed a government to replace that of Pol Pot, which resulted in the Chinese invasion of the northern Vietnamese border in that same year. Chinese troops withdrew after one month. The Khmer Rouge guerrillas, backed by the Chinese, fought on, even after the withdrawal of Vietnamese forces from Cambodia. Random acts of guerrilla violence are still common in much of Cambodia. Mass graves of innocents slaughtered by the Khmer Rouge have been found along Vietnam's Cambodian border.

After the fall of the Soviet Union, Vietnam put in place a policy of renovation (**doi moi**). This called for economic reform and opening of the country to the rest of the world. On February 3, 1994, President Clinton lifted the US trade embargo against Vietnam. The American Embassy in Hanoi and Vietnamese Embassy in Washington, DC, resumed diplomatic relations. The problem of American soldiers still classified as **Missing In Action** from the Vietnam War remains an issue of great concern. Numerous joint US-Vietnamese military working groups have met since the early 1990's to resolve the remaining outstanding cases. In 1996, former President George Bush visited Vietnam to meet with officials about locating MIAs. Many still remain unaccounted for, and groups searching for the American servicemen are not satisfied.

CURRENT EVENTS

Today, Vietnam is a dynamic nation in the midst of limited and controlled free-market reforms. Faced with problems of rapid population growth and urban crowding, the government is taking many steps to further economic and social development. The industrial countries quickly acknowledged Vietnam's new policies and is responding with economic aid. In 1993, the United Nations granted funds for the resettlement of thousands of Vietnamese refugees from Cambodia. The World Bank and the International Monetary Fund have pledged ongoing support.

Vietnam is governed by a president, vice-president, and cabinet. The national political and legislative authority is the National Assembly, which holds sessions twice each year. The Standing Committee of the National Assembly conducts daily affairs. The government is still Communist, however, and the Politburo still calls the shots. The government imposes censorship in all media. Yet personal freedom and economic potential of individuals have taken giant strides forward – although there are still concerns regarding political and religious freedoms.

Vietnam strives for universal literacy. Education is free at all levels and classes are conducted in Vietnamese and the languages of each minority people. Hanoi University is the national institution of higher education, with smaller universities throughout the country.

6. PLANNING YOUR TRIP

Vietnam is a surprisingly easy country for travelers. After years of relative isolation from western tourists the floodgates are open, and travelers are rushing in to become acquainted with this beautiful country and its warm people. Likewise, the Vietnamese people are extremely happy to have foreign guests.

The country is undergoing great change, and the tourism industry is making strides to meet demands of western travelers. New hotels, restaurants and services spring up everywhere. The number of taxis in Ho Chi Minh City and Hanoi is on a steady increase. Vietnam Airlines delivers international and domestic service with reasonable standards of excellence. This is great for today's traveler, because while changes are taking hold, the charm of tradition still permeates society. Many who leave Vietnam say "I'm glad I came here now, before everything changes."

Making plans, schedules and reservations are not necessary, although doing so may ease your mind. You can simply arrive, and find your way around without much trouble. Many Vietnamese speak English, especially those who work in the hotel and travel industries.

Most travelers have limited time and follow a well-trodden path from Ho Chi Minh City, north to Hue or Hanoi. They find the greatest restricting factor is time. You may have to choose cities to miss, but the sacrifice is made up if really enjoy those you do see. The best advice comes from travelers, and you will meet many. They will give you the latest scoop on an ever-changing scene.

BEFORE YOU GO

WHEN TO GO

Vietnam lies in a monsoon zone which is different from other Asian countries. Polar winds give the north of Vietnam (above the 18th parallel) cold winters and year-round high humidity. The climate in the north is tropical, and that of the south is subequatorial. The monsoon season, from May to October, is felt primarily on the northern coast, which is prone to flooding.

The summer months are tourist season in Vietnam, although travelers visit year-round. For most of the country this season brings the most turbulent weather. During the summer, temperatures as well as prices rise, and rain falls (especially in May and September). The mild climate makes the country ideal for winter travel. Winter also brings lower prices in some areas. The south is hot all year (average temperature 27°C), and the north has cool winters.

Vietnam has three main climactic zones—south, central and north—which have varying wet and dry seasons. A visit between November and March gives you the best chance of dry weather. Regardless of when you go, bring an umbrella and rain coat, since the weather is best defined as temperamental.

The south, which is subequatorial, experiences wet season from June through October, with the dry season falling from December to April. Temperatures are always high here, never dipping below 20°C.

The central region includes the mountainous Central Highlands and coastal areas. In the southern regions of the Central Highlands, around Dalat, dry season runs from November through March, although humidity is always high, and light showers possible. Along the coastal resorts, from Phan Thiet to Nha Trang, summer is dry. Temperatures are high year-round, ranging from 18°C to 40°C.

The north has the most dramatic seasonal changes with cold winters and hot summers. Typhoon season lasts from May to October. The Northern Highlands become scorching hot in the summer, and during the winter, from November through March, become quite cold. Frost and near 0°C temperatures are common. As a rule of thumb, for every 100 meter increase in elevation, the temperature decreases by one-half degree centigrade.

WHAT TO PACK

Vietnam is a casual country, so simple clothes are appropriate for most any occasion. The year round heat and humidity in the south make lightweight cotton separates the best choice. Streets are often dirty, so expect that your shoes will get a good deal of wear.

In the north and the Central Highlands, the temperature is cool enough for sweaters and light jackets during much of the year. In the Northern Highlands, especially during the winter, cold weather clothes (such as long johns, down vests or jackets) are necessary.

Should you want to trek in the Central or Northern Highlands, bring a pair of hiking boots. Otherwise, lightweight canvas walking shoes or athletic shoes are sufficient.

As when you travel in any foreign country, a pair of shower thongs is essential to keep your feet away from fungus in the bathroom and to guard against nasty diseases such as worms. The thick-soled variety with Velcro straps give you the best protection (and least amount of splashing). Some travelers wear these as walking shoes. It is considered inappropriate to wear shoes inside a home. And for this reason, hotels often provide a pair of slippers; but unless you are staying at a high-end establishment they may be at least slightly used.

Bring an adequate supply of any medication you use regularly or may need. Most travelers have some stomach problems, regardless of how in tune they are to Asian countries, so bring diarrhea and digestive medicine. Mosquito repellent is essential during most times of the year in the south. Sunscreen should be worn daily. The hot, humid climate allows most women to forget about applying make-up, so you will not be alone if you go without your mascara and lipstick.

Cash is the easiest way to pay for most things, as dollars are accepted in many places. Credit cards can be used in large cities and most tourist areas. Travelers checks are difficult to exchange. There are no ATMs in Vietnam yet. Wear your valuables in a small travel purse under your clothes as a safeguard against theft.

Bottled water and film, a tourist's staples, are found easily throughout the country. In Ho Chi Minh City and Hanoi you can even pick up a new camera if in need of one. Toiletries such as shampoo, shaving cream and even designer cologne are available in markets in most cities. So the bottom line is pack light. Bring only the essentials, and pick up what you need as you go.

CUSTOMS - CANADA

When returning to Canada, no duty is charged on up to $300 Canadian of goods (for personal use) once a year if you leave the country for more than 7 days or on up to $100 Canadian several times a year if you leave the country for more than 48 hours. An adult can bring in 1.14 liters of alcohol or 8.5 liters of beer. For those 16 years of age and over, up to 200 cigarettes, 400 grams of tobacco, and as many as 50 cigars can be brought in.

CUSTOMS - UNITED STATES

You will be relieved to know that the US government no longer imposes a spending limit on US citizens visiting Vietnam.

When returning to the US, no duty is charged on up to $400 dollars worth of goods (for personal use) and quantities of up to 400 cigarettes, 100 cigars or 100 grams of tobacco, and 1.5 liters of alcohol.

You will be asked to declare everything you have purchased when you return to the US. The customs forms will be handed out on your flight.

CUSTOMS - VIETNAM

You must fill out customs forms before arrival. Thesewill be passed out to you on your flight. Every form asks for your contact address in Vietnam. You need one passport-sized photo for the "entry form," and are required to carry documentation of immunization (the yellow international immunization card).

Customs policy strictly regulates items which are brought into (and taken out of) the country. The Vietnamese will not allow you to bring more than $5,000 in cash. You must declare video equipment and "cultural material." Books, tapes, or anything which may be considered "cultural information" may be seized upon entry or exit. However, confiscation of these items seldom occurs. Gifts may not have a value of more than $50. You may not bring in weapons, explosives or flammable materials, drugs or items which reflect a negative attitude toward "Vietnamese tradition."

Be warned that penalties against transporting restricted items are severe. The airports at Ho Chi Minh City and Hanoi are equipped with X-ray machines which meet international standards, and therefore will not harm film or computer equipment.

You may not take the currency, Vietnamese dong, out of the country. Video tapes purchased in Vietnam require a special customs stamp. No antiques may be taken out of the country. Certain items considered valuable by the government and some gemstones require a special permit. The beautiful blue ceramics which many buy in Hoi An and Hue may be confiscated as "antique," regardless of the authenticity of the claim. Arguing about your rights to hold on to your possessions will not get you anything except delayed and possibly fined.

Usually travelers encounter more difficulties leaving, not entering the country. And those on extended stays, such as those with business visas, may be scrutinized more closely. Save baggage claim tickets for your exit; you are not supposed to take out more baggage than you brought.

When traveling on international flights, an airport tax of $8 will be charged to each person. Domestic flights have a $1.50 airport tax.

HOTELS

Vietnam has the "Field of Dreams" theory about hotels and tourists: if you build them, they will come. Hotels of all sizes and classes are springing up in every city. Currently, the 50,000 available rooms in the country are more than enough to handle the 1.2 million annual visitors.

More travelers come to Vietnam each year, but it is still a traveler's market for accommodation.

You may make hotel reservations by phone or fax. To save money on your long-distance bill, you may want to make reservations while traveling. Simply call the hotel of your choice two or three days in advance.

There are few hotels which could fit the five-star classification. This means that four-star hotels are charging prices which may seem too high for what you get. These hotels often fall short on amenities such as sports facilities, to which luxury travelers are accustomed.

Tourist-class travelers are luckiest on the cost spectrum. Many small, new hotels with competitive prices (from $15 to $50 per night) are opening every day.

Budget travelers are perhaps the hardest hit by the hotel boom. Super cheap accommodations (under $10 per night) do not have much competition, since most new places are vying for the tourist-class dollars. So budget accommodations are often dirty, in disrepair, and unpleasant. You may be able to find a decent double room in a tourist hotel for the price you would pay for two budget singles.

So you should expect to find a clean room with a western-style bathroom for a reasonable price. Rooms in a hotel are designated by classes, from first to fourth. Third and fourth class rooms probably will be in a less desirable location in the hotel, like on an outer wing, and may not be renovated. Often the only difference between first and second class rooms are amenities such as the television and refrigerator—first class rooms are fully loaded, second class are not. Take the best combination of comfort and economy.

Do not be afraid to bargain, especially if you plan to stay more than a few days. It is the policy of most hotels to offer a discount to guests who stay one week. You may be able to shave a bit more off the price if you do not take breakfast at the hotel. Some hotels have renovated and unrenovated wings. Rooms in the older part may be considerably less than the advertised rate.

Traveling solo can be significantly more expensive than going with a friend. The cost difference between single and double rooms is nominal; often the rates are the same. Usually children under 12 may stay without charge when traveling with parents.

Advertised rates may not include the government tax of 10 percent or the hotel's service charge, which may be from 5 to 10 percent. If you use a credit card, expect from 3 to 5 percent to be added onto your bill. Be certain to ask about these charges before you check in.

Of course, it always pays to be a careful consumer. Check a room before you decide to stay and clarify the price in writing. If you are not comfortable with the surroundings, move on. Most cities have at least a few hotels. Beware of taxi drivers who insist on taking you to their choice of hotel. They are probably getting a kick-back for delivering guests, and you may not be getting the best accommodation for your money.

The plethora of new hotels opening throughout Vietnam make it fairly easy to find a good, clean room at a reasonable price. Unless you choose to go the extreme budget route, a room will have a new, tiled bathroom with hot water. Most rooms in new or renovated hotels have satellite television, international phone lines (IDD), refrigerator, private bath, hot water and air-conditioning. Many hotels have installed full-size bath tubs.

After settling in, flipping on the satellite TV and indulging in a hot bath, its tea time. You will find a thermos of hot water (which should be changed daily), a tea service, and a jar of tea leaves. On your way out remember to drop off your clothes to be laundered. Charges range from 20 to 75 cents per item. Most hotels have modern washing machines, so clothes are not treated too harshly. Only the roughest of budget hotels with common baths attempt to restrict guests from washing their own clothes by hand.

IMMUNIZATIONS

Consult with a physician well in advance of your trip, since some immunizations require a few weeks to become effective. At this time, no immunizations are required for Americans to enter the country, but some are strongly recommended – particularly if you're traveling to remote, rural areas where there may be some risk of malaria infection. (See the immunizations sidebar below.)

You should have your doctor record immunizations on a yellow International Immunization Record, which you should bring on your trip. Vietnamese immigration requests that the immunization card be presented upon entry, even though they don't require any immunizations. It should show a record of childhood immunizations including polio, tetanus, diphtheria and all boosters.

RECOMMENDED IMMUNIZATIONS

- *Immune Globulin: take just before travel begins.*
- *Oral Typhoid Booster: must be taken every three years.*
- *Japanese B Encephalitis: a series of three injections taken over one month.*
- *Malaria pills: taken two weeks prior to the trip, during the trip and four months after return.*

There is **malaria** in Vietnam in rural areas. It is carried by mosquitoes, but may also be transferred by other means, such as blood transfusions. You may be told that malaria is only present at altitudes under 1,200 meters. While this would be a comfort while in the Dalat region, which is thick with mosquitoes and at an elevation of 1,500 meters, the fact remains that malaria is endemic to the entire country. Flu-like symptoms accompany malaria, including fever and muscle aches. Kidney failure and death may result if the disease is left untreated.

The most common prevention of malaria includes taking a weekly pill (mefloquine is commonly prescribed, but check with your physician) two weeks before the trip, each week while traveling, and four weeks after leaving at-risk areas. Finishing the prescription is important since malaria may break- out months after infection.

It takes multiple bites to spread malaria; when in mosquito-infested areas protect yourself against bites. Spray insect repellent on clothes and wear cover on as much skin as possible. Also keep in mind that mosquitoes feed primarily at night and are found in concentrations around stagnant water. Flies may spread diseases, so, if for no other reason than health, avoid swarms of flies.

You are at a higher risk of infection from **Japanese encephalitis** during the rainy season. Mosquitoes that bite in the afternoon and evening are more likely to carry the disease. The symptoms vary widely, and may be non-existent. Major complications may arise from this disease, and all travelers planning extended stays in rural areas should consider immunization.

Dengue fever is present is Vietnam, however there are no immunizations against the disease. It is a viral infection, transferred by mosquito-bite, may take over one month to break out, and has symptoms similar to those of the flu. The only tell-tale sign of this affliction is fever.

Cholera, which is commonly transmitted by poor hygiene in food handling, remains a major threat. A doctor may prescribe antibiotics for treatment of cholera. You can ask your doctor at home for a prescription of wide-spectrum antibiotics which would work against cholera. Bring the pills with you on your trip, as the same drugs you would get from your pharmacist may not be available in Vietnam.

Hepatitis is another serious threat. Hepatitis A is generally transferred by contaminated food, water, and substandard sanitation. Hepatitis B may be contacted sexually or through contact with infected blood. Symptoms are similar to those of the flu, and may range from mild to severe. Jaundice may or may not appear. Immunizations are available for both Hepatitis A and B.

Typhoid is caused by bacteria and also transmitted by unsanitary conditions. Shellfish may carry typhoid. Vaccinations can be given orally or by injection. The oral treatment requires pills taken once weekly over the period of one month, and should begin at least two weeks before departure.

In the last year, 38 people died of **rabies** in Hanoi alone. Most dogs you encounter, despite their haggard appearance, will not be aggressive. The best prevention of rabies is to avoid all animals, including dogs, cats and monkeys. A rabies vaccination is available. However, this will merely reduce your chances of getting rabies. If you are bitten seek medical attention at once.

The US government provides up-to-date health information, including recommended vaccinations, through a 24-hour hotline at *404/332-4559*. Some county health departments offer information and travel vaccination clinics.

The Centers for Disease Control and Prevention (CDC) provides the most current information about traveler's health concerns on the Internet (http://www.cdc.gov/travel/travel.html). The US Government publishes *Health Information for International Traveling*, which gives specifics about immunization requirements, and how to stay well. This book costs $6 and is available from the *Superintendent of Documents, U. S. Government Printing Office, Washington, DC 20403, Tel. 202/783-3238*.

PASSPORTS & VISAS

You must have a valid US passport and visa to enter Vietnam. Obtaining the visa takes about two - four weeks and can be done through a travel agent or the Vietnamese Embassy in the United States, *Embassy of Vietnam, 1233 20th Street NW, Suite 501, Washington, DC 20036, Tel. 202 861 0737*. Rush delivery is possible.

The **tourist visa** application is a short form which requires two pictures and submission of a passport, or three pictures and a copy of the passport photo page. Your passport must be valid for at least nine months after your date of departure from Vietnam. The visa application requires the name and address of your contact in Vietnam (this simply may be the hotel where you will stay upon arrival) and flight numbers.

Tourist visas permit a 30-day stay and the fee is $25. Should you enter by seaport at either Nha Trang or Danang an additional $10 is charged. The Vietnamese government no longer grants visa extensions. Although tourist visas are single entry, it is possible to leave the country (to go to Angkor Wat, for example) and return. The paperwork for such trips is usually done through a travel agency or tourist bureau after arrival in Vietnam. Should a tourist stay beyond expiration of a visa, high fines and/ or detention may be imposed.

Former citizens of Vietnam (called Overseas Vietnamese or *Viet Kieu*) may receive a tourist visa or residence permit for a visit. It may be possible to extend the trip for up to six months from the date of arrival. Former citizens of Vietnam should keep in mind that the Vietnamese government considers them citizens of Vietnam. This means that you may not have ready access to US Embassy officials should the need arise, and the US Embassy might not be notified if you are arrested or hurt.

Business visas are becoming increasingly difficult to obtain. Approval from either the State Committee for Cooperation and Investment in Hanoi or the Vietnam Chamber of Commerce and Industry in Hanoi is mandatory and must be done through a sponsor in Vietnam. Business visas range from $40 to $100. Extensions must be handled by the Vietnamese sponsor. Contact the Embassy of Vietnam for specifics.

You may also get a visa at a Vietnamese embassy in Asia. The process may take a few hours or a few days depending on the time of year.

Travel permits are still necessary in some regions of Vietnam. Often these permits require that you are accompanied by a government-approved guide. Arrangements for these permits are made through a travel agent or tourist agency after arrival in Vietnam. Entering a region without a travel permit when one is required is grounds for expulsion from the country.

Carry at least two extra photos in case you have the misfortune of losing your passport. If you plan to apply for other visas bring two photos for that. Since Vietnam relies on heavy bureaucracy to regulate tourism, it is a good idea to travel with a few precautionary documents. Bring copies of the front page of your passport (showing photo and passport number). Should you need to apply for an exit (replacement) visa, these are required. Also, if journeying to more remote areas of the country you may feel safer turning over a copy (instead of your passport) to your hotel or regional police.

The US Embassy in Hanoi, *7 Lang Ha Street, Dong Da District, Tel. (84 4) 8431500*, is not there to be of assistance with your travel plans, permits and visas, except if you are in the country for diplomatic, business or educational purposes.

TRAVEL ADVISORIES

Vietnam is not expected to go through turmoil, since the government is stable and the economy growing. Seasoned travelers know to keep abreast of the latest events in a their region. The US government issues notices about countries which may be particularly dangerous for American tourism due to political, social or economic unrest. These notices are free to the public. For the latest travel advisories posted contact the *Bureau of Consular Affairs of the US State Department, Tel. 202/647-5225* or automated *fax 202/647-3000*. You may also log on to the computer bulletin board at *Tel. 202-647-9225*.

Background Notes, which offers information about history and society, is published by the US Department of State for each country in the world. The price varies, but runs around $1. *Safe Trip Abroad* offers advice on minimizing risks while abroad ($1). For either of these publications contact the Superintendent of Documents at the *US Government Printing Office, Washington, DC 20402, Tel. 202/783-3238* or your regional government bookstore.

GETTING TO VIETNAM

BY AIR

Flight availability to and from Vietnam is generally not a problem, with the exception of flights in and out of Asia during Tet—Chinese Lunar New Year.

The following international airlines serve Vietnam from the west coast of North America: **Cathay Pacific**, **Eva Air**, **Japan Airlines** and **Korean Airlines**. Most flights connect through Hong Kong or Bangkok. Plans are in the works for direct service from San Francisco to Ho Chi Minh City. The Asian carriers Malaysian Air, Philippine Airlines, Thai Airways and Vietnam Airlines, provide connections through Asia.

Vietnam Airlines offers joint service with Cathay Pacific using Boeing 767s and Airbus 320s on European routes. Cathay Pacific offers direct flights between New York and Hong Kong. Japan Airlines, which has direct flights from the west coast of the US to Japan, has connections to Ho Chi Minh City. Emirates Airways and British Air connect Europe with Vietnam.

BY CAR

You may cross the land border between Cambodia and Vietnam by car, but have your visa in order before you arrive at the border crossing.

BY CRUISE SHIP

Vietnamese ports-of-call are being added to many Asian cruise routes. Over 10,000 people visited Vietnam by cruise ship in 1995. The ease of touring by day, and returning to the ship's familiarly posh surroundings has obvious advantages.

During a limited season Cunard, *Tel. 800/5-CUNARD*, operates cruises which stop at Vietnamese ports. Princess Cruises, *Tel. 800/421-0522*, have routes in Southeast Asia and Australia with ports of call in Ho Chi Minh City and Danang. Holland America Lines, *Tel. 800/426-0237*, included ports of call in Vietnam in 1996, however future itineraries are uncertain.

BY TRAIN

You can enter from China by train through Dang Dong, Vietnam. The Vietnamese and Chinese trains use different size track, so you must change trains at the border. The trip from Hanoi to Ping Xiang, China takes 52 hours and a one-way ticket costs $186. In order to re-enter Vietnam, you must cross at Dang Dong.

STUDY TOURS & LEARNING VIETNAMESE

There are no study-abroad programs in Vietnam. To undertake serious language study, you should enroll in a university program. In some cases simple housing may be arranged. For more information contact **Hanoi University**, *90 Nguyen Trai, Hanoi, Tel. (84 4) 8581426*, which conducts programs for the study of Vietnamese.

Expatriates most commonly hire private-language tutors. Cost for a tutor ranges from $5 to $6 per hour. **Lotus College**, *53 Nguyen Du Street, District 1, Ho Chi Minh City, Tel. (84 8) 8290841*, arranges hourly lessons. In Hanoi, contact the **Vietnamese Language Center** at Hanoi Foreign Language College, 1 *Pham Ngu Lao Street, Hanoi, Tel. (84 4) 262468*.

An institute which has an excellent reputation for intensive study programs is the **Hanoi Foreign Language College**, *Thanh Xuan Dong Da Street, Hanoi, Tel. (84 4) 8262468*.

A few private-language schools have opened. You will find advertisements for these schools in English-language newspapers and magazines published in Vietnam.

TRAVEL AGENTS & SPECIALISTS

There are no travel agents in Vietnam. Instead travel offices, regulated by the provincial and local governments, offer services. You will be able to book hotels and tours, rent cars with drivers, and obtain information about restaurants and recreational facilities in the area. These offices do not handle plane reservations, and usually can not help with train schedules. Information about airlines is best obtained from the office of each individual airline. Vietnam Airlines has a centralized reservation system, which has limited information about other carriers.

Currently the Vietnamese authorities most strongly encourage travel by tours or cruise ships. In fact, they go so far as to implement policies (such as visa regulations) to control free-spirited backpackers from entering and leaving on whims.

TOUR PACKAGES TO VIETNAM

Tours solve the problems of dealing with unreliable transportation, questionable restaurants, and the language barrier. You can find all sorts of tours—from simple trekking journeys to elaborate cruise packages. The following is a sampling of tour companies which offer trips to Vietnam. All 800-numbers are toll-free in the United States.

Abercrombie & Kent International, *Tel. 800/323-7308*, has cruises and tours which include Vietnam. The 21 day Images of Indochina package includes Angkor Wat in Cambodia, and Laos. These trips are designed for travelers who prefer luxurious vacations, even when voyaging through rough areas.

Adventure Center, *Tel. 800/227-8747*, takes small groups to off-the-beaten path destinations. They specialize in bringing travelers in contact with the culture and indigenous people. Trips to Vietnam include trekking, bicycle-riding and boat trips.

Chinasmith, *Tel. 800/USC-HINA*, offers an all-inclusive package for a 12-day tour from Ho Chi Minh City to Hanoi. They can make arrangements for cities not included in the package.

Intrepid Tours, *Tel. 800/558-2522*, has 10-day tours which include Hanoi, Hue, Danang and Ho Chi Minh City, with optional extensions to Cambodia and Laos.

TBI Tours, *Tel. 800-223 0266*, offers a 13-day tour of Vietnam which includes three days in Bangkok, and a 20-day tour of all the countries of Indochina.

Adding Vietnam on to Your Tour Package

If you plan to take a tour of the Orient and would like to spend part of your time in Vietnam, consider an "add-on" package. These are mini-tours which usually originate in Asia, designed to add only a few days to a trip. Generally you may purchase an add-on only if you are taking a tour with the same company which offers it.

Cathay Pacific offers "Discovery Tours" which originate in Hong Kong. DER Tours, *Tel. 800/937-1235, Fax 800/860-9944*, offers tour extensions to Vietnam from Hong Kong. Singapore Airlines, *Tel. 800/742-3133*, offer add-ons to their tour packages. These originate from Singapore and go to either Hanoi or Ho Chi Minh City.

Arranging Your Own Tour

If you can gather a group of five to ten who want to travel together, you may find it most economical to arrange your own tour. Should you form your own group, engaging the services of a native tour agency may be the best way to minimize expenses and maximize ease of travel. The government operates tour agencies in most major cities, and the larger agencies can put together a tour for your group. Communicating by fax allows you to ignore the time difference.

Voiles Vietnam, 17 *Pham Ngoc Thach Street, District 3, Ho Chi Minh City, Tel. (84 8) 8296750 or 8231589 or 8231590, Fax (84 8) 8231591*, operates sailing and scuba trips for small groups originating in Ho Chi Minh City. The proprietors have lived in Vietnam for years and can arrange specialized private tours to any part, or all, of the country. They speak French and English and offer unsurpassed service at reasonable prices.

Should you prefer to arrange your tour from the United States, here are two companies in the US: Brenden Tours, *Tel. 800/421-8446*, for airfare and accommodations in Danang, Hanoi, Ho Chi Minh City, Hue and Nha Trang. You can book four or seven-day land packages for Vietnam from Japan & Orient Tours, *Tel. 800/377-1080*.

TRAVEL PROFESSIONALS IN VIETNAM

Danang Hotel Tourist Company, *3-5 Dong Da Street, Danang. Tel. (84 51) 823431 or 823122 or 824555 or 823258, Fax (84 51) 823431*. This company offers some of the most comprehensive tour packages ranging from four days to two weeks. Tours originate in Ho Chi Minh City, Hanoi and Danang. They specialize in arranging tours for French and American veterans.

Fidio Tourist, *73-75 Dong Khoi Street, District 1, Ho Chi Minh City. Tel. (84 8) 811561, Fax (84 8) 223571*. Arranges adventurous trips such as scuba diving, trekking in the highlands and safaris. Itineraries range from nine to thirty days.

Lam Dong Province Tourism Office, *4 Tran Quoc Toan Street, Dalat, Tel. (84 63) 822125 or 822304 or 822520, Fax (84 63) 822661*. This company arranges motorcycle tours through the mountains of Vietnam. In the Central Highlands trip from Dalat to Kontum, you visit and sleep in minority villages. Other itineraries include Danang Truong Son mountains.

Saigon Tourist, *49 Le Thanh Ton Street, District 1, Ho Chi Minh City. Tel. (84 8) 8230101 or 8295834 or 8298914, Fax (84 8) 8224987 or 8225516*. The government tourist authority in the south, Saigon Tourist arranges everything from car rentals and individual reservations to comprehensive bus tours. One of their specialties is "shore excursion" package trips designed for passengers on cruise ships at a port-of-call.

T & T Co. Ltd., *9 Dong Khoi Street, District 1, Ho Chi Minh City. Tel. (84 8) 8299363 or 8251564, Fax (84 8) 8295832*. If the 16-day cross-country motorcycle journeys are not to your liking, this company has more standard bus or car travel. Short tours include weekends at the beach and mountain-climbing.

Vietnam Travel Bureau, *140 Dong Khoi Street, District 1, Ho Chi Minh City. Tel. (84 8) 8251471, Fax (84 8) 8290386*. In addition to tours of

Vietnam, excursions to Phnom Penh and Angkor Wat, Cambodia and Vientiane, Laos can be arranged through the Vietnam Travel Bureau.

Voiles Vietnam, *17 Pham Ngoc Thach Street, District 3, Ho Chi Minh City. Tel. (84 8) 8296750 or 8231589 or 8231590, fax (84 8) 8231591.* Sailing up the Mekong River or along the coast of Vietnam aboard a beautiful oriental junk is probably one of the most pleasurable ways to see Vietnam; this, as well as private tours by car, can be arranged.

GETTING AROUND VIETNAM

The most overwhelming aspect of traveling through Vietnam is the long periods of time required to travel short distances. The public transportation system—slow trains, highways in disrepair, and break-down-plagued buses—leave travelers lacking their most valuable commodity, time. Careful planning and a relaxed pace are the essential elements of a good trip.

Getting around Vietnam in not as difficult as it was just a few years ago, when travel permits were required for most cities. Regardless of how independent you may want to be, eventually you will probably join a tour of some sort.

"Cafe" tours are a Vietnamese phenomena. These are restaurants which provide transportation and budget tours throughout the country. These tours cater specifically to English-speakers. You simply go to the cafe and sign on for the scheduled tours; reservations are not necessary.

BY AIR

Vietnam Airlines serves 16 domestic cities, and is the only airline that operates within Vietnam. The airline is in a constant state of upgrading and improving its facilities and service. There are two main booking offices in Ho Chi Minh City, *116 Nguyen Hue Street, Tel. (84 8) 8292118* and *15B Dinh Tien Hoang Street, Tel. (84 8) 8299910*; one in Danang, *35 Tran Phu Street, Tel. (84 52) 821130 or 822094*; and one in Hanoi, *1 Quang Trung Street, Tel. (84 4) 8250888 or 8268913*.

You can make reservations, but advance booking does not lower fares. Excursion and group rates are not available, although the Vietnam Airlines timetable states such fares are offered. For an idea of cost, the flight between Ho Chi Minh City and Hanoi takes two hours and costs $175; Hue to Hanoi takes one-and-a-half hours and costs $89. Round-trip tickets cost the same as two one-way fares.

BY BUS

Regular buses serve the entire country. They are often overcrowded and over-loaded, with baskets, animals and packages strapped to the top. Passengers sit on wooden benches and if lucky, get to be by the open window. The ride might be rough, but many travelers report it is pleasant, and the only way to really get in touch with the country. As is the case in many communist countries, foreigners must pay prices that are higher than those charged to Vietnamese passengers.

Bus trips are slow and unpredictable. Usually you must show up early, around 6 am, to get a seat. The driver then waits until enough travelers arrive to make a profitable trip. On the road, the old buses often break down or blow tires.

BY CAFE TOUR & OPEN TICKET BUS

The popular "cafe" tours are building an infrastructure of tourist-class bus transportation. A few cafes compete in this arena; all offer reasonable service. **Sinh Cafe** in Ho Chi Minh City and **Queen's Cafe** in Hanoi are the largest tour operators and have the best reputation for consistent satisfaction. The cafes have affiliates in the cities on the tour schedules, many of which offer local tours.

Examples of destinations of cafe tours include budget trips to the Mekong Delta or Halong Bay, and day-long mini-van tours of the DMZ or the Perfume Pagoda outside Hanoi. The tours are inexpensive and circumvent the travel permits that are still required in some areas. Many travelers hire cars and guides to reach the remote highlands more easily. None of these arrangements must be made in advance. These tours offer some of the best and most exciting ways to explore Vietnam and allow you to simply show up, then make plans.

THE OPEN TICKET BUS ROUTES

The different cafes that run open ticket bus service follow basically the same route. You can take the buses along the reverse route from Hue to Ho Chi Minh City as well.

Ho Chi Minh City to Dalat: the 120 kilometer trip takes about 5 hours.

Dalat to Nha Trang: the 214 kilometers takes at least 6 hours.

Nha Trang to Hoi An: the longest journey on the route takes 11 hours, and covers 530 kilometer route.

Hoi An to Hue: the 120 kilometers trip on windy mountain roads takes at least 6 hours.

The "Open Ticket" bus is a popular means of traveling between Ho Chi Minh City and Hue. One inexpensive ticket ($35) allows you to go to Dalat, Nha Trang, Hoi An, Danang and Hue. The catch is that it takes one day of travel between each city. Full-size motor coaches, mini buses and vans make the trip, and they do not run at night. This is the preferred mode of transport for increasing numbers of travelers, and you are sure to make friends along the way.

BY CAR

Car travel allows you to see Vietnam's beautiful rural areas. You can experience the fishing villages and farming hamlets that many travelers never see. Sights such as Cham ruins and remote highland villages are also accessible.

At the present time it is not possible to rent a car and drive in Vietnam. Tourists can hire a car with a driver, and this can be the most efficient way to see the country. A few points should be considered if you hire a car and driver.

Be certain to meet the driver or guide before you are scheduled to leave in order to make sure you can communicate. Agree upon how much freedom you have in the agenda. Can you alter the plans once on the road? Reach an understanding about making stops. You should be able to request a photo or rest stop whenever necessary. Know the specifics of what you are expected to pay. Usually the set fee for meals and room for a driver or guide is $15 per day. The driver should pay any tolls or fines as well as gas and repair. The driver is also responsible to have all travel permits and insurance papers. Generally you pay half the cost at the outset, and the final half upon arrival. Always get receipts and remember to tip your driver and guide. Clarify all of this and any questions you may have before you set-out, to ensure a comfortable journey.

Even if you have your own driver and guide, some areas (especially the Central Highland cities) require you to hire a local guide for sightseeing. The government-approved local guides charge about $20 per day, and are hired through the local tourist authority. You are expected to buy your guide lunch or dinner. There are stiff fines for attempting to sidestep the formality. These guides usually speak fluent English and have a good deal of information about local history and folklore. However, they take tourists only to set, approved areas.

In general the roads are rough. Over half the roads were considered very poor in a recent government survey. Flooding is a common danger. Tourist cars stay on the main highways, as there are areas considered unsafe due to bandits. When traveling by car, expect long periods of time with no chance of food or toilets. Often the road-side cafes are fly-infested and unclean. (You have the freedom to choose your stops by car, but not by bus.) Along the coastal highways you will find snacks and water sold almost everywhere. When in the Central Highlands it is best to bring your own supplies.

Twelve highways run through Vietnam, but not all are in good condition. The main drag and best known highway is Highway 1, built in conjunction with Americans during the war. It runs from the Chinese border in the north through Hanoi, to Ho Chi Minh City and south to Go Dau Ha. Highway 19 runs from Qui Nhon to Pleiku, and may be the best quality stretch of road in the country. Highway 14 connects Hue to the cities of the Central Highlands. Highway 20 connects Ho Chi Minh City (from Dau Giay, about 85 km north of Ho Chi Minh City) to Dalat. Highway 20 then dips south connecting Dalat to the coastal town of Phan Rang.

HIGHWAY 14

As you leave Buon Ma Thout you pass through the rhythmic lines of rubber trees, then these give way to coffee plants. The women of this region wear long skirts and wrap their heads in colorful scarves. You may see them coming home from the fields carrying anything from farm equipment to babies in the baskets on their backs. North of Buon Ma Thout the road is in generally in good condition; the greatest hazards being children, chickens and dogs sitting and playing in the street. The gently rolling landscape and pine trees give way to palm trees. Ny Than is a mini-metropolis with two gas stations, a pharmacy and post office all on the highway.

BY MOTORBIKE

Motorbikes are not just for the Vietnamese. Many tourists just cannot resist the call of the open road. Some tourists buy motorcycles, ride to the other end of the country and sell them. Most of the motorcycles available are old, and a bit rough. You should be handy with a wrench before undertaking such a journey.

Notices of vehicles for sale appear on bulletin boards of the Sinh Cafe (Saigon) and Queen's Cafe (in Hanoi). For freewheeling fun without the commitment, rent motorbikes for local day trips. Keep in mind the nasty law that stipulates foreign drivers are responsible for any accident in which they are involved.

BY TRAIN

The Vietnamese trains are old, but they still get you where you are going. There are six classes of seats, the most expensive, the air-conditioned soft berth, is available between Ho Chi Minh City and Hanoi and costs nearly as much as a flight ($160). Tickets can be purchased at train stations or some travel offices. You must pay cash for train tickets.

THE SIX CLASSES ON VIETNAMESE TRAINS

Special soft berth: two-bed compartment with air-conditioning
Soft berth: Four beds in one compartment
Hard berth: Six beds with no padding in one compartment
Soft seat: the seats are small and can be uncomfortable on long trips.
Hard seat: wooden bench seats
Common car: benches run under the windows; many passengers sit on the floor.

The hard seats often fill up and can get very crowded. Prices for sleepers vary; low berths are the most desirable, and top berths are terribly hot in the summer. You must make reservations about four days in advance for soft berth tickets. During periods of increased travel, such as the Tet Holiday, more cars are added to accommodate passengers.

On long hauls, simple meals of greens, meat and rice may be available on the train. At most stops vendors come aboard selling baskets of bread and snacks. Sometimes kids will run along the top of train cars to make the selling rounds.

The trains are relatively safe, and more reliable than buses. Tourists report few inconveniences traveling by rail. At places, the train moves excruciatingly slowly. Keep the wire window covers down at all times; some people pitch rocks at passing trains, others may reach or crawl in the window.

Passengers taking the overnight Hanoi/Hue route are pleased with the service. Overnight trains connect Hanoi with Lao Cai, the Chinese border town closest to Sapa. This train now continues into China, making the border crossing a simple task.

The Reunification Express runs between Hanoi and Ho Chi Minh City. The trip takes 38, 42 or 46 hours. Making your way along the north/south routes is easy; service from east to west is almost non-existent with the exception of the Hanoi-Haiphong line in the north. Tickets are available from railway stations and tourist offices.

You can cross the Chinese border by train through Dang Dong (in Vietnam). The Vietnamese and Chinese trains use different size track, so you must change trains at the border. The trip from Hanoi to Ping Xiang, China takes 52 hours and a one-way ticket costs $186. In order to re-enter Vietnam you must cross at Dang Dong.

The government is working in cooperation with foreign interests to improve tourist rail lines. A line is planned to connect Dalat to Ho Chi Minh City. Fortification of bridges, upgrading track, and adding new cars are among future projects.

GETTING AROUND CITIES

Cities do not have extensive public transportation systems yet. Foreigners are not allowed to ride city buses.

BY BICYCLE

Bicycles are a popular form of transportation for the Vietnamese, although motorbikes are overtaking bicycles in larger cities. This is an inexpensive way to get around a city. Most serious bicyclists do not travel on the highways because the major routes are often dangerously crowded.

If you plan to ride a bicycle, keep in mind that bicycle helmets cannot be found in Vietnam; you must bring your own. The drawbacks to bikes are the chaotic streets and pollution.

BY CYCLO

The most popular and visible mode of transport is the **cyclo**. These three-wheeled bicycles are peddled by a driver and can carry one or two passengers. Riding by cyclo is not only a romantic mode of travel, but it is down right fun. During rush hour in Ho Chi Minh City you are in for an exciting ride, as your cyclo driver weaves through the bustling traffic.

In Ho Chi Minh City, tourists often hire cyclos by the hour to tour the pagodas. A fair price falls between $1 and $2 per hour. You should be able to get just about anywhere within a city for $1 (11,000 dong).

Set the price before you take the ride. Cyclo drivers are earning a bad reputation. Some drivers try to get more than the agreed fare after the ride by arguing that there was a misunderstanding. Another scam is the driver turning down a dark alley and stealing your purse or pack.

BY FOOT

You will have no problem getting around most cities on foot. Walking is the best way to get a feel for the city and its inhabitants. Most people combine walking with occasional cyclo rides to sights that are far off the beaten path.

It is important to drink plenty of water, since the heat can dehydrate you pretty quickly as you're tromping around.

BY TAXI

On short rides, a taxi may cost less than a cyclo. So many taxi services have begun service in the past year that regulation is a problem, especially in the North. Be certain that the meter is on or the price is set.

There is no need to be overly cautious, however. Overall, cyclo and taxi drivers are friendly; some of your best conversations may be with them.

7. BASIC INFORMATION

AIRLINE OFFICES IN VIETNAM

Should the urge strike you to fly off to another Asian destination, or perhaps to Europe, here is a list of major airlines you can contact, with both their Hanoi and Ho Chi Minh City offices:

- **Air France**, *1 Ba Trieu Street, Hanoi. Tel. (84 4) 8253484; 130 Dong Khoi Street, Ho Chi Minh City. Tel. (84 8) 8290981*
- **Asiana Airlines**, *143 Ham Nghi Street, District 1, Ho Chi Minh City. Tel. (84 8) 8222685, Fax (84 8) 8222710*
- **Cathay Pacific**, *27 Ly Thuong Kiet Street, Hanoi. Tel. (84 4) 8267298; 58 Dong Khoi Street, District 1, Ho Chi Minh City. Tel. (84 8) 8223203*
- **China Southern Airlines**, *29 Ly Thai To Street, Hanoi. Tel. (84 4) 8269233, Fax (84 4) 8269232; 52B Pham Hong Thai Street, District 1, Ho Chi Minh City. Tel. (84 8) 8291172, Fax (84 8) 8296800*
- **China Airlines**, *132 Dong Khoi Street, District 1, Ho Chi Minh City. Tel. (84 8) 8251388, Fax (84 8) 8251390*
- **Eva Air**, *129 Dong Khoi Street, District 1, Ho Chi Minh City. Tel. (84 8) 8224488, Fax (84 8) 8223567*
- **Garuda Indonesia Airlines**, *106 Nguyen Hue Street, Ho Chi Minh City. Tel. (84 8) 8293644, Fax (84 8) 8293688*
- **KLM Royal Dutch Airlines**, *244 Pasteur Street, District 3, Ho Chi Minh City. Tel. (84 8) 831990, Fax (84 8) 8231989*
- **Lufthansa**, *134 Dong Khoi Street, District 1, Ho Chi Minh City. Tel. (84 8) 8298529, Fax (84 8) 8298537*
- **Malaysia Airlines**, *15 Ngo Quyen Street (Hotel Metropole), Hanoi. Tel. (84 4) 8268821, Fax (84 4) 8266920; 116 Nguyen Hue Street, District 1, Ho Chi Minh City. Tel. (84 8) 8242885, Fax (84 4) 8242884*
- **Pacific Airlines**, *100 Le Duan Street, Hanoi. Tel. (84 4) 8515356; 27B Nguyen Dinh Chieu Street, District 1, Ho Chi Minh City. Tel. (84 8) 8230930, Fax (84 8) 8231248*
- **Philippine Airlines**, *4A Le Loi Street, District 1 Ho Chi Minh City. Tel. (84 8) 8292113*

• **Quantas Airlines**, *24 Ly Tu Trong Street, District 1, Ho Chi Minh City. Tel. (84 8) 8293257, Fax (84 8) 8292218*
• **Royal Air Cambodge**, *16 Ho Huan Nghiep Street, Ho Chi Minh City. Tel. (84 8) 8907302, Fax (84 8) 8299462*
• **Singapore Air**, *15 Ngo Quyen Street (Hotel Metropole), Hanoi. Tel. (84 4) 8268888, Fax (84 4) 8268666; 6 Le Loi Street, District 1, Ho Chi Minh City. Tel. (84 8) 8231583, Fax (84 8) 8231554*
• **Thai Airways**, *25 Ly Thuong Kiet Street, Hanoi. Tel. (84 4) 8266893, Fax (84 4) 8223465; 65 Nguyen Du Street, District 1, Ho Chi Minh City. Tel. (84 8) 8292810, Fax (84 8) 8223465*
• **Vietnam Airlines**, *1 Quang Trung Street, Hanoi. Tel. (84 4) 8250888, Fax (84 4) 8248989; 116 Nguyen Hue Street, Ho Chi Minh City. Tel. (84 8) 8292118*

BUSINESS HOURS & HOLIDAYS

Offices are generally open from 7 am to 4:30 pm. Most commercial businesses open early and close by 6 pm. Markets and small stores may begin to open as early as sunrise. Restaurants usually shut-down during the afternoon and reopen for dinner, which is served early, between 6 - 9 pm.

As more tourists enter the country, more establishments keep longer hours. Restaurants and bars which stay open late are not uncommon. Shops in tourist areas usually keep extended hours. Offices of foreign companies usually keep regular western hours of 9 am to 5 pm.

Government offices and museums open at 7:30 am, close for one hour during lunch and remain open until 4:30 pm. Saturday is a normal work day for most, and a half-day for some. Sunday is the day-off.

Both the Gregorian and Chinese calendars are used in Vietnam. The Chinese calendar begins in the Gregorian year 2637 BC. The year 1997 in the Chinese calendar is 4635.

Every 60 years represents a cycle in the Chinese calendar. In 1985 the seventy-eighth cycle began. Within these 60-year cycles are smaller periods of 10 years (repeated six times) and 12 years (repeated five times). Ten year periods correspond to natural elements and 12 year periods to the Chinese zodiac.

Tet, or the traditional New Year celebration, is the most important holiday of the year. It begins about three days before Lunar New Year; families spend four to seven days together. The date of Tet varies on the Gregorian calendar, falling toward the end of January or beginning of February. Businesses which rely on tourists, such as hotels, shops (in major tourist centers) and restaurants remain open during Tet.

OBSERVED PUBLIC HOLIDAYS

*January 1: **New Year Day***
*February 3: **Vietnamese Communist Party Founding Day***
*end of January: **Tet**, the traditional New Year Celebration*
*April 30: **Liberation Day** (the anniversary of the fall of Saigon)*
*May 1: **International Worker's Day** (May Day)*
*May 19: **Ho Chi Minh's Birthday***
*September 2: **Independence Day***

COST OF LIVING & TRAVEL

Vietnam is gearing up for and trying to cater to luxury travelers. There is no need to spend a lot of money to have a good time. The most memorable parts of your travel experience—having a cool, fresh coconut cut open for juice, taking a boat ride in the Mekong, trekking through the northern highlands—will be the least taxing on your budget.

For an average of $30 per night you can find comfortable accommodation; and you can spend less than half of this if you give up amenities such as air-conditioning and television. Two to three is an ideal number for traveling here. Often hotels charge the same for a single or double.

Transportation can be the largest part of a budget. Airline tickets are not cheap in the country, or to foreign destinations. Having ample time to take trains, tourist and local buses and for walking will cut expenses dramatically. Moreover, the less time spent in the air means there will be more time to see the countryside and meet people.

Renting a car requires that you hire a driver as well. This will cost about $50 per day. Tours available though cafes in Hanoi and Ho Chi Minh City offer reasonably priced excursions to most of the popular destinations.

Food is an affordable treat in Vietnam. An average meal costs only a few dollars. For about ten dollars you will have a superior meal. Imported alcohol is the easiest way to make your meal cost more than it needs to. The good local beer is cheap. Incidental expenses such as bottles of mineral water, add up.

ELECTRICITY

Electricity may be either 220 volts or 110 volts and run on either a plug with two straight, parallel prongs or two round prongs. The round-prong plugs are the most common. Grounded plugs also vary, with the third prong being oval. Adapters for Hong Kong are of no use, while certain adapters from Bangkok work in Vietnam.

Brownouts and blackouts, which used to happen daily in some areas, are much less frequent today. Many better hotels and restaurants have their own generators which kick on about five to ten minutes after power goes down. Power surges are a problem, and when operating a computer you should always guard against these with a power surge protector.

Many of the wires hanging over the street, in restaurants, and shops are live, so exercise caution.

EMBASSIES & CONSULATES IN VIETNAM

These are some major embassies and consulates you may have need of while you're in Vietnam:

- **Embassy of Australia**, *66 Ly Thuong Kiet Street, Hanoi. Tel. (84 4) 8252763 or 8261904;* **Consulate**, *5B Ton Duc Thang Street, District 1, Ho Chi Minh City. Tel. (84 8) 8296035*
- **Embassy of Belgium**, *50 Nguyen Thai Hoc Street, Hanoi. Tel. (84 4) 8230688;* **Consulate**, *236 Dien Bien Phu Street, District 3, Ho Chi Minh City. Tel. (84 8) 8294526*
- **Embassy of the United Kingdom**, *16 Ly Thuong Kiet Street, Hanoi. Tel. (84 4) 8252610;* **Consulate**, *261 Dien Bien Phu Street, District 3, Ho Chi Minh City. Tel. (84 8) 8298433*
- **Embassy of Cambodia**, *71 Tran Hung Dao Street, Hanoi. Tel. (84 4) 8253788;* **Consulate**, *41 Phung Khac Khoan Street, District 3, Ho Chi Minh City. Tel. (84 8) 8292751*
- **Embassy of Canada**, *39 Nguyen Dinh Chieu Street, Hanoi. Tel. (84 4) 8265840;* **Consulate**, *203 Dong Khoi, Suite 303, District 1, Ho Chi Minh City. Tel. (84 8) 8242000*
- **Embassy of the Peoples' Republic of China**, *46 Hoang Dieu Street, Hanoi. Tel. (84 4) 8253736;* **Consulate**, *39 Nguyen Thi Minh Khai Street, Ho Chi Minh City. Tel. (84 8) 8292457*
- **Embassy of France**, *57 Tran Hung Dao Street, Hanoi. Tel. (84 4) 825719;* **Consulat**, *27 Xo Viet Nghi Tinh Street, Ho Chi Minh City. Tel. (84 8) 8297231*
- **Embassy of India**, *58-60 Tran Hung Dao Street, Hanoi. Tel. (84 4) 8253409 or 8252644;* **Consulate**, *49 Tran Quoc Thao Street, Ho Chi Minh City. Tel. (84 8) 8294498 or 8231539*
- **Embassy of Indonesia**, *50 Ngo Quyen Street, Hanoi. Tel. (84 4) 8257969;* **Consulate**, *18 Phung Khac Khoan Street, Ho Chi Minh City. Tel. (84 8) 8223799*
- **Embassy of Japan**, *61 Truong Chinh, Hanoi. Tel. (84 4) 8527924;* **Consulate**, *13-17 Nguyen Hue Street, District 1, Ho Chi Minh City. Tel. (84 8) 8225314*

- **Embassy of Laos**, *40 Quang Trung Street, Hanoi. Tel. (84 4) 8268724*; **Consulate**, *181 Hai Ba Trung, Ho Chi Minh City. Tel. (84 8) 8299272*
- **Embassy of Malaysia**, *82 Van Phuc Quarter Block A3, Hanoi. Tel. (84 4) 8253371*; **Consulate**, *53 Nguyen Dinh Chieu, Ho Chi Minh City. Tel. (84 8) 8299023*
- **Embassy of Myanmar** (formerly Burma), *Van Phuc Diplomatic Quarter A3, Hanoi. Tel. (84 4) 8253369*
- **Embassy of The Philippines**, *27B Tran Hung Dao Street, Hanoi. Tel. (84 4) 8257948*
- **Embassy of Singapore**, *41-43 Tran Phu Street, Hanoi. Tel. (84 4) 8233966*; **Consulate**, *5 Phung Khac Khoan Street, Ho Chi Minh City. Tel. (84 8) 8225173*
- **Embassy of South Korea**, *29 Nguyen Dinh Chieu Street, Hanoi. Tel. (84 4) 8226677*; **Consulate**, *107 Nguyen Du Street, Ho Chi Minh City. Tel. (84 8) 8225757*
- **Embassy of Thailand**, *63-65 Hoang Dieu Street, Hanoi. Tel. (84 4) 8235092*; **Consulate**, *77 Tran Quoc Thao Street, District 3, Ho Chi Minh City. Tel. (84 8) 8222637*
- **Embassy of the United States**, *7 Lang Ha, Hanoi. Tel. (84 4) 8431500*

ETIQUETTE

Vietnamese people are very gracious and polite people. And they make every effort to have foreign guests feel comfortable. Most places you go to eat will have knives and forks (in addition to chopsticks), for example. The Vietnamese attempt to respect other cultures. Tourists should reciprocate by understanding that things work differently than they may be used to. For example, the buses may not run on schedule, misunderstandings may arise, expectations may not be met. Losing your temper does not help a situation; smiles and patience work better as a way to cross cultural barriers and are far more effective.

From the workers' simple outfits in the rice fields to western-style business suits in the city, the dress of Vietnamese men and women is conservative. Long sleeved shirts and long pants are worn. Tourists wearing shorts are usually tolerated, unless you enter an area that is culturally sensitive, such as a mosque. Keep in mind that although tolerant, people may be judgmental. There is a Vietnamese phrase "*tay ba lo*" which denotes a traveler who is not culturally sensitive or aware.

Unfortunately, you can not expect hospitality at every turn. There are still problems with the police taking petty bribes (especially in the north). Cyclo and taxi drivers have been known to overcharge customers. Petty crime, like pick-pocketing, is common in Ho Chi Minh City. The best defense against such incidents is caution. Don't allow your trip to be ruined over the growing pains of a newly open economy.

FESTIVALS

The many ethnic groups which make up Vietnam keep their traditions intact. Their celebrations offer insight to the unique culture of each region. The dates vary each year; approximate months of the festivals are given below. Lunar months are approximately twenty-eight days and the first day of the first lunar month begins on Tet, so if you know what day Tet is in a given year, you can better approximate the date of the festival.

January

Lieu Doi martial arts competition in Ha Nam Ninh features different forms of traditional fighting (on the second day of the first lunar month).

The Keo people have a temple festival which is celebrated in Vu Thu District of the Thinh Binh Province.

The Festival of Dong Da Hill in Hanoi (on the fifth day of the first month of the lunar year), celebrates the 1789 military defeat of Chinese invaders by King Quang Trung.

Bani Sec people conduct Cham celebrations of Tet (on the sixth day of the first lunar month).

February

In the central highland town of Buon Ma Thout elephant races are held by the Mnong people (on the tenth day of the first lunar month).

The Lim festival in Ha Bac is marked by children meeting on the riverbank and in pagodas to sing traditional songs and features the "Quan Ho" folk song contest (on the thirteenth to the fifteenth days of the first lunar month).

Tay Ninh celebrates the arrival of spring on Ba Den mountain (on the fifteenth day of the first lunar month).

The Trung Sisters are honored in a festival at the Hai Ba Trung Temple in Hanoi (on the fifth and sixth days of the second lunar month).

March

Traditional ceremonies and folk songs are performed at the Hang Kenh Communal House in Haiphong during a three-day festival (from the sixteenth to the eighteenth days of the second lunar month.)

Vinh Phu the Hung Temple festival marks the coming of spring (on the tenth day of the third lunar month).

April

The Love Market (on the twenty-seventh day of the third month of the lunar year) in Khau Vai, Ha Giang Province, is the annual courtship meeting place for the area Tay, Nung, Giay and Hmong peoples. Khau Vai is a 24 kilometer drive from the provincial capital, Meo Vac.

Traditional celebration of Tet for the Khmer people is held throughout the Mekong Delta (on the second day of the fourth lunar month).

The defeat of the An invaders is marked with the performance of a play in the Giong festival in Hanoi (on the ninth day of the fourth lunar month).

July

The Lan Ong festival: ancient rites, traditional theater performances, and cock fights (on the thirteenth day of the seventh lunar month).

August

A buffalo fighting festival is held in Haiphong (on the ninth day of the eighth lunar month).

The Tran Hung Dao temple in Ho Chi Minh City conducts the Tran Hung Dao celebration (on the twentieth day of the eighth lunar month).

October

The Ghe Ngo rowing festival is celebrated on the waterways of Soc Trang in the Mekong Delta. This is a Khmer tradition (on the fourteenth day of the tenth lunar month.)

GETTING MARRIED

In order to marry a Vietnamese citizen in Vietnam you must receive the approval of the municipal or provincial People's Committee. This is done by registering the marriage. A foreigner must present a valid birth certificate, documentation that he or she is not married and not infected with a sexually transmitted disease or HIV. And finally, certification that he or she is free of mental disease must accompany the registration.

After all this is submitted, a police check is run. If the applicant is clean, the People's Committee takes over. Once the Chairman of the People's Committee signs the registration, the couple has seven days to present their passports and be registered in the "marriage registration book." The entire procedure takes about three months.

A marriage may be registered at a consular office (although the consul does not perform the ceremony). This should take about 45 days. In order for the marriage to be legally binding in Vietnam, the Vietnamese citizen must register the marriage with the People's Committee.

HEALTH CONCERNS

Vietnamese doctors are well-trained. However, medical facilities lag about 20 years behind Western standards. In small towns it may be difficult to find a clinic and impossible to find an English-speaking doctor.

Pharmacies are easy to find and sell various imported brands of common medication. However, there are no standards in place for regulation of medication, so buyer beware. Medicine boxes often stand in glass cases exposed to the baking sun. Also, fake medication is not uncommon. Since high quality medical supplies may be hard to come by, travelers often bring their own, including antibiotics, anti-diarrhea tablets and syringes. Be certain to have a valid prescription label on medication that can not be bought over-the-counter in order to guard against hassles at customs.

Before you leave home, check with your **health insurance** company about coverage in Vietnam. It may be necessary to buy supplemental coverage for the trip. The Vietnamese government runs a program which provides assistance with emergency evacuations of foreigners. You may purchase traveler's health insurance in Vietnam which will cover the cost of treatment at government-run clinics. Generally medical facilities demand payment in cash at the time of treatment.

In order to maintain your health, drink plenty of water. (Bottled water, that is; not even residents drink tap water.) The tropical climate allows for easy **dehydration**. Take it easy for the first week; exhaustion brought on by climate, change of food and jet lag can seriously weaken the immune system. Curbing alcohol intake and exposure to the sun will help ease the adjustment. The country's high humidity may aggravate allergies (especially sensitivity to mold and dust) and asthma.

A common ailment of travelers, even those who have spent time in Asia, is **diarrhea**. Over the counter medication and drinking plenty of fluids should curb most cases in a few days. You should see a doctor if symptoms persist more than three days.

No matter how small the town, you are likely to see educational billboards illustrating the perils of **HIV** infection, which is becoming an increasingly more serious problem. To guard against HIV, practice very safe sex and use only imported condoms. Bring syringes should you need an injection. Blood used in transfusions is not screened, and is very risky. Travelers should also avoid going to a dentist, or getting acupuncture, manicures or pedicures. Barbers and hairdressers, especially those who cut hair on the street or in markets, often do not sterilize their instruments.

Refer to Chapter 6, *Planning Your Trip*, for recommended **immunizations** and information on the diseases that you need to be aware of in Vietnam.

HOSPITALS

In the event of an emergency, a foreigner can receive treatment at hospitals in major cities and clinics throughout the country. In some cases it may be necessary to provide proof of the ability to pay for services.

For foreigners living abroad, the **Asia Emergency Assistance** (AEA), *230 Nam Ky Khoi Nghia, Ho Chi Minh City, Tel. (84 8) 8298520, Fax (84 8) 8298551*, provides emergency medical assistance to its members. Clinics throughout the country offer care which meets international standards. The staff operate an around-the-clock emergency hotline. For membership information contact AEA, Representative Office, *65 Nguyen Du Street, District 1, Ho Chi Minh City.*

The **SOS IMC Medical Center**, *151-153 Vo Thi Sau, District 3, Ho Chi Minh City. Tel. (84 8) 8294386, Fax (84 8) 8242846, 24 hour Emergency line (84 8) 8242866*, is an international assistance service agency and clinic which arranges medical treatment and consultations by foreign doctors.

In the event of emergency, the official hospital for foreigners is **Cho Ray Hospital** in Ho Chi Minh City at *201 B Nguyen Chi Thanh Street, Tel. (84 8) 8554137, 8554138, emergency number: 8554137, extension 115.* Cho Ray has English speaking staff.

In Ho Chi Minh City there is a centrally-located **Emergency Clinic** at *125 Le Loi, District 1, Tel. (84 8) 8292071 or 8291711 or 8225966*, which is open 24 hours per day and has English-speaking staff.

Other hospitals designated to treat foreigners include: **Thong Nhat Hospital**, *1 Ly Thuong Kiet Street, Tan Binh District, Ho Chi Minh City, Tel. (84 8) 8642141, emergencies: 8640339, extension 15*; and for pediatric treatment: **Gralle Hospital**, *33 Nguyen Du Street, District 1, Ho Chi Minh City, Tel. (84 8) 8298385.*

Medical Treatment in Hanoi

The **AEA** has an office in Hanoi: *4 Tran Hung Dao, 4th Floor, Hanoi, Tel. (84 4) 8213555, Fax (84 4) 8213523.*

The hospital for foreigners is the **International Department of Bach Mai Hospital**, *Giai Phong Street, Tel. (84 4) 8522083 or 8522089.*

The **Viet Muc Hospital**, *48 Trang Thi Street, Hanoi, Tel. (84 4) 8253531*, operates 24 hour emergency surgery facility and has English speakers on staff.

And the **Friendship Hospital**, *1 Tran Khanh Du, Hanoi, Tel. (84 8) 8252231*, maintains rooms for foreigners.

MAGAZINES - ENGLISH LANGUAGE

A slick, glossy magazine with in-depth reading on interesting cultural issue that carry economic impact is the *Vietnam Economic Times* (subscriptions, *Tel. (84 4) 8452411, Fax (84 8) 8451888*). Examples of past articles include a feature about the commercial trade of ethnic minority artisans, and a cover-story about the business concerns of returning overseas Vietnamese. This monthly costs $5 per issue.

Vietnam Today (subscriptions: EBSCO Services, *PO Box 1943, Birmingham, AL, 35201-1943, USA, Fax 205/991-1479*) is a business-oriented magazine which claims to be the "only publication completely independent of any other organization." It is published in Singapore and distributed worldwide. In addition to economics articles, the Night & Day section has restaurant and movie listings and a photo society page.

MONEY & BANKING

Credit cards and travelers checks may be used in most tourist destinations throughout Vietnam. Most hotels and some restaurants and shops accept credit cards. However, standard practice is to charge a 3 percent fee directly to the customer for any transaction. Travelers checks may be exchanged at banks and hotels; fees from 2 to 5 percent are charged.

The easiest form of payment is US dollars. Although the laws stipulate that all transactions must be made in Vietnamese **dong**, dollars are universally accepted. Prices are often given in dollars, not dong. An establishment may accept your dollars, and simply change them to dong at their own exchange desk. Always ask for the rate in dong and pay with the currency which offers the best exchange.

DOLLAR-DONG EXCHANGE RATE
$1 US = 10,900 Dong

The exchange rate is currently 10,900 dong to one US dollar. In some cases better rates are given when exchanging foreign currency bills of large denomination. People leaving exchange offices with bags of money is not an uncommon sight, since the largest denomination bill is 50,000 dong. Dong are cumbersome and dealing in such large quantities can be confusing.

Western Union has money transfer offices in Vietnam. Cash can be wired from the Untied States and received in Vietnamese dong. The money may be picked-up at a Western Union office or delivered to the recipient. A telegram may be included with the transfer.

NAMES

Vietnamese names are written with the family name first. A separating name may come next; for women this is usually "Thi," for men "van, ngoc, and xuan" are the most common. The person's given name is written next.

NEWSPAPERS - ENGLISH LANGUAGE

There are a number of English-language newspapers in Vietnam, published both in Hanoi and Ho Chi Minh City. Most publications are sponsored, at least in part, by a government agency.

The nation's only English-language daily is *Viet Nam News*. The articles in this paper cover economics, politics, and international news with an emphasis on the region. The back page is devoted to sports. At 3,000 dong (27¢) per issue, you can afford to read it every day. For subscriptions, contact the paper at: *79 Ly Thuong Kiet Street, Hanoi, Tel. (84 4) 8260987.*

Vietnam Investment Review focuses on economics and the articles emphasize development and foreign investment activity in Vietnam. The weekly includes a pull out section called "Time Out" that gives information about new restaurants and cultural activities, mostly about Hanoi. Each issue costs $2 at the newsstand. Contact their Subscription Department at: *175 Nguyen Thai Hoc Street, Hanoi, Tel. (84 4) 8450537, Fax (84 4) 8457937.*

POST OFFICE

Mail service from Vietnam is slow and expensive. Post offices are easily found throughout the country, and most hotels sell postage stamps. Express Mail Service (EMS) guarantees domestic delivery within 48 hours, and international delivery to 30 countries from two to 10 days. Private mail services such as DHL, Federal Express and UPS have offices in Ho Chi Minh City and Hanoi.

Larger post offices offer international pay-by-use phones, fax transmission and special services such as flower delivery. If you need to receive mail, have it marked *poste-restante*, and the post office will hold it. You can pick it up upon presentation of identification.

Although service is improving, some problems persist. In small towns stamps may be removed after letters are mailed. To guard against this, mail letters only when you can watch the attendant cancel the stamps, or purchase only postage that is applied by machine to your letters.

RADIO

The national radio station, **Voice of Vietnam**, broadcasts on multiple channels in a variety of languages including languages of the H'mong and

Khmer. English, French and Spanish broadcasts are regularly scheduled. English language broadcasts for expatriates on Channel 5 (1242 KHz) run daily at 6:30 am, 5 pm, 7:30 pm, and 8:30 pm.

SHOPPING

Both silk weaving and the art of lacquerware are native crafts of Vietnam. Vietnamese silk is of extremely fine quality. You can purchase silk either from the roll, or have clothes tailor-made in Ho Chi Minh City, Hoi An, Danang or Hanoi. Hoi An has a booming tourist-made tailor industry.

For more information about shopping, see each destination chapter throughout the book.

STAYING OUT OF TROUBLE

Traveling in Vietnam is often a hassle-free experience for those who exercise reasonable caution. For this reason many women travel alone without feeling threatened or harassed. However, as more foreigners enter the country, theft and violence begins to increase. Ho Chi Minh City is notorious for drive-by snatchings of sunglasses and cameras. Pickpockets often work in groups and abound in tourist areas, especially around markets. A common scam is for a child to distract a tourist with a friendly conversation, while another lifts your wallet.

There is no need to be overly cautious. Simply be mindful of your belongings, especially at crowded intersections, and carry valuables securely.

While traveling through Vietnam it becomes easy to forget that you're in a communist country. In some areas foreigners are regarded as suspicious. Undercover police may monitor the actions of foreigners. Play it safe, don't take photographs of military or police installations. In the North you may be asked to refrain from taking pictures from trains or of government buildings.

Foreigners are held responsible for injury and damage to Vietnamese when involved in a traffic accident, regardless of fault. There are no fair and equitable guidelines for compensation, and the government has the right to detain foreigners until payment is furnished.

Vietnamese people are quiet and reserved. They are not used to obnoxious revelers or bar-room brawlers. Consequently, they do not hesitate to call the police should trouble arise. And the police do not hesitate to throw foreigners in jail.

Illegal drugs are a problem in Vietnam, especially in the North. Undercover police are reportedly on the beat, attempting to curb the sale of drugs. The Vietnamese government has a no tolerance policy for drug smugglers. For those who attempt to transport illegal substances penalties are harsh.

If you're an American citizen and you wind up in jail, immediately contact the **US Embassy**, *7 Lang Ha Street, Dong Da District, Hanoi, Tel. (84 4) 8431500*. The US has an agreement with Vietnam that guarantees the right of incarcerated citizens to contact the consular office, although establishing contact may be difficult. The consular office cannot act as a legal representative, but can aid in finding legal assistance and contacting the family of the incarcerated person. In Vietnamese jails, prisoners must reimburse the government for the cost of meals.

Overseas Vietnamese who are American citizens may be denied contact with US officials should a problem arise, because dual citizens are legally considered Vietnamese by the Vietnamese government in most legal aspects.

STOLEN PASSPORTS

Never leave your passport in a hotel room, unless you can lock valuables in a safe. In the case of a lost or stolen passport contact the consular office immediately. Once you receive a new passport you must obtain an exit visa in order to leave the country. When applying for an exit visa at the immigration office in either Ho Chi Minh City or Hanoi, presenting a photocopy of the original visa may save senseless days of delay. A departure ticket is also required for the issue of an exit visa.

Carry copies of the photo page of your passport to use as identification if you are stopped by authorities. That way you will not lose control of your documentation. Hotels are required to present the passports of all guests to the local police station every evening for registration. Leaving your passport with the hotel reception desk is generally safe, although some tourists prefer to use a photocopy. Never leave an original passport as a guarantee for a rental (of a motor-scooter, for example). Refusing charges or responsibility for damage is much harder if your passport is being held.

TELEGRAMS & FAXES

Telegrams may be sent via Western Union. It is easier to send a fax because most hotels have fax machines. On average hotels charge $7 for the first page and $5 for each additional page to send a fax to the United States, and slightly less to Europe. Receiving a fax may cost up to $1 per page.

Charges for sending domestic faxes run from $1 to $2 per page. Service charges may be tacked onto the rates.

TELEPHONES

Yellow pay phones in Ho Chi Minh City and Hanoi operate with cards purchased at post offices. These phones can make international and domestic long distance calls.

Long-distance rates from Vietnam are probably the highest on the planet. The best international rates are found at Post Offices, which have pay-per-call phone rooms and fax service. Collect calls may be made from post office phones for a small fee. You may not call collect from private phones.

Most hotels now have international direct dial (IDD) lines. To call out of the country dial "00" plus country code, area code and phone number. To make a domestic long-distance call simply dial "01" plus the area code and phone number. International long-distance carriers do not yet provide calling card access numbers for Vietnam.

To reach a domestic operator from anywhere in the country dial "101," and to reach an international operator dial "110."

Mobile telephones which offer nationwide service are available in **Ho Chi Minh City**, *750 Dien Bien Phu Street, District 10, Tel. (84 8) 8351410*; **Hanoi**, 44H Lang Ha Street, *Tel. (84 4) 85366960*; and **Danang**, *101 Tran Phu Street, Tel. (84 51) 820666.* The connection fee is 2,200,000 dong and does not include the phone. Monthly fee runs $30 plus air time.

TELEPHONE CITY CODES

Ban Me Thout 50	Lai Chau 23
Bai Chay 33	Lao Cai 20
Ca Mau 78	Long Xuyen 76
Cantho 71	My Tho 73
Dalat 63	Nha Trang 58
Danang 51	Ninh Binh 30
Haiphong 31	Phan Rang 68
Ha Long Bay (Quang Ninh) 33	Phan Thiet 62
Hang Chau 76	Pleiku 59
Hanoi 4	Qui Nhon 56
Hoi An 51	Soc Trang 73
Hue 54	Son La 22
Kien Giang 77	Vinh 38
Kontum 60	Vinh Long 70
	Vung Tau 64

TELEVISION

Three national television stations and a number of regional channels broadcast in Vietnam. Most stations cut off in the late evening. Satellite television is common and most hotels place a satellite TV as standard equipment rooms. BBC, CNN, Star TV and MTV Asia may be received by satellite.

TIME

All of Vietnam is in the same time zone, Greenwich Mean Time (GMT) plus seven hours. So, at midnight in New York City, it is 11 am in Vietnam. Vietnam does not observe daylight savings time.

TIPPING

Tipping is a relatively new institution in Vietnam. Giving a tip to your waitperson is often greatly appreciated. In some cases, especially family-run establishment, a tip is graciously declined. In better restaurants a standard 15 percent tip is expected.

You should tip your guides and drivers what you feel is appropriate for the service offered, keeping in mind that the salary of a guide may be less than $200 per month. On group tours, a hat is discretely passed around the bus for contributions to the tip.

WATER

Even the Vietnamese generally don't drink the water. Foreigners may become violently ill from tap water. Urban water supplies are chlorinated, so once boiled the water should be safe. Therefore the water in tea, coffee and soup does not pose a problem. Some of the more expensive hotels have safe water supplies. However, to be certain of your well-being, it is always safer to brush your teeth with bottled water.

Expatriates in Ho Chi Minh City say that ice cubes which have holes in the middle are produced with safe water, while those which do not should be avoided. Blocks of ice are not only made with questionable water, but often carried on the backs of bicycles or left on the street. Most tourists stick to canned or bottled drinks. You may ask for a drink to be cooled before it is served.

Bottled water is readily available, and the domestic spring water La Vie (from the Mekong Delta) is excellent.

Another source of unsafe water is raw food. Don't eat salads or other uncooked vegetables, or unpeeled fruit. Even the fresh herbs and bean sprouts served with every bowl of soup can effect your stomach. Eating only cooked food and using caution with fruit and vegetables will make your stay much more comfortable.

WEIGHTS & MEASURES

Vietnam uses the European standard metric system.

MORE INFORMATION, PLEASE!

Destination Vietnam is a glossy magazine published bi-monthly in San Francisco, California. In-depth articles by some of the leading authorities on travel in Vietnam offer excellent insight for the traveler or enthusiast. An annual subscription costs $20 or individual issues $5. For more information contact **Global Directions Incorporated***, 58 Genebern Way, San Francisco, California, 94122, Tel. 415/333-3800, Fax 415/333-6888. Or cruise their Web site at: http://www.well.com/www/gdisf.*

The **Gioi Publishers** *in Hanoi offers books dealing with tourism, history and business in eleven languages, including English.* **New Vietnam***, a monthly magazine covers economy, foreign investment, history and tourism. Contact them at 46 Tran Hung Dao Street, Hanoi, Vietnam, Tel. (84 4) 8254542 or 8253841, Fax (84 4) 8269578.*

8. SPORTS & RECREATION

The outdoors beckons travelers, especially the spectacular and varied landscape of Vietnam. There are many ways to enjoy sports and fitness, both in cities and the countryside.

Finding supplies for your favorite sport can be difficult. If you inquire with the company or club that sponsors an activity, you will probably be able to rent what you need. For camping and biking, bringing your own equipment is a sure solution.

BICYCLE TRIPS

Bicycling through the beautiful countryside of Vietnam is a popular diversion. There's no secret to venturing around on two wheels—just do it. Recent magazines glamorize the country-long route from Ho Chi Minh City to Hanoi. However, the main road, Highway 1, is so small and crowded that cyclists often spend more time watching oncoming traffic than enjoying the countryside.

Easier and safer roads can offer better routes. A long-time expatriate and biking enthusiast offered her inside information about the best roads for weekend journeys. "The main highways are obstacle courses. The small roads lead through towns and along farmland and provide an escape. Bottled water and food are easy to find, so you don't need to load yourself down with supplies...I thoroughly enjoyed riding from Mytho to Ben Tre and back to Saigon."

The mountain roads around Dalat are in good condition, have beautiful scenery and the weather here is mild. The Mekong Delta roads are flat and accessible directly from Ho Chi Minh City.

Superior mountain and racing bikes are not available, nor are accessories such as durable helmets. You can bring your bike by plane. Airlines often will provide bicycle boxes, or you can buy one from a pro shop.

GOLF

Golf is one of the most popular sports in Asia, and it is catching on in Vietnam. In the last few years new courses have opened. You can usually rent golf clubs at the courses.

In Hanoi

The **Dong Mo** Golf Course set amid mountains and forest, is about 50 kilometers from Hanoi. The course has 18 holes. For more information, contact *Son Tay Tourist Company, Dong Mo Tourist Center, Ha Tay Province. Tel. (84 34) 8332279.*

In Ho Chi Minh City

Vietnam Golf Club, *Thu Duc Town, Ho Chi Minh City. Tel. (84 8) 896756.* This club, in the Ho Chi Minh City suburb Thu Duc, has a full 18 hole course plus driving range. The reasonable prices make this a favorite of those in the Ho Chi Minh City area.

Song Be Golf Club, *Thuan Giao Commune, Than Au District, Song Be Province (this is the location of the actual golf course). The business office is located at 245B Nguyen Dinh Chieu Street, District 3, Ho Chi Minh City.* The Song Be project began as a golf resort, and is turning into the never-ending development scheme. Currently, there are plans for a club house, luxury hotel, residential community and two casinos in Song Be. Actually, one casino already opened and had to temporarily shut down due to lack of customers.

Song Be Golf Club has an 18 hole that rates par 72. This is indisputably the finest golf course close to Ho Chi Minh City. The club is open to members and guests. For information on playing at the Song Be Golf Club, contact *The Asian Hotel, 146-150 Dong Khoi Street, District 1, Ho Chi Minh City. Tel. (84 8) 8296979, Fax (84 8) 8297433.*

The **New World Hotel**, *76 Le Lai, District 1, Ho Chi Minh City.* The New World Hotel has a **putting range** for the use of guests and members of the hotel.

In Dalat

Dalat's golf course was first built in the 1920s as a nine-hole course. Today it is expanded to 18 holes and is one of the premier golf facilities in Asia. The club boasts bent grass fairways, scenic holes and excellent, cool weather. The course spans 7,009 yards and rates a par 72. You will be challenged by lakes that weave through ten holes.

The original club house from the 1920s was renovated into a modern pro-shop and cafe. A new resort club facility is under construction.

Weekday green's fees are $65 per player and weekend fees are $85. You can rent clubs for $20 and shoes $8. The caddie fee the $8, and carts are not available. You can use the driving range fee for $5.

In Phan Thiet

The **Ocean Dunes Resort and Golf Club** is under construction. The spectacular golf course, with its many sand dunes, has ocean views from many of the holes.

RUNNING

Hash House Harriers, *Floating Hotel, 1a Me Linh Square, District 1, Ho Chi Minh City*. The Hash House Harriers is an infamous group of expatriates who hold serious weekend runs. The group usually takes a bus to the country, then runs and walks along a course of rural roads and country trails. The Ho Chi Minh City meeting point is the Floating Hotel at 2:30 on Sundays. Check message boards in area restaurants for more information. In Hanoi the runs take place at 4 pm on Saturdays. Fliers at the Metropole announce the weekly meeting point. A $5 donation to the club is requested.

Both Hanoi and Ho Chi Minh City hold annual **marathons**. In 1996, 450 runners from Vietnam and around the world participated in the first Ho Chi Minh City Marathon. City streets closed as runners made their way through the usually congested intersections. People gathered on the sidewalks to cheer the participants.

People of all ages and backgrounds ran. Some of the top runners who make the international circuit ran, as did many residents, disabled people and foreign expatriates. The marathon is held toward the end of January.

Phan Dinh Phung Stadium, *8 Vo Van Tan, District 3, Ho Chi Minh City. Tel. (84 8) 8224355*. This indoor stadium has adjoining track and basketball courts.

SAILING

The world of yacht racing has Vietnam on its map. The **Hong Kong Vietnam Yacht Race** enjoyed its first sailing in 1996. Seventeen boats raced the course that is billed as the fastest off-shore competition in Asia. Unruly winds that characterize the Vietnamese waters make the race a challenge even for the world's most skilled sailors. In 1996, the sleek boats ended the race in Nha Trang.

In The Mekong

Voiles Vietnam, *17 Pham Ngoc Thach Street, District 3, Ho Chi Minh City. Tel. (84 8) 8296750, Fax (84 8) 8231591*. Voiles Vietnam operates a reproduction of an oriental junk boat. Sailing trips up the Mekong River or along the southern coast can be arranged. The boat comfortably accommodates 10 guests plus a full crew.

In Nha Trang
      Nha Tran Sailing Club, *72-74 Than Phu Street, Nha Trang. Tel. (84 58) 826528, Fax (84 58) 821906*, rents sailboards, not sail boats. The cost for a board is $5 per hour. Jet skis are available for $40 per hour.

In Phan Thiet
      Hai Duong Resort, *Coco Beach, Mui Ne Peninsula, Phan Thiet. Tel. (84 62) 823591 or 848401 or 848402, Fax (84 62) 823590. Singles/doubles $60.* This popular beach-side resort has sail-boards and jet-skis for rent.

SCUBA DIVING & SNORKLING

The beautiful coast of the South China Sea boasts clear blue water, coral reefs and a variety of fish. Nha Trang is rich in coral reefs. Snorkeling is very popular, especially because it is impossible to jump into the inviting sea without wanting to catch a glimpse of what lives on the bottom.

Equipment-intensive sports such as scuba diving are brand new to Vietnam. Few companies have equipment and divers that have western certification.

In Nha Trang
      Nha Trang Ship Chandler Company, *74 Tran Phu Street, Nha Trang. Tel. (84 58) 821195*. Snorkeling and skin diving areas abound of the coast of Nha Trang. You can rent equipment and get information from this tourist office.
      Voiles Vietnam, *17 Pham Ngoc Thach Street, District 3, Ho Chi Minh City. Tel. (84 8) 8296750, Fax (84 8) 8231591*. This company arranges luxury scuba diving trips aboard an oriental junk boat. The trip includes sailing from Ho Chi Minh City, up the coast to Nha Trang.

SOCIAL GROUPS

The **American Chamber of Commerce**, *30 Le Thanh Ton #105, District 1, Ho Chi Minh City, Vietnam. Tel. (84 8) 8295892, Fax (84 8) 8296087.* "Am Cham" maintains an active, although unofficial office in Ho Chi Minh City. Membership includes newsletters, monthly luncheons and special functions. AmCham Vietnam provides a great way to be active in the dynamic ex-pat business community and ease bouts of homesickness. The Fourth of July bash draws hundreds of ex-pats. Overseas (non-voting) memberships are available.

SPECTATOR SPORTS

Phu Tho Horse Racing, *2 Le Dai Hanh Street, District 11, Ho Chi Minh City. Tel. (84 8) 8551205*. Betting is a popular obsession in Vietnam. The national lottery recently restricted winning numbers from being announced over the radio in order to discourage illegal wagers on the outcome.

If you would like to partake in some legal betting, just visit the race track. The horses are far smaller than in other parts of the world. On Saturday mornings you can watch jockeys lead their horses to the track through the streets of District 11.

Phan Dinh Phung Stadium, *8 Vo Van Tan, District 3, Ho Chi Minh City. Tel. (84 8) 8224355*. This indoor stadium hosts a variety of sporting events including international volleyball and soccer matches.

SWIMMING

In Hanoi

The Army Sports Club, *19 Hoang Dieu Street, at the Citadel, Hanoi*. This is a national fitness center with a pool for lap swimming. Monthly dues are under $10.

International Club, *35 Hung Vuong Street, Hanoi. Tel. (84 4) 8252310*.

Thang Loi Hotel, *78 Yen Phu Street, Hanoi. Tel. (84 4) 8268211*.

In Ho Chi Minh City

International Club, *285b Cach Mang Thang Tam, District 10, Ho Chi Minh City*. The club allows non-members to use the pool for a daily fee.

Lam Son Pool, *342 Tran Binh Trong, District 5, Ho Chi Minh City*. This public pool is competition size, and a good place for a serious workout.

The Worker's Club, *55b Nguyen Thi Minh Khai, District 3, Ho Chi Minh City*. For the French this was the Circle Sportif. In the park next to Reunification Hall you can enjoy the outdoor swimming pool, clay tennis courts and volleyball courts at reasonable prices. Day passes for swimming cost 15,000 dong. Or simply stroll along the park's garden-lined pathways.

Saigon Floating Hotel, *1A Me Linh Square, Bach Dang Wharf, District 1, Ho Chi Minh City. Tel. (84 8) 8290783, Fax (84 8) 8297441*. The pool is a popular spot for expatriates and visitors alike. The high cost of daily visits ($10 per day) is the only deterrent to spending an afternoon here.

The Palace Hotel, *56-58 Nguyen Hue Street, District 1, Ho Chi Minh City. Tel. (84 8) 8292860 or 8292862 or 8291520*. Use of the pool is $1. The renovation in the hotel may keep the pool closed sometimes.

TENNIS

Tennis is less popular than badminton in Vietnam. There are a few public courts in Ho Chi Minh City and Hanoi. You will find tennis courts at some hotels.

In Hanoi

Ba Dinh Club, *Hoang Van Thu Street, Hanoi. Tel. (84 4) 8253024.*

Khuc Hao Sports Club, *1B Le Hong Phong Street, Hanoi. Tel. (84 8) 8232287.* This club has tennis courts and exercise classes.

Worker's Cultural Palace, *Tran Hung Dao Street, Hanoi.* This is the local athletic facility, which is open to residents and visitors.

Youth Club, *5 Tang Bat Ho Street, Hanoi Tel. (84 4) 8255533.*

In Ho Chi Minh City

The Rex Hotel Tennis Center, *141 Nguyen Hue, District 1, Ho Chi Minh City. Tel. (84 8) 8292185.* The two cement courts are lit for night play. Equipment is available for rent. Reservations made through the Rex Hotel

Saigon Floating Hotel, *1A Me Linh Square, Bach Dang Wharf, District 1, Ho Chi Minh City. Tel. (84 8) 8290783; Fax (84 8) 8297441.* The hotel has courts in the front, along the wharf.

The Worker's Club, *55b Nguyen Thi Minh Khai, District 3, Ho Chi Minh City.* For the French this was the Circle Sportif. This large complex offers many forms of recreation including outdoor clay and cement tennis courts and volleyball courts at reasonable prices.

In Vung Tau

Rex Hotel *(Thang Loi Hotel), 1 Duy Tan Street, Vung Tau. Tel. (84 64) 852135 or 852612.* The Rex Hotel in Vung Tau has tennis courts available to guests and visitors.

TREKKING

Most tourists stay on the beaten path. A few are enticed by the magnificent variety of the landscape to set out to explore the countryside. Currently camping equipment can not be purchased in Vietnam. So if you plan overnight treks, bring your own gear.

Throughout the country, tracts of land have been reserved for use as national parks. However, there are not yet camp sites. The only area where foreigners currently hike and camp on their own is in the Northern Highlands by the town of **Sapa**.

In the Northern Highlands

The best way to enjoy and learn about life in the Northern Highlands is by trekking around the mountains. This is one of the few areas in the country where no central tourist authority attempts to control or limit the activities of tourists.

The most convenient place to begin your walk is from the mountain town of Sapa. From here you can take off in any direction and come upon villages of the Hmong and Dao tribes. The minority people are friendly and welcoming to foreigners. Many adventurous tourists have stories about being invited into a family's house for a meal or to spend the night.

The country's tallest mountain peak, Fanxipan, is just outside Sapa. Many enjoy the three day hike to the top, even when heavy clouds restrict the view.

There are no tents to be rented in Sapa. The weather is cool from October to March, and often rainy, so bringing your own tent is advised. You can arrange for a guide in Sapa. You will sleep in minority people's homes or under the stars with your guide.

Some of the guest houses in Sapa can arrange for a guide to take you through the mountains or to Fanxipan Mountain. The **Auberge Dang-Trung**, *Sapa Town, Lao Cai Province, Tel. (84 20) 871243*, has a manager who speaks English and provides excellent and reliable service.

In the Central Highlands

In the Central Highlands, trekking is more difficult. The weather and environment is less hospitable than in the northern mountains. Also the tribes people are not as welcoming. If you stop at a village, the people are likely to ask you for money, instead of inviting you to dinner. And travel permits and guides are required of all visitors, regardless of the method of transportation.

Gialai Travel Service Center, *124 Le Loi Street, Pleiku. Tel/Fax (84 59) 824891*, specializes in tours to the Bahnar and Jarai tribes. The staff specializes in arranging treks on foot, by bicycle or elephant. Special tours for veterans can be arranged. Overnight treks cost from $55 to $65 per night, per person. This price includes a guide.

WORKING OUT

In Hanoi

The **Army Sports Club**, *19 Hoang Dieu Street, at the Citadel, Hanoi.* This is a military and public gym with a pool. Monthly dues are less than $10, which is probably less than you would pay for a couple of workouts at a private facility.

In Ho Chi Minh City

World Gym, *26 Le Thanh Ton, District 1, Ho Chi Minh City. Tel. (84 8) 8295950.* This club is not affiliated with the chain in the US. The city's first private gym has fitness equipment, weight machines and saunas. This club has limited membership but allows visitors to use the facilities for a daily fee.

Omni Saigon Health Club, *251 Nguyen Van Troi Street, Ho Chi Minh City. Tel. (84 8) 8449222.* The Omni has a full gym with a range of fitness machines. You can relax in the beautiful outdoor pool after your workout.

9. FOOD & DRINK

FOOD

The cuisine of Vietnam is unlike any other Asian food. The aromatic lemon grass, delicate rice noodles and fragrant cilantro mark the cuisine. After every meal, green tea is served. Meals are eaten early, with lunch around noon and dinner at 6 p.m.

The day starts with *pho* or Hanoi soup, Vietnam's answer to ham and eggs. The big bowls of long rice noodles, thinly-sliced meat and fragrant broth are garnished with fresh cilantro and bean sprouts. The broth takes hours to prepare and has a soft taste and pungent aroma all its own. You will find pho served on the street at food stands and at restaurants at all times of the day.

Another breakfast favorite, *banh bo* are Chinese breakfast dumplings. They are a real treat of sweet bread quick-boiled around spicy minced meat. These are sold by street vendors in nearly every city.

Com (rice), the staple of the Vietnamese diet, comes in a variety of forms and is eaten in nearly every meal. Prepared rice is either hard, which is preferred in the north, or sticky, the type westerners know. Rice noodles come in all sizes, from the thick chewy variety used in *bun bo* (specialty of Hue), to the super-fine vermicelli used in salad rolls.

Rice paper is a tissue-thin form of noodle used to make salad rolls. These are similar to spring rolls, but stuffed with noodles, fresh vegetables and seafood or meat. At some restaurants you receive all these ingredients on plates and roll your own salad rolls. Dip the rolls in fish sauce, *nuc mam*,

NOODLE SPECIALTIES

Bun bo is a dish prepared in the cuisine of Hue. The thick bun bo noodles are served on a bed of lettuce with mint and topped by beef fried with citronella and peanuts. A sour chili sauce is poured on at the table.

Cau lau, thick, fried noodles, can be prepared in Hoi An only. The recipe calls for well water from that city.

which usually comes in a small bowl on the side. Fried spring rolls are called *nem rán* and are also eaten with fish sauce.

Fruit

Tropical fruit is grown in abundance. Four types of mangoes, durian, longan, and rambutan are among the exotic fruit that you can eat daily. The small native bananas are packed with flavor.

Meat

Either beef or pork is eaten at every meal for most Vietnamese. Domestic beef is rather tough. The best beef is imported from Australia, and due to the high price this is not easy to find. Domestic chicken is generally good. Duck and squab are served at fancy establishments.

Vietnam has a very special form of barbecue that is cooked at the table. Clay pots of hot coals are brought and each person grills up the meat or seafood and rolls it into spring rolls. You could say it is the Vietnamese version of Mexican fajitas.

Seafood

This is the country for seafood lovers. For centuries, Vietnamese fisherman cast their nets to bring in some of the best fresh fish to be found. This has given cooks ample opportunity to perfect their skills with seafood.

Fish and seafood specialties are eaten throughout the country. Nha Trang has good, fresh shrimp, crab and squid. Spicy shrimp wrapped around sugarcane has a tantalizing mix of flavors. Outside Nha Thang where crab farms line the highway, road-side restaurants serve whole boiled crab covered in tamarind sauce.

The most famous seafood is probably Hanoi's fried fish, *cha ca*. Cha ca Street in Hanoi pays tribute to the dish, first served here by the Doan family about 100 years ago. Cha ca is made of pieces of fish filet, first grilled then fried. A tangy sauce rounds out the exotic taste.

Tofu

Tofu (bean curd) takes many forms in Vietnam. Soft cheese tofu has a creamy texture and rich taste. Firm tofu is used in soups, and the hard variety is fried in vegetable dishes.

Vegetarian

Buddhist monks are strict vegetarians and the tradition of vegetarian cooking is found throughout the country. Hue vegetarian food is particularly flavorful, since it is complemented by flavors from the traditional regional cuisine.

Other Delicacies

Another specialty of the central coast are savory pancakes called *ban xeo*. These are mixtures of vegetables, meat and rice batter which are fried until crispy and rolled into spring rolls. You will see these made on the street in Nha Trang, and they are delicious with fish sauce. In Hue, a similar pancake is called *banh khoi*.

For those with a taste for gastronomic adventure, Vietnam will not disappoint. Dog, *cho*, is considered a delicacy. Although its illegal in many other parts of Asia, you can find restaurants which serve dog in Vietnam. It is more common in the north than in the south. A meal of dog is usually partaken of by men only.

Another meal reserved for men is cobra. Often the dinner is more of a ceremony with live snake brought to the table. The snake is killed and drained of its blood, which is mixed with rice wine and drunk. The eldest man in the group has the honor of eating the snake's heart while it is still beating. This ensures longevity and strength.

In the Mekong Delta alligator is a delicacy. A Frenchman attested that alligator tastes a bit like chicken. Then again, the same has been said of cobra. For a taste unlike any other, try a plateful of bat or turtle. Restaurants specializing in Chinese food may prepare these exotic dishes.

French Influence

There is no need to switch to a completely native diet if you don't want to. The French left a strong impression on Vietnamese cooking. Fresh baguettes are delicious and ubiquitous. Pancakes, popular for breakfast, are actually thick crepes filled with fresh fruit. The pate and yogurt, also French legacies, are excellent.

DRINK

Mineral water is available throughout the country. La Vie water is bottled at the source in the Mekong Delta city of Mytho. Phan Rang produces refreshing carbonated mineral water called Danh Thanh.

Vietnamese **coffee** is some of the strongest in the world. Each demi-tasse is prepared individually with a drip filter, and served in a glass. In most parts of the country, if you order milk you will receive sweetened condensed milk in your glass. It is potent and sweet as candy.

In the north and some tourist areas you may receive instant "American" coffee and may even get real milk. Or you might wind up with an instant, sweetened international coffee drink.

Fragrant **green tea**, che tuoi, is consumed either hot or cold. Jasmine or lotus blossoms may be mixed in to add flavor. Special tea ceremonies mark occasions such as engagements and weddings. Tea is offered after every meal, and drinking tea is a way of solidifying a friendship or business meeting.

Western **alcohol** is available in most cities—you can even get frozen margaritas in Ho Chi Minh City—although quite pricey. Whisky is popular, especially among Asian businessmen. French table wine that is decent at best is served in some restaurants.

Regional Wine

The regional wines of Vietnam are inexpensive and easy to find:

Dalat makes sweet **strawberry wine**, that is good as a dessert. In Hue, the tradition of wine-making begun by the Nguyen kings is kept alive in **Ruon Minh Mang**, the potent regional wine.

In the central and southern regions **rice wine** is an everyday drink. The tribes people of the Central Highlands make **jar wine** which they drink through bamboo straws straight from large ceramic jars. The wine of **Sapa** is full-bodied and resembles sherry.

In Ho Chi Minh City, sample a bottle of Russian-Vietnamese "champagne," **Rosvietvina Moskovske Igrixtoe**, made without aging in Vietnam. Strong stuff!

THE BEERS OF VIETNAM
BGI - *Mytho*
Halida Beer - *brewed in Hanoi with Carlsberg*
Son Han - *Hoi An*
Huda Beer - *brewed in Hue, in cooperation with Tuborg Beer*
Imperial Stout Beer - *Hue*

10. BEST PLACES TO STAY

MODERN HOTELS

HO CHI MINH CITY

CONTINENTAL HOTEL, *132-134 Dong Khoi Street, District 1, Ho Chi Minh City. Tel. (84 8) 8299255 or 8299201 or 8294456, Fax (84 8) 8290936. Singles $104 to $174, doubles $126 to $195. Rates include tax, service charges and breakfast. Credit cards accepted.*

The Continental harks back to the genteel style of the French Colonial period. This elegant white French hotel was home-away-from-home for Somerset Maughm when his travels brought him to Saigon. Graham Greene stayed in the building across Dong Khoi Street that used to be the annex of the Continental. The 87 rooms are impeccably furnished. Built in 1880, the rich decor remains true to the building's legendary history.

The Continental Shelf, one of the cafes where correspondents hung out during the war, used to be in the hotel. Guido's, the Italian restaurant downstairs, is one of the oldest foreign-run restaurants in the country.

DALAT

DALAT PALACE (HOTEL SOFITEL), *12 Tran Phu Street, Dalat. Tel. (84 63) 825444. Singles/doubles $120 to $350.*

If you allow yourself only one indulgence on your entire trip this should be it. The Dalat Palace was the grande dame of accommodations when it was built in 1922. Today it has regained its status as the foremost luxury resort of the country. The Palace offers the most tranquil surroundings in Dalat, on a hill which overlooks the city. The interior is nothing short of extraordinary.

The Dalat Palace has the best night spot to be found. Larry's Bar is a most pleasant evening spot for a drink and conversation. Depending on how many guests are at the hotel, the bar will either be full and lively or quiet. The warm, rustic atmosphere is reminiscent of a French wine cellar.

Golfers will be far more taken-in by the extraordinary golf facilities. The 18-hole Dalat golf course is a paradise for the avid golfer and novice alike. First laid out by the French as a nine-hole course, the Acor Group revamped the greens and expanded it to a full 18 holes. A shuttle runs from the hotel to the nearby golf course.

Standing on the bent grass fairway under misty pines, it seems you are playing golf at the top of the world. Dalat's cool, moist climate allows the entire course to maintain perfectly manicured bent grass tees, fairways, and greens. The course spans 7,009 yards and rates a par 72. You will be challenged by lakes that weave through ten holes, then indulge in wide, sprawling greens. A shuttle runs from the hotel to the near-by golf course.

HANOI

THE METROPOLE, *15 Ngo Quyen Street, Hanoi. Tel. (84 4) 8266919. Singles/doubles $220 to $450. Credit cards accepted.*

The Bluet family, legendary French hoteliers, opened the Metropole in 1911, during the golden days of colonial rule. Its elegance remains stately and reminiscent of by-gone days. The lovely restaurant serves delicious French food. The hotel has been renovated in the graceful European tradition. Just a few blocks from the Metropole stands the Opera House, which was built in the same period.

In 1992, the Metropole was restored to its former elegance by Pullman-Sofitel, after nearly 40 years of being run as a state enterprise. This is the only true luxury hotel you will find in Hanoi. The Metropole is often booked-up far in advance. You should make reservations over one month before you travel.

PHAN THIET

HAI DUONG RESORT, *Coco Beach, Mui Ne Peninsula, Phan Thiet. Tel. (84 62) 823591 or 848401 or 848402, Fax (84 62) 823590. Singles/ doubles $60.*

Nestled in a grove of swaying palms, half-way between Phan Thiet and Mui Ne Beach are the bungalows of Hai Duong Resort. This is the first and only deluxe bungalow accommodation in the country. And it sits on the most beautiful stretch of beach on the Vietnamese coast.

The European couple (he is French, she is German) who own and run the resort brought a Swiss chef to work with the Vietnamese cook to create the cuisine for the restaurant. The restaurant is decorated in hand-carved

Vietnamese furniture. The rooms are large and comfortable, with air-conditioning and rattan furniture. Each bungalow has a sitting room and patio overlooking the beach. The bungalows can sleep a family of four (the rate for four people is $120 per night).

The Hai Duong truly is a resort, with recreation such as sailing, snorkeling, jetskiing. Bicycles and motor bikes also available for rent.

NHA TRANG

BAO DAI VILLAS, *Tran Phu Street, Nha Trang. Tel. (84 58) 81049, Fax (84 58) 81471. Singles/doubles $25 to $70.*

This is one of the most attractive settings imaginable for a vacation stay. Once a vacation residence for the Emperor Bao Dai, the five spacious villas perched on a hill overlooking the harbor are now a hotel. The villas were built in 1920, and retain their period decoration. During the war, the elite of the South Vietnamese government used the villas. The hotel is also a museum, and open to the public.

The distance from the city (6 kilometers) allows you to completely enjoy the beauty of the setting without the noise and hassles of an urban environment. The hotel restaurant serves the freshest and most delicious seafood in the city. Boats are available for rent at the hotel, as are bicycles and cars. The hotel provides all services on a cash-only basis.

COLONIAL ACCOMMODATIONS

The hotels in this section are holdovers from the French colonial era, offering a glimpse of years gone by.

DALAT

BIET THU HOTEL, *28 Tran Hung Dao, Dalat. Singles $25/doubles $50.*

Biet Thu is Vietnamese for "villa". This pink villa dates from the colonial era and was probably the private vacation home of a French family. A stay here will truly take you back in time. Today it is run as a mini-hotel. The rustic feeling is charming. The rooms are very large and comfortable, with simple and clean bathrooms. Beds are low to the ground and the wooden floors are the original. The reception desk sells snacks, but there is no food available.

Of the French villas that line Tran Hung Dao Street, this is the only one currently open. Most are in the process of being renovated into mini hotels.

HUE

GOVERNMENT GUEST HOUSE, *5 Le Loi Street. Singles $25/doubles $40 to $60.*

The estate-like hotel was built in 1865 for visiting French government officials. The 16 large rooms with high ceilings and beautiful wood moldings transport you to genteel bygone days. Remember, this place offers charm, not grandeur. The hotel is surrounded by a substantial lawn and garden and sits right on the Perfume River. There is no restaurant, but this is a minor inconvenience, easily outweighed by the unique surroundings.

For a perfect sunset, sip tea on the large balcony off the main hall. Rooms have refrigerators and televisions. People traveling solo during the off-season may be able to get a slight reduction in the price.

NHA TRANG

THE GRAND HOTEL, *44 Tran Phu Street, Nha Trang. Tel. (84 58) 822445 or 826944 or 826940, fax (84 58) 825395. Singles $18 to $64/doubles $23 to $68.*

This solid yellow building has been a hotel since its opening in the early 1930s. From the outside you would guess it's a government building. The hotel does not offer enough to get away with the top-end prices. That is to say the $23 dollar double is a good deal and the $64 single is near robbery.

While the rooms are renovated, the decor is far from first-class. Budget rooms are available for $10 per night (with a private bath and fan, but no air-conditioning.)

SAPA

HAM ROUNG GUEST HOUSE, *Sapa Town, Lao Cai Province. Tel. (84 20) 871305, 871304, 871251, 871312, Fax (84 20) 871303. Single/doubles $15.*

The yellow houses are colonial villas. The location is ideal—halfway up the hill that overlooks the city—and just a few steps from the market. Satellite television, a novelty in Sapa, is standard in the clean and comfortable rooms. The hot water in the showers is unreliable, and there is no heating in the rooms, which poses a problem during the chilly winter months,

The hotel restaurant serves a variety of food. Live snakes kept in a cage outside by the parking area are prepared as the specialty of the house.

THE UNTOUCHED ISLANDS

Looking for a true "get away from it all" experience? Try any of these islands for a memorable escape! You won't be staying in the lap of luxury, but you will see a Vietnam that most other tourists will not.

CON DAO ISLANDS

As more and more weary expatriates choose Phu Quoc Island as their retreat, Con Dao Islands, becomes increasingly appealing. Con Dao has thick vegetation and rolling hills. The coral reefs off the shore are great for snorkeling. Con Dao consists of 14 islands lying 180 kilometers south of Vung Tau, in the South China Sea.

Con Son, the largest island in the archipelago, is only 20 square meters and has a population of 2,000. Regardless of the season you should have no problem getting a room at the only hotel on the island: **PHI YEN HOTEL**, *Tel. (84 64) 30168. Singles/doubles $20*. The hotel is as remote as the island itself. There are no amenities, but if you want to see this beautiful island, this is your only option. Rent a bicycle or motor bike to explore the island.

You can get to Con Son by hiring a boat from Vung Tau or Nha Trang. The trip from Vung Tau takes over 10 hours; from Nha Trang the journey is longer.

PHU QUOC ISLAND

A trip to Phu Quoc means getting away from it all. With over 40 kilometers of empty beaches, the island attracts tourists and expatriates alike. The beaches are deserted but for the fishing boats that work the clear water.

The most popular sport for vacationers here is reading since the electricity on the entire island shuts down every night at 10 pm. Fishing and the production of fish sauce are the main industries Peppers are grown on small farms. Phu Quoc is about 150 kilometers west of the Mekong Delta town of Rach Gia. The island is close to Cambodia, but it is safe. You can reach Phu Quoc by a ten hour ferry ride for less than $5. Vietnam Airlines flies to Phu Quoc from Ho Chi Minh City.

The only hotel on the island is **HOUNG BIEN HOTEL**, *Tel. (84 8) 846113, singles/doubles $20*.

PHU QUY ISLAND

The windy retreat of Phu Quy invigorates the senses with its pristine coastline and burly breezes. If you want to get in touch with the real life and people of Vietnam, this trip will be your most valuable. Phu Quy is a small island 80 kilometers from mainland Vietnam. The island supports a fishing village that is a gem of untouched culture. The people here are charmed by foreign visitors.

The only way to reach Phu Quy is to hire a boat from Vung Tau, Phan Thiet or Nha Trang and it could take a few days. The journey is truly for only the adventurous who want to go where tourists do not tread.

There are no hotels on the island, but visitors have been able to rent rooms with a local family. If you have camping gear, you can find a sheltered area on the beach. The conditions are rugged and you must be prepared to rough it.

11. HO CHI MINH CITY

Residents of **Ho Chi Minh City** still say "Saigon" when they refer to their home. The name Saigon is derived from the ancient language of the Khmer people who first settled the region. After the fall of Saigon in 1975, it was renamed in honor of President Ho Chi Minh, who died before the country was reunited.

Modern Ho Chi Minh City (**HCMC**), founded in the seventeenth century, is the nerve center of the south. A dramatic mix of modern and traditional, the city is in flux. Peddlers wearing straw hats kneel on street corners under steel and concrete construction sites. The buzz of motorbikes swirls through the air into the night.

The city center is undergoing dramatic construction, with high-rises blossoming on nearly every street corner. Neon signs and advertisements encroach on the French colonial charm.

ARRIVALS & DEPARTURES
BY AIR

Tan Son Nhat Airport (*airport information, Tel. (84 8) 8443179*) lies just minutes from the city center. When you fly into Tan Son Nhat airport at Ho Chi Minh City you feel like you are landing at the edge of the world. Don't fear, the airport is, in many ways, the least developed part of the city—at least, it looks that way. There are no terminals; in fact there is not much of a building. Fortunately this makes things easy; just get through immigration, pick up your bags and go out the door. The Saigon Tourist booth by customs offers an accommodation service. They maintain lists of most levels of hotels, from moderately-priced to expensive.

Shuttles Between the Airport & the City

A private shuttle service, Saigon Star Transport, *Tel. (84 8) 8645809*, runs **Skybus** mini-vans between the city's luxury hotels and the airport. Skybus leaves the airport every half-hour from 8 am to 7 pm; the ride costs 77,000 dong ($7).

Taxis Between the Airport & the City

Saigon Taxi, the airport taxi service affiliated with the national tourist agency, Saigon Tourist, provides rides to the city center for $8. Look for drivers wearing white shirts with dark blue ties congregating just outside the main doors, they will help you navigate through the anxious crowd pushing toward the doors to get a snapshot or first glimpse of relatives and friends. The meters tally the fare in dong, but you may pay in dollars.

Most taxi drivers speak English and may try to convince you to change your plans to stay at a different hotel. They may tell you that your hotel is dangerous, too expensive or far from restaurants, and so on. They get a kickback from the hotels they work with, which are usually not the best establishments.

HO CHI MINH CITY TAXI SERVICE

Airport Taxi (white cars), Tel. (84 8) 8446666
Cholon Taxi (green cars), Tel. (84 8) 8226666
Saigon Taxi (purple cars), Tel. (84 8) 8424242
Saigon Taxi (green cars), Tel. (84 8) 8448888
Vina Taxi (yellow cars), Tel. (84 8) 8422888

BY TRAIN

Trains run from Ho Chi Minh City to points north. The train follows the coast and does not go through Dalat or the Central Highlands. The best place to get train information is at the main station. The ticket office can make reservations and give you information about all train service in Vietnam. You must purchase tickets in cash.

Main (Hoa Hung) Train Station, *1 Nguyen Thong Street, Tel. (84 4) 8230105 or 8230106.*

Railway Ticket Office, *275C Pham Ngu Lao Street, District 1, Ho Chi Minh City; Tel. (84 8) 8292118. Train information Tel. (84 8) 8945543.*

ORIENTATION

Of the 17 administrative districts, most visitors see only District 1, the historical area, and District 5, *Cholon* or Chinatown. Districts 3 and 10 border District 1 and have some good restaurants and hotels.

District 1

The central business district and tourism center is District 1. Hotels, restaurants, bars and clubs abound. The city's main shopping street, Dong Khoi is found in District 1. This was the center of life for the

American soldiers who came to Saigon during the War. The French colonial hotels, the Majestic and the Continental are here, as well as the Notre Dame Cathedral and Main Post Office.

Since tourists spend most of their time in District 1, the area is full of newspaper sellers and kids pushing packs of gum.

District 3

For a taste (and smell) of everyday life in Ho Chi Minh City take a walk through District 3. This business and residential zone is packed with shops and apartments. Perhaps because traffic noise is so deafening in the commercial center's small streets and alleyways, or simply because they are not accustomed to tourists, cyclo drivers beckon with only a hand gesture.

Amid the shoe repairmen squatting on the street and pushcarts delivering wood, new shopping-mall-style stores like Le Chic Jeans are cropping up.

District 5

District 5, Cholon, is the city's Chinatown. Overseas Chinese have lived in Cholon for generations and maintained their traditions. To walk through the market is to take an exciting step into China. You can find good, inexpensive Chinese food throughout the area.

GETTING AROUND TOWN

There is a public bus transportation system in Ho Chi Minh City, but it is unavailable to foreigners.

By Bicycle

The do-it-yourself version of cyclo travel is bicycle rental. Truly brave travelers may choose to rent motor bikes. Unfortunately, as of yet there are no helmets to be rented. Some hotels can arrange motor bike rental, or try **Ky Hoa Tourism**, *16 The 3rd of February Avenue, District 10, Ho Chi Minh City, Tel. (84 8) 8225187.*

By Cafe Tours

No, these aren't tours of the local cafes, but tours arranged by the cafes. There are a number of cafes in Ho Chi Minh City that run local and long-distance tours; Sinh Cafe has the most professional operation. Open ticket bus service to Hue is also available.

Contact them at:
• **Sinh Cafe**, *179 Pham Ngo Lao Street, District 1, Ho Chi Minh City. Tel. (84 8) 8355601.*

By Car and Driver

Since foreigners are not permitted to drive in Vietnam, you must hire a car with a driver. Most hotels can arrange this, or you may go to one of many tourist offices.

- **Eden Tourist**, *114 Nguyen Hue, District 1, Ho Chi Minh City; Tel. (84 8) 8295417 or 8295417.*
- **Saigon Tourist Car Rental Office**, *34 Ton Duc Thang Street, District 1, Ho Chi Minh City; Tel. (84 8) 8295952,* and an annex at *46 Nguyen Hue, District 10, Ho Chi Minh City; Tel. (84 8) 8224496.*
- **Youth Center Tourist Office**, *1 Pham Ngoc Thach, Ho Chi Minh City. Tel. (84 8) 8294345.*

By Cyclo

Traveling by cyclo through the streets of Ho Chi Minh City can only be described as exciting. The thick traffic provides an obstacle course for the intrepid cyclo drivers who seem to know no fear. During rush hour (at its peak around 6 pm on weekdays), the traffic congestion is so bad it may be quicker to walk than take a cyclo in the city center.

The best time to take a cyclo ride is in the twilight of early morning, when the streets are relatively clear of cars and the lights are coming on across the city.

By Mini-bus

Saigon Star Transport, *Tel. (84 8) 8645809,* operates minibuses between selected hotels and the city center as well as Cholon (District 5). The one-day pass costs 44,000 dong ($4).

By Taxi

Taxis provide a convenient way to get around town and an escape from the heat and pollution of downtown Ho Chi Minh City. Taxi rates are not regulated in HCMC, but the variations in charges among the main taxi companies is slight.

When you take a taxi, be certain that you have a legitimate taxi service. Some of the taxis that operate without affiliation to larger companies may overcharge or deliver you to the wrong address.

WHERE TO STAY
Expensive
District 1
   CENTURY SAIGON HOTEL, *68A Nguyen Hue Ave, District 1, Ho Chi Minh City. Tel. (84 8) 8292959 or 8231818; Fax (84 8) 8292732 or 822958; US Tel. 800 256 5533. Singles $115 to $185; doubles $170 to $195. Credit cards accepted.*
   The 109 room luxury Century Saigon is part of the Century family which operates hotels throughout Asia. The rooms are rather generic, but very comfortable since the recent renovation. The French restaurant has good, simple dishes.
   CONTINENTAL HOTEL, *132-134 Dong Khoi Street, District 1, Ho Chi Minh City. Tel. (84 8) 8299255 or 8299201 or 8294456; Fax (84 8) 8290936. Singles $104 to $174; doubles $126 to $195. Rates include tax, service charges and breakfast. Credit cards accepted.*
   This elegant, white French hotel was home-away-from-home for Somerset Maughm when his travels brought him to Saigon. Graham Greene stayed in the building across Dong Khoi Street that used to be the annex of the Continental. Built in 1880, the rich decor remains true to the building's legendary history. The Continental Shelf, one of the cafes where correspondents hung out during the war, used to be in the hotel. Guido's, the Italian restaurant downstairs, is one of the oldest foreign-run restaurants in the country. The Continental has 87 rooms.
   KIM DO HOTEL, *133 Nguyen Hue Street, District 1, Ho Chi Minh City. Tel. (84 8) 8225914 or 8225915 ; Fax (84 8) 8225913 or 8291026. Singles $119 to $179; doubles $134 to $199; suites $319 to $479. Breakfast included. Credit cards accepted.*
   New hotel has elegant French-influenced decoration. The 135 rooms meet the highest standards. The hotel features a health club, a bar, two cafes and a restaurant. The location is excellent, just a few blocks away from the restaurant and shopping district. In the morning you can look out upon Nguyen Hue Street and watch the badminton games at dawn.
   MAJESTIC HOTEL, *1 Dong Khoi Street, District 1, Ho Chi Minh City. Tel. (84 8) 8295517 or 8295514; Fax (84 8) 8295510. Singles $130 to $195; doubles $150 to $215; suites $295 to $575. Rates include tax, service charge and breakfast.*
   The stately Majestic, built in 1924 is a pleasure to visit. This elegant hotel is located close to the Saigon River. The beautiful lobby bar and restaurant features a piano player at most times of the day. Each of the 120 rooms is tastefully appointed. The two restaurants have excellent food. The Majestic is a restful retreat from the crowded city.

NEW WORLD HOTEL, *76 Le Al Street, District 1, Ho Chi Minh City. Tel. (84 8) 8228888 or 8295314; Fax (84 8) 8230710; in the United States Tel. 800 538 8882. Singles/doubles $185 to $250; suites $300 to $850. Credit cards accepted.*

New World Hotels are known throughout Asia as premier establishments. The immense 541 room hotel is Vietnam's largest and one of the few in the city to offer a drive-up entry. The New World boasts the highest standards in security and accommodates dignitaries such as former President and Mrs. Bush. Six restaurants, a sports club and business center are all on site. Rooms on the Dynasty Club floors have access to a private lounge and meeting facilities.

Although the staff strives to build a reputation of excellence in service, the New World comes across as cold and lacking personality. Besides the health club, fitness facilities include an outdoor swimming pool, driving range and tennis courts.

MERCURE HOTEL, *79 Tran Hung Dao Street, District 1, Ho Chi Minh City. Tel. (84 8) 8242525 or 8242555; Fax (84 8) 8242602; in the US 800 SOFITEL. Singles/doubles $95 to $137; suites $189 to $230. Credit cards accepted.*

The Mercure has the sophistication of European standards. The location leaves you too far for a comfortable walk to most restaurants. The overall ambiance of this 104 hotel appeals to those who want European-style surroundings. The Mercure has baby-sitting service, 24-hour room service and a fantastic French Restaurant.

THE METROPOLE, *148 Tran Hung Dao Street, District 1, Ho Chi Minh City. Tel. (84 8) 8322021 or 8322022 or 8391043; Fax (84 8) 8322019. Singles $86 to $109; doubles $95 to 120; suites $119 to $149. Breakfast and service charge included. Credit cards accepted.*

The 94 room Metropole offers impeccable service. The rooms are simple yet comfortable. The hotel is located on the main street that connects Cholon (Chinatown) to central Saigon. The hotel has a nice health club and swimming pool. This is a convenient choice for travelers who have cars.

NORFOLK HOTEL, *117 Le Thanh Ton, District 1, Ho Chi Minh City. Tel. (84 8) 8295368; Fax (84 8) 8293415. Singles $85 to $125; doubles $100 to $140; suites $180 to $220. Breakfast included. Credit cards accepted.*

This 47 room hotel is an Australian/Vietnamese joint venture and strives to satisfy both tourists and business travelers. Baby-sitter, business center and secretarial services are available. Fitness room has a variety of weight machines. The restaurant is known for excellent Australian rib-eye and lamb.

THE REX, *141 Nguyen Hue Street, District 1, Ho Chi Minh City. Tel. (84 8) 8293115 or 8292185 or 8296046; Fax (84 8) 8291469 or 8296536. Singles $73 to $100; doubles $81 to $136; suites $136 to $800. Credit cards accepted.*

The Rex is a campy escape. The Asian decor was applied rather heavy-handed, with carved furniture, wood-paneled walls and red carpet throughout the common areas. The kitsch is the charm of this place. The banquet hall-restaurant puts on shows. The roof top restaurant is famous, both for its elaborate garden and as a meeting place for foreign correspondents during the war. The downstairs lounge is refreshingly cool and has international news on its televisions. Each of the 207 rooms feature an in-room fax, as well as the standard amenities. The Rex has its own tennis courts.

SAIGON FLOATING HOTEL, *1A Me Linh Square, Bach Dang Wharf, District 1, Ho Chi Minh City. Tel. (84 8) 8290783; Fax (84 8) 8297441. Singles/doubles $150 to $300. Credit cards accepted.*

The Floating Hotel is originally from Australia. The 182-room boat-hotel floats on the Saigon River. When you step into the lobby, you feel as though you are entering the set of the Love Boat. The center-piece of decoration is a chrome-and-glass spiral stair case. You can enjoy the pool even if you are not a guest (for a charge of $10). A rumor is floating around town that the hotel is soon to move from the Saigon River, on to bluer waters.

SAIGON PRINCE, *63 Nguyen Hue Street, District 1, Ho Chi Minh City. Tel. (84 8) 8222999; Fax (84 8) 8241888. Singles/doubles $180 to $210; suites $350. Credit cards accepted.*

The Saigon Prince offers the ultimate in Oriental luxury. The hotel is furnished in Japanese elegance, with no detail overlooked. Each of the 203 rooms has a view of the city. The comfortable rooms are furnished with simple style. The health facilities feature an indoor pool and steam rooms. Japanese sushi chef prepares the food for the hotels Japanese lounge.

WINDSOR HOTEL, *193 Tran Hung Dao Street, District 1, Ho Chi Minh City. Tel. (84 8) 8357848; Fax (84 8) 8357889. Singles/doubles $90 to $174/ suites $198 to $220. Credit cards accepted.*

The spacious rooms, amenities and friendly management gives the Windsor an American atmosphere. Half of the 64 rooms are apartments with kitchenettes. Most of the Windsor's guests are business travelers. In addition to the gymnasium, the hotel has a library.

District 3

SOL CHANCERY SAIGON, *196 Nguyen Thi Minh Khai Street, District 3, Ho Chi Minh City. Tel. (84 8) 8299152; Fax (84 8) 8251464. Singles/doubles $150 to $200. Credit cards accepted.*

All rooms are apartment-style suites and elegantly furnished. The hotel offers full facilities, 24 hour room service and is located next to a the large, tranquil Van Hoa Park.

District 5
HOTEL EQUATORIAL, *242 Tran Binh Trong Street, District 5, Ho Chi Minh City. Tel. (84 8) 8390000; Fax (84 8) 8390011. Singles/doubles $180 to $215; suites $310 to $980. Credit cards accepted.*
The Equatorial is the only true luxury hotel in Cholon. The opulent lobby offers a preview of the 334 rooms, which are spacious and well decorated. The hotel has Japanese and Chinese restaurants, and a cafe that serves American specialties. The hotel's conference facilities are the best in the city. This is an excellent choice for those who value fitness facilities in a hotel. The pool is large and inviting; the gym is well-equipped with free-weights and machines.

Phu Nhuan District
THE OMNI, *251 Nguyen Van Troi Street, Phu Nhuan District, Ho Chi Minh City. Tel. (84 8) 8449204; Fax (84 8) 8449202. Singles/doubles $180 to $260/suites $300 to $800. Credit cards accepted.*
This 248 room luxury hotel offers a haven from the congested city. You will not be disappointed by the attentive service and the exquisite decoration of the Omni. The decor is a mix of modern elegance and old French grace. The hotel offers a floor reserved for business travelers, which has meeting rooms and a receptionist. The restaurants serve excellent Japanese and Cantonese food and the Cafe Saigon has French coffee and pastries. The hotel has a full health club and grand outdoor swimming pool.

Moderate
District 1
AMERICAN HOTEL, *(Mogambo Cafe) 20 Bis Thi Sach, District 1, Ho Chi Minh City Tel. (84 8) 8251311. Singles/doubles $30 to $45.*
This mini-hotel with a popular restaurant on the ground floor is run more like a youth hostel than hotel. You will not have much privacy here. The unorganized staff has been reported to walk into occupied rooms without warning. The hotel is within stumbling distance from the bar district.
ASIAN HOTEL, *146-150 Dong Khoi Street, District 1, Ho Chi Minh City. Tel. (84 8) 8296979; Fax (84 8) 8297433. Singles $72 to $97; doubles $87 to $112. Credit cards accepted.*
The Asian Hotel is a 47-room, well-run deluxe hotel, conveniently located on the main shopping street between the Notre Dame Cathedral

and the Saigon River. This hotel is often the choice of Asian business travelers, and it has a business center. There is no charge for children less than 12 years of age who stay with their parents. The restaurant on the ground floor serves Oriental specialties.

BACH DANG HOTEL, *33 Mach Thi Buoi Street, Distinct 1, Ho Chi Minh City. Tel. (84 8) 8251501; Fax (84 8) 8230587. Singles/doubles $40 to $100. Credit cards accepted.*

The Bach Dang is close to the Saigon River and Me Linh Square, in the heart of the concentration of restaurants and shops. Full amenities—including air conditioning, and modern baths—offset the modular furniture and stale atmosphere.

BONG SEN HOTEL, *117-123 Dong Khoi Street, District 1, Ho Chi Minh City. Tel. (84 8) 8291516 or 8290545; reservations Tel. (84 8) 8291721; Fax (84 8) 8298076. Singles/doubles $60 to $90; suites $150 to $200. Rates include service charges, tax and breakfast. Credit cards accepted.*

This 136-room hotel is located a few blocks south of the National Theater, offering clean, comfortable surroundings, recently renovated rooms, and a good breakfast buffet with European and Vietnamese food.

CARAVELLE HOTEL, *19-23 Lam Son Square, District 1, Ho Chi Minh City. Tel. (84 8) 8293704 or 8293708; Fax (84 8) 8296767 or 8299746. Singles/doubles $30 to 180. Breakfast included. Credit cards accepted.*

The old 115-room Caravelle stands across the square from the Continental Hotel. The decor is stuck somewhere between the 1970s and 1990s, and the staff is a bit lackadaisical. Round-the-clock construction on the site next-door may be a nuisance in some rooms.

HUONG SEN HOTEL, *66-68-70 Dong Khoi Street, , District 1, Ho Chi Minh City. Tel. (84 8) 8291415 or 8290259 or 8299400; Fax (84 8) 8290916. Singles $38 to $95; doubles $50 to $95. Breakfast included. Credit cards accepted.*

The Huong Sen is a comfortable 50 room hotel. The service is very good and the standards of the hotel are high. The Oriental decor is tastefully done. The rooms have electronic safes, mini-bars and complimentary fruit. There is a full business center and a doctor on 24-hour call.

KIM LONG HOTEL, *58 Mac Thi Buoi Street, Ho Chi Minh City. Tel. (84 8) 8228558 or 8228678; Fax (84 8) 8225024. Singles $40; doubles $50.*

The new mini-hotel of 12 rooms has a good location. Fresh, clean rooms and attentive service make the Kim Long a good choice for people seeking reasonably priced modern facilities.

THE MONDIAL HOTEL, *109 Dong Khoi Street, District 1, Ho Chi Minh City. Tel. (84 8) 8296291 or 8296296; Fax (84 8) 8296273. Singles $55 to $105; double $88 to $121. Rates include tax.*

This small, older hotel has warmth and comfort with its decorative mix of European and Asian styles. The 40 rooms have the amenities and decoration of a large deluxe hotel. Yet the small size allows a coziness that you miss at a bigger place.

NAM PHUONG HOTEL, *46 Hai Ba Trung Street, District 1, Ho Chi Minh City. Tel. (84 8) 8224446 or 8299766; Fax (84 8) 8297459. Singles $55; doubles $75.*

The small hotel is new, but somehow already has a musty feel. The most notable amenity is an elevator. The location is convenient and the rooms are standard.

THE PALACE HOTEL, *56-58 Nguyen Hue Street, District 1, Ho Chi Minh City. Tel. (84 8) 8292860 or 8292862 or 8291520; Fax (84 8) 8244229 or 8244230. Singles $43 to $120; doubles $58 to $140. Credit cards accepted.*

The Palace Hotel is palatial only in size. Its 150 rooms are best described as shabby around the edges. Services of the hotel include sauna rooms and massage, swimming pool and two restaurants. Currently the hotel is undergoing partial renovation, which should spruce up the overall appearance.

RIVERSIDE HOTEL, *18 Ton Duc Thang, District 1, Ho Chi Minh City. Tel. (84 8) 8224038 or 8297492 or 8231117; Fax (84 8) 8251417. Singles $60 to $100/doubles $75 to 115/ suites $130 to $250. Breakfast included. Credit cards accepted.*

The 77 room hotel is close to the Saigon River. The staff is not particularly attentive, so if service is a priority choose another hotel. The building has plenty of French colonial charm, but it does not carry through to the rooms. Some of the rooms are quite small. The terrace on the roof offers a lovely view of the river. Full tourist services are available; the hotel restaurant has adequate food.

District 3

LIBERTY HOTEL, *167 Hai Ba Trung Street, District 3, Ho Chi Minh City. Tel. (84 8) 8294227 or 8294229 or 8298822; Fax (84 8) 8290919. Singles $41 to 130; doubles $55 to $130. Breakfast included. Credit cards accepted.*

This 52 room hotel offers full service. It is a cozy place and is located two blocks from Notre Dame Cathedral, rather close to District 1, where you will find most of the city's restaurants. The hotel has two restaurants and a dance club. Shows of traditional music are often held.

District 5

DONG KHANH HOTEL, *2 Tran Hung Dao B Street, District 5, Ho Chi Minh City. Tel. (84 8) 8350678 or 8350838; Fax (84 8) 8352427. Singles $65 to $75; doubles $79 to $89; suites $149 to $167. Breakfast included.*

This is a large tourist hotel in the heart of Chinatown. Staying here gives you an interesting perspective of the city, since you are far from the

French-influenced District 1, yet still in the center of a thriving neighborhood. The 81 rooms have standard amenities and the hotel is furnished entirely in Chinese decor.

HANH LONG HOTEL, *1027-1029 Tran Hung Dao Street, District 5, Ho Chi Minh City. Tel. (84 8) 8350251 or 8351087; Fax (84 8) 8350742. Singles $50 to $95; doubles $60 to $105. Tax, service charge and breakfast included.*

This simple hotel with basic amenities offers discounts of 20 to 40 percent during low season. The restaurant serves good Chinese food.

Budget
District 1
CHAMPAGNE HOTEL, *129-133 Ham Nghi Ave, District 1, Ho Chi Minh City. Tel. (84 8) 8224912; Fax (84 8) 8230272 Singles/doubles $30.*

Despite the name, the 38-room hotel is nothing to celebrate. The rooms are clean and very basic. The lobby is run down. There are better hotels in this price range available.

DONG KHOI HOTEL, *12 Ngo Duc Ke Street, District 1, Ho Chi Minh City.*

The Dong Khoi was a favorite of budget travelers before it closed for renovation. The hotel is a beautiful French colonial building. The hotel will be a superior one when it reopens in 1997; the rates and telephone number are not yet available.

LE LE HOTEL, *171 Pham Ngu Lao Street, District 1, Ho Chi Minh City. Singles/doubles $20 to $40.*

The Le Le Hotel is a modern, tourist hotel just across the street from the Sinh Cafe. If you plan to take the cafe tours, this is the most convenient place to stay. The rooms are generously large and have comfortable bathrooms and satellite television. The hotel will hold your bags while you travel outside the city. Be careful to agree on what you will be billed for before you check in. Although this hotel is new they have already earned a reputation for attempting to overcharge.

MINH CHAU ACCOMMODATION, *75 Bui Vien Street, District 1, Ho Chi Minh City. Tel. (84 8) 8331288. Singles/doubles $10 to $15.*

Minh Chau offers simple rooms for rent, either with or without air-conditioning. The family that runs Minh Chau is very friendly. The rooms are clean and have hot water and private bathrooms. The front door is closed in the evening, but you can ring the bell to be let in.

VANG LANG HOTEL, *290 Hai Ba Trung Street, District 1, Ho Chi Minh City. Tel. (84 8) 8201354; Fax (84 8) 8201355. Singles $36 to $56; doubles $40 to $60. Breakfast included.*

With only thirty rooms, the Van Lag sells itself as a "home away from home." The staff caters to foreigners, and it is indeed a very nice, modern establishment. Rates include breakfast; a 3.6 percent fee is added for credit card payment.

District 3

EVERGREEN HOTEL, *261b Hai Ba Trung Street, District 3, Ho Chi Minh City. Tel. (84 8) 8298875 or 8299523 or 8201579; Fax (84 8) 8291835. Singles $35 to $40; doubles $45 to $55. Credit cards accepted.*

Mainly used by business travelers, this small, clean hotel is located in the bustling business district. It is outside of the tourist areas, but a good place for the price. The small, informal lobby offers no restaurant or coffee shop. You can send and receive faxes at the front desk. Rooms are comfortable with modern bathrooms and window air-conditioning.

Phu Nhuan District

LONDON HOTEL, *216 Phan Dung Luu Street, Phu Nhuan District, Ho Chi Minh City. Tel. (84 8) 8443344, 8421117, 8421118. Singles/ doubles $30.*

This is a simple, large hotel with a restaurant, located near the airport. The karaoke bar is generally not too lively.

WHERE TO EAT

Expensive
District 1

ASHOKA, *Indian, 17a-10 Le Thanh Tan Street, District 1 Ho Chi Minh City. Tel. (84 8) 8231372. Hours 11 am to late. Credit cards accepted.*

The atmosphere transports you from Indochina straight to India, where you can enjoy the Mogul specialties of the north. The chef specializes in tandoori dishes, which slow cooked in clay pots. Try a few plates and share with friends.

AUGUSTIN, *French, 10 Nguyen Thiep Street, District 1 Ho Chi Minh City. Credit cards accepted.*

The small restaurant serves excellent French food. You can enjoy a bottle of French wine with your meal.

CARMARGUE, *French, 116 Cao Ba Quat Street, District 1, Ho Chi Minh City. Tel. (84 8) 8243148. Credit cards accepted.*

The restaurant is located in gorgeous white villa. The simple elegance of the surroundings enhances the delicious food. Dine outside under the stars or upstairs overlooking the courtyard. The comfortable bar is a tranquil setting for coffee and drinks.

LE CAPRICE, *French, 5 Ton Duc Thang Street, The Landmark Building, 15th floor, District 1, Ho Chi Minh City. Tel. (84 8) 8228337. Credit cards accepted.*

You will have a great view of the Saigon river from this posh eatery. Excellent French-influenced Western cuisine is served in an elegant atmosphere. This is a favorite spot for business lunches. Three course lunch for $12. Live piano music in the evening.

LE CHALET SUISSE, *French, 211a Dong Khoi Street, District 1. Tel. (84 8) 8293856 or 8293838; Fax (84 8) 8242901. Credit cards accepted.*

You'll think you stepped from the equator, into the Alps when you enter this chalet-style restaurant. The bar has two (yes two) happy hours, from noon to 2 pm and from 4 pm to 7 pm.

LOTUS COURT, *Chinese, The Omni Hotel, 251 Nguyen Van Troi Street, Phu Nhuan District, Ho Chi Minh City. Tel. (84 8) 8449204. Credit cards accepted.*

The Cantonese restaurant in the Omni Hotel serves the finest Chinese food in the city. The chef from Hong Kong prepares a full-range of succulent specialties, including extraordinary dim sum. The vegetarian dishes are excellent.

MAXIM'S, *Chinese, 15 Dong Khoi Street, District 1, Ho Chi Minh City. Tel. (84 8) 822554.*

Despite reports of raves over the food, the Chinese dishes are average at best and are less impressive than the atmosphere. Maxim's retains the grandeur the bygone pre-liberation era. Live music accents dinner.

NEW WORLD HOTEL DELI, *International, Shop No. 6, 76 Le Lai, District 1, Ho Chi Minh City. Tel. (84 8) 8228888 ext. 2122.*

The deli is one of the few places to get imported cheese, like camembert and brie, Italian deli meat, hand-made ice cream and fresh bread and pastries. Wine, tea and other gourmet goodies are also available.

RESTAURANT 180, *International, 180 Nguyen Van Thu Street, District 1, Ho Chi Minh City. Tel. (84 8) 8251673. Daily 7 am to 11 pm.*

This is the place to go if you just need to eat steak. The restaurant imports their meat from Australia. Other dishes include pasta and standard Western fare. The steak is good, but the rest of the menu is merely adequate. Champagne brunch is featured on Sunday.

SANTA LUCIA, *Italian, 14 Nguyen Hue, District 1, Ho Chi Minh City. Tel. (84 8) 8226562. Credit cards accepted.*

Santa Lucia is a trendy Italian eatery with artistic decor. As one of the newer places, it is very popular. The Italian food is very good, but perhaps not as flavorful as the whole dining experience. The restaurant truly feels international.

WINDSOR HOTEL GOURMET DELI, *Western, 193 Tran Hung Dao Street, District 1, Ho Chi Minh City. Tel. (84 8) 8251 503 Open 10 am to late.*

For a delectable sugar fix visit the Gourmet Deli in the lobby of the Windsor hotel. Pastry, bread cookies and cakes are baked every day. Special orders accepted for weddings or birthdays.

Moderate
District 1
   ANNIE'S PIZZA, *Western, 59 Cach Mang Thang Street, District 1, Ho Chi Minh City. Tel. (84 8) 8392577. Daily 11 am to 3 pm and 5 pm to 11 pm.*
   Annie's was the first place to bring delivery to food service in Ho Chi Minh City. For this, the expatriate community shows Annie's undying loyalty. This pizza parlor also dishes out hamburgers, sausage rolls and desserts. Annie's is located just across from the Notre Dame Cathedral
   BASKIN ROBBINS, *Western, 128A Pasteur, District 1, Ho Chi Minh City.*
   Here you will find glorious Baskin Robbins ice cream shipped all the way from the United States.
   BAVARIA, *German, 20 Le Anh Xuan, District 1 Ho Chi Minh City. Tel. (84 8) 8222673.*
   If you find yourself in the midst of Saigon's mad streets suddenly craving some truly German food such as schnitzel or wurst, jump into your lederhosen and cyclo over to Bavaria. You can even practice your German during happy hour from 4 pm to 7 pm.
   BRODARD CAFE, *International, 131 Dong Khoi Street, District 1, Ho Chi Minh City.*
   This cafe has been in operation for decades. Although the government took over after the French owner left some twenty years ago, the atmosphere and menu remains much the same. European dishes such as spaghetti and Vietnamese standards compose the menu. This is a very popular place with locals.
   BUFFALO BLUES, *Western, 72A Nguyen Du Street, District 1 Ho Chi Minh City. Tel. (84 8) 822874. Daily 11 am to 1 am. Credit cards accepted.*
   Pub food, barbecue, European and Vietnamese food and set menus. Sunday brunch served. Lively weekend nights with live jazz. Happy hour every day from 11 am to 8 pm.
   JIMMY'S, *Western, 57 Nguyen Du, District 1, Ho Chi Minh City. Tel. (84 8) 8223661.*
   American-style food like standard spaghetti, simple steak as well as Vietnamese food. Across from the Notre Dame Cathedral.
   LA BIBLIOTHEQUE, *Vietnamese, 84 Nguyen Du Street, District 1, Ho Chi Minh City.*
   Not only is this one of the most unique places in the world to eat, but the food is exemplary. Madame Dai, a former lawyer, opened her home to the hungry masses about twenty years ago. Patrons dine among the tomes of Madame Dai's personal library. This is a favorite of tourists and locals alike. But the eight tables fall far short of meeting demand, so stop by during the morning to make a reservation. Madame Dai's house is located two blocks from Notre Dame Cathedral. Ring the bell and wait to

fill out a reservation card. Madame Dai charges $15 for a four course dinner; the cook will make seafood for people who do not eat meat.

LE COUSCOUSSIERE, *Moroccan, 24 Nguyen Thi Minh Khai Street, District 1, Ho Chi Minh City. Tel. (84 8) 8299148.*

Huge servings of Moroccan couscous with chicken or lamb are the trademark of this middle eastern restaurant. You will not go away hungry.

LE PIERROT GOURMAND, *French bakery, 19 Le Thanh Tan Street, District 1, Ho Chi Minh City. Tel. (84 8) 89081565.*

This small out of the way cafe has the best French pastries south of Hanoi. Sandwiches, light food and breakfast served. The specialty here is home-made ice cream.

LE PETIT BISTRO, *European, 58 Le Thanh Ton, District 1 Ho Chi Minh City. Tel. (84 8) 8230219; Fax (84 8) 8293619.*

This place features an extensive selection of European wine and cheese as well as Bass Ale on tap. Perfectly prepared dishes include pork steak gratine and quiche Lorraine. Happy hour runs from 4 pm to 7 pm.

LEMON GRASS, *Vietnamese, 4 Nguyen Thiep, District 1, Ho Chi Minh City. Tel. (84 8) 8220496.*

Lemon Grass is probably the best Vietnamese restaurant you will find. Traditional dishes are given tasty modern flare, and the menu always features irresistible specials. The four course lunch menu is very popular with the business community.

MOGAMBO AMERICAN BAR, *Western, 20 Bis Thi Sach, District 1, Ho Chi Minh City. Tel. (84 8) 825311.*

When you're in the mood for a chili-cheese burger, head over to this jungle-theme restaurant. One of the reasons that the hamburgers are the best in town is that Mogambo's uses beef imported from the United States. This also accounts for the price of $8. The catsup tastes just like home, too.

SAIGON TIMES CLUB, *Vietnamese, 37 Nam Ky Khoi Nghia Street, District 1 Ho Chi Minh City. Tel. (84 8) 8298676.*

The atmosphere is very informal here. A bar with pool tables by night, the Saigon Times Club dishes up some of the best Vietnamese food in the city by day.

SPAGO, *Western, 300 Dong Khoi, District 1, Ho Chi Minh City.*

A trendy corner restaurant with a menu that includes "French-style" hamburgers and frozen margaritas as well as large tasty salads, good soup and pasta dishes. Skip the fried cheese, which looks like frozen fish sticks. Dine on the balcony for a surreal view of the motor bikes zipping by under a Southwestern-style mural.

Save room for dessert, or at least look at the menu which offers tropical ice cream dishes like the Casablanca (here's ow it's described: *"He is looking at you kid... Two layers of ice cream topped whipped cream. It will make your heart pounding.*") Sample local ice cream flavors like mango, soursop, durian and avocado.

TEX-MEX, *Tex-Mex, 24 Le Thanh Ton, District 1, Ho Chi Minh City. Tel. (84 8) 8295950.*
The only place in town to chow down on guacamole or chips and salsa. The cooks here manage to replicate Tex-Mex favorites. The standard French-influenced Vietnamese specials are also served. At night, the Tex-Mex bar outshines the food service.

VIETNAM HOUSE, *Vietnamese, 93 Dong Khoi Street, District 1, Ho Chi Minh City.*
The Vietnam House serves excellent modern Vietnamese dishes. Influences from all over the country make this menu special. Live piano music is featured nightly.

District 3

RUSSIAN RESTAURANT (RESTAURANT A), *Russian, 361/8 Nguyen Dinh Cheieu Street, District 3, Ho Chi Minh City. Tel. (84 8) 8359190.*
Borscht, blintzes and caviar galore. Should you yearn for Azerbaijani specialties, the Russian Restaurant can fill the craving.

SAIGON STAR RESTAURANT, *Western, in the Saigon Star Hotel, 204 Nguyen Thi Minh Khai, District 3, Ho Chi Minh City. Tel. (84 8) 8230260.*
For those of us who can't get up early enough for brunch, the Saigon Star has a weekend dinner buffet. For $10 you can choose from steak, chicken and seafood with salad and one drink.

Inexpensive
District 1
Thi Sach Street is lined with Vietnamese cafes which serve good, inexpensive food.

CAFE MAX AMERIQUE, *Coffee house, desserts, 144 Hai Ba Trung Street, District 1, Ho Chi Minh City. Tel. (84 8) 8296616. Hours 9 am to 10 pm.*
Coffee house which features ice cream, deserts and snacks.

DINH CONG TRANG, *Vietnamese, Hai Ba Trung near the Tan Dinh Market, District 1, Ho Chi Minh City.*
This grungy pit stop serves up some of the tastiest Vietnamese pancakes in the city. The pancakes here are a rice-batter crepe with vegetable and special sauce.

GIRVAL CAFE, *Vietnamese, Lam Son Square, District 1, Ho Chi Minh City.*
The Girval is a step back in time. The cafe first opened its doors in 1955, and today looks as it probably did then. It remains popular and the food is very good and cheap. The crowd is interesting. A few locals come here, and it is very popular with travelers and expatriates who do not favor

the new, trendy places. The pastry shop next door sells rich and tempting desserts.

MANHATTAN, *fast food, 17 Nguyen Van Chiem Street, or 147 Pham Nu Lao, District 1, Ho Chi Minh City.*

Both locations serve hamburgers and fries that are fast and cheap. The double cheeseburger is no Big Mac, but it will fill you up for under $2. The adventurous can try fried chicken or pizza.

MARGHERITA, *Western, 14 Pham Ngu Lao Street, District 1 Ho Chi Minh City. Tel. (84 8) 8230105.*

Inexpensive and quick Vietnamese food and simple Western dishes like spaghetti and pizza.

RESTAURANT 13, *Vietnamese, 13-19 Ngo Duc Ke Street, District 1, Ho Chi Minh City. Tel. (84 8) 8291417.*

This is where expatriates and locals alike go for traditional Vietnamese food. Entrees average around $2. The outside tables on the sidewalk give you a genuine Vietnamese dining experience. The salad rolls are excellent. The specialty of the house is clay pot mushrooms.

SAWADDEE, *Thai, 252 De Tham, District 1, Ho Chi Minh City. Tel. (84 8) 8322494.*

The food here is authentic Thai. Most dishes can be prepared vegetarian. The red walls and open-air dining add to the heat of the curry. But the informality of this restaurant is part of the charm

THIEN MAN, *Vietnamese, 53 Nam Ky Khoi Nghia, District 1, Ho Chi Minh City.*

The name means "southern sky." This diner was frequented by American soldiers during the war, and has remained open and popular since.

THUAN TUAN, *3/6 Nguyen Van Thu, District, 1 Ho Chi Minh City. Tel. (84 8) 8244051.*

Vietnamese food with international flavors borrowed from Russian, Arab and French cuisine. Lamb is the specialty here. French wine served.

District 3

HUONG VIET, *Vietnamese, 81 Cao Thang Street, District 3, Ho Chi Minh City. Tel. (84 8) 8391714.*

This simple eatery is no longer a well-kept secret. Now tourists and expatriates get down and dirt cheap for authentic Vietnamese food.

RESTAURANT 39, *Vietnamese, 39 Nguyen Trung Truc, District 3, Ho Chi Minh City.*

Sit outside like the locals at this cafe near the Reunification Palace which serves excellent, traditional Vietnamese dishes.

SEEING THE SIGHTS

A good place to use as a landmark while touring Ho Chi Minh City is the National Theater, which stands in the heart of the French colonial area of District 1. Begin your visit in **Le Son Square**, the plaza in front of the National Theater. This area is the setting for the fictional bomb attack in Graham Greene's novel *The Quiet American*.

Le Loi Street runs south from Le Son Square. This is a center of shopping and commerce. At the intersection of Le Loi and Nguyen Hue Street is a small park; at the far end of which stands the People's Committee Building, built in 1901. This is the main government administration offices and is not open to the public. This area is also the hot spot for young Vietnamese to cruise on their motor bikes. The vendors by the Rex Hotel give the park a carnival-like atmosphere in the early evenings. The statue of Ho Chi Minh sits stoically amid the chaos in the center of the park.

Returning back to Le Son Square, Dong Khoi Street runs east-west. **Dong Khoi Street** was the promenade for the French colonists and later for the French and American soldiers who were stationed here. The Continental Hotel, to the west of Le Son square, is one of the gems of colonial architecture. Further west you will find Notre Dame Cathedral. Following Dong Khoi east leads past the main area for souvenir shopping, to the Saigon River.

The French Buildings

The **National Theater**, *Dong Khoi Street, Tel. (84 8) 8291249*, stands close to the mid-point of the stretch. The French colonial theater is in disrepair, but it is only cosmetic. The charm has not worn off the walls although the paint is peeling. Regular performances that include local and traditional singing are held here during the week. The Sunday jazz performances feature local bands that sing in a variety of styles in both Vietnamese and English. The shows are good and held every Sunday at 3 pm to 5 pm.

Continuing down Dong Khoi, past the French colonial Hotel Continental you will find **Notre Dame Cathedral**, *Dong Khoi Street, District 1, Ho Chi Minh City, Tel. (84 8) 8294822*. Notre Dame Cathedral was built from 1877 to 1883, intended as a place of worship for the French colonial community. However, it was not given the name Notre Dame until 1959. Today, a large Vietnamese Catholic community worships at Notre Dame Cathedral. The cathedral is probably the most memorable landmark of the city, as it marks the center of the old French colonial area.

The red brick building, although incongruous to an Asian city, adds a special flavor and romantic touch to the city. Many couples get married

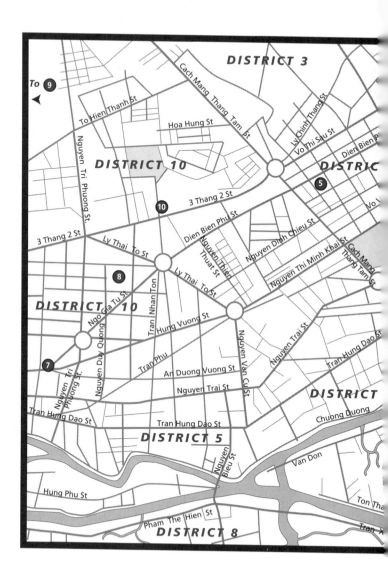

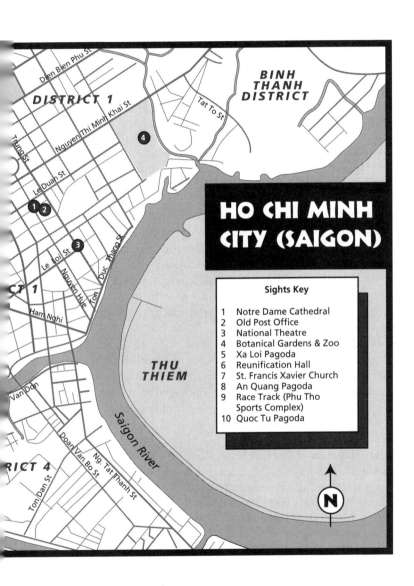

HO CHI MINH CITY (SAIGON)

Sights Key

1 Notre Dame Cathedral
2 Old Post Office
3 National Theatre
4 Botanical Gardens & Zoo
5 Xa Loi Pagoda
6 Reunification Hall
7 St. Francis Xavier Church
8 An Quang Pagoda
9 Race Track (Phu Tho Sports Complex)
10 Quoc Tu Pagoda

BINH THANH DISTRICT

DISTRICT 1

THU THIEM

DISTRICT 4

Saigon River

Dien Bien Phu St
Tat To St
Nguyen Thi Minh Khai St
Truong St
Le Duan St
Le Loi St
Nguyen Hue
Ton Duc Thang St
Ham Nghi
Van Don
Doan Van Bo St
Ng. Tat Thanh St
Ton Dan St

at the cathedral, and you will see the wedding parties, in western-style formal clothes, posing for pictures in front of cathedral by the statue of the Virgin Mary. The twin red-brick towers stand 40 meters tall. The cathedral stands on the square at the end of Dong Khoi Street.

The **Old Post Office**, another piece of the former French life of Saigon, stands across from Notre Dame Cathedral. This is still used as the main post office, and is where to go to buy stamps, send faxes or buy cards.

Two blocks south of the Cathedral you will find the former Presidential Palace of South Vietnam, **Reunification Hall**, *106 Nguyen Du Street, District 1, Ho Chi Minh City, Hours: Daily from 7:30 am to 10:30 am and 1 pm to 3:30 pm. The admission fee is 40,000 dong ($3.66).* On April 30, 1975, North Vietnamese tanks ploughed through the gates of Reunification Hall, then known as the Presidential Palace. This marked the fall of Saigon.

Reunification Hall is the most striking landmark of the Vietnam War, since it stands nearly as it was at the time of reunification in 1975. The South Vietnamese President Thieu left the furnishings and decor untouched when he fled the country and went into exile. The downstairs building was constructed in 1962 as a military command center for the South Vietnamese government. You can see the maps that Thieu's commanders used to track the war. The underground war rooms are open to visitors.

The building has an even deeper history. In 1873, the Norodom Palace, the residence of the French governor of Vietnam, was built in this spot. The President of South Vietnam, Ngo Dinh Diem resided in Norodom Palace until air raids severely damaged it in 1962. After that, Norodom Palace was razed and the present building put up.

Museums

The **Art Museum of Ho Chi Minh City**, *97 Pho Duc Chinh Street, Ho Chi Minh City, Tel. (84 8) 8222577,* is a disappointingly small assortment of paintings which mimic European styles.

The large **Botanical Garden and Zoo**, *1 Thong Nhat Avenue, District 1, Ho Chi Minh City, Tel. (84 8) 8298146, admission $1,* offer a refreshing escape from the city. The 130 year old zoo, built by the French, houses exotic Asian animals. Many of the animals are endangered species that you will not be able to see outside of Vietnam. The main entrance to the zoo is at Le Duan Street and Nguyen Binh Khiem Street. A bridge dating from 1927 leads to the Botanical Gardens.

The Botanical Garden is a large park which provides a quiet retreat from the city. The gardens were originally the work of a French botanist, Louis Pierre, who oversaw the construction. The flora is from all regions of Indochina, and many beautiful flowers decorate the grounds, including orchards. It is a good place to spend a few hours just relaxing in the shade of large trees.

The **History Museum**, *1 Thong Nhat Avenue, District 1, Ho Chi Minh City, Tel. (84 8) 8298146, hours: Tuesday through Sunday, 8 am to 11:30 am and 1 pm to 4 pm; admission $1*, is located on the grounds of the Botanical Gardens. The bright yellow Oriental-style building was built in 1929 by the French Societe d'Etudes Indochinoise. The exhibits trace ancient history from the Bronze Age thorough the Cham and Vietnamese empires. The bronze artifacts from the Dong Son culture fill an entire room and are beautiful examples of the high-level of development in the ancient Viet lands. Water puppetry performances are held here on weekends.

The **Revolution Museum of Ho Chi Minh City**, *65 Ly Tu Trong Street 114 Nam Ky Khoi Nghia Street, Ho Chi Minh City, Tel. (84 8) 8299741, hours: 8 am to 11:30 and 1:30 to 4:30 daily; admission 10,000 dong*, contains a collection consisting primarily of a photographic chronicle of the people and places that paved the bumpy road to a unified, communist nation. The beautiful white building dates from 1890. Some of the photographs provide a fascinating glimpse of life in Saigon at the turn of the century. Modern artifacts include items from the Vietnam War.

The national tribute to women, the **Women's Traditional House**, *202 Vo Thi Sau Street, District 3, Ho Chi Minh City. Tel. 8298056*, focuses on the importance of women in the armed conflicts of Vietnamese history.

War Crimes Museum, *28 Vo Van Tan Street, District 3, Ho Chi Minh City. Hours 8 am to 12 pm and 2 pm to 5 pm, Tuesday to Sunday. The admission charge of $.50 includes a pamphlet in English which outlines the displays*.

The grounds are a chilling testimony of the country's turbulent history and stands amid the remains of destroyed armament. Exhibits inside present the Vietnamese view of their sacrifices and struggles for independence. The exhibits in the museum chronicle atrocities committed by foreign powers against the Vietnamese people. Although the collection is blatantly disturbing, many foreigners visit the War Crimes Museum and find it extremely worthwhile. During the Vietnam War, this building housed the United States Information Agency.

One of the more unusual museums is the **Ho Chi Minh Museum Annex** located at *1 Nguyen Tat Thanh Street, District 4, Ho Chi Minh City, Tel. (84 8) 8291060*. This marks the sight where in 1911, the 21 year-old Ho Chi Minh took a job on a ship and thus began three decades of travels across the world. Many photographs and personal items are on display. The building that holds the collection was once a shipping office. The museum is on Nha Rong Wharf. The street bears Ho Chi Minh's given name, Nguyen Tat Thanh.

Temples & Pagodas

The best way to see the pagodas of Ho Chi Minh City is to hire a cyclo, car or motorbike and have your driver act as a guide. Most of the temples are quite a distance from each other. You could easily spend an entire day visiting pagodas, and I would recommend devoting at least a half-day.

Temples & Pagodas: District 1

The **Ngoc Hoang Pagoda**, *73 Mai Thi Luu Street, Ho Chi Minh City*, is a sanctuary that honors Ngoc Hoang and dates from 1909. It is full of large wooden statues of traditional Chinese gods of nature, including the Sun God and Moon God. A statue of Ngoc Hoang with his guardians are at the center of the sanctuary,

Another temple of interest is **Phung Son Tu Pagoda**, *338 Nguyen Cong Tru Street, Ho Chi Minh City*. This Buddhist temple honors Ong Bon, the guardian of happiness. It was constructed in the 1940s. The Chinese influence is evident in the decoration of this pagoda which is in continual use.

The national hero, Tran Hung Dao, repelled the invading Chinese in the 13th century. The **Tran Hung Dao Temple**, *36 Vo Thi Sau Street, Ho Chi Minh City, Tel. (84 8) 8293079*, is built in his honor. This is one of the smaller temples you may see, but it is worthwhile since it is purely Vietnamese, in all aspects including its decoration and dedication.

Temples & Pagodas: District 3

Vinh Nghiem Pagoda, *339 Nam Ky Khoi Nhgia Street, District 3, Ho Chi Minh City, Tel. (84 8) 8441153*. This large, modern pagoda has a collection of exceptional woodcarvings of sacred animals and statues of the Buddha. The decorations show influences that are distinctly Japanese. The central shrine stands 15 meters (49 feet) high and is 35 meters (115 feet) in length. The impressive bell tower was built in 1971.

Xa Loi Pagoda, *89 Ba Huyen Thanh Quan Street, District 3, Ho Chi Minh City, Tel. (84 8) 8292438, hours 7 am to 11 am and 2 pm to 5 pm*. Sermons are delivered at 8 am and 10 am every Sunday. Although the Xa La Pagoda is relatively modern (built in 1956), the seven story bell tower and vivid paintings make this a worthwhile place to visit. The Sakyamuni Buddha is portrayed in the statuary and frescoes.

Temples & Pagodas: District 5

Ho Chi Minh City's Chinatown area is full of tradition and beauty. The pagodas of the area are true to their Chinese heritage. The **Chau Ba Bhau Pagoda**, *118 Trieu Quang Phuc Street, District 5, Ho Chi Minh City*, is one of the most visited pagodas. The decoration remains virtually untouched since the time of the opening of the temple, in the late 1800's. The pagoda is dedicated to the Chinese Fertility Goddess.

Phuoc An Hoi Quan Pagoda, *184 Hung Vuong Street, District 5, Ho Chi Minh City,* is a vibrant shrine. Smoke from spiral incense fills the hall and the intricate shrines around the altar appear dazzling. A statue of Ong Bon is the centerpiece of this Chinese pagoda.

Thien Hau Pagoda, *710 Nguyen Trai Street, District 5, Ho Chi Minh City, Tel. (84 8) 8555322.* Thien Hau is the Chinese Sea Goddess, and the patron of this temple. Statues depicting Thien Hau and her sea-borne entourage decorate the sanctuary. The pagoda was built in the early 19th century. Thick incense smoke fills the air every day and offerings are burnt in the large urns in front of the pagoda.

Temples & Pagodas: District 10

An Quang Pagoda, *243 Su Van Hanh Street, Ho Chi Minh City. Tel. (84 8) 8351243 or 8357437.* This pagoda is reportedly the home of the monk Quang Trang, famous for his advocacy of peace during the Vietnam War. He was the resident monk at the pagoda during the war, then was imprisoned for a brief period by the government after the reunification.

Temples & Pagodas: Tan Binh District

The **Giac Lam Pagoda**, *164 Lac Long Quan Street, Tan Binh District, Ho Chi Minh City, Tel. (84 8) 8642012,* was built in 1744 by a descendent of the Chinese Ming dynasty. The Chinese influence of Confucianism and Taoism are strong in the decorative detail of this building. The bodhi tree in front of the pagoda was brought from Sri Lanka. The wooden sanctuary is used regularly for ceremonies; traditional religious music is played at various times throughout the day.

Other Houses of Worship
District 1

The only Hindu temple in Vietnam is the **Mariamman Temple**, *45 Truong Dinh, Ho Chi Minh City*. This late-19th century temple is still used by Vietnamese, Chinese and Tamil-Indian Hindus. The central figure is the goddess Mariamman and her guardians. Stairs to the left of the main entrance lead to the two towers.

The Central Mosque, *66 Dong Du Street, Ho Chi Minh City*, has four minarets that are visible from the upper stories of down town buildings. The Islamic decoration is simple and lovely. The building was constructed in 1935. You can stop in to partake in a vegetarian lunch for $2. Simply ask at the gate.

RELIGIOUS SERVICES

Buddhism

Xa La Pagoda, 89 Ba Huyen Thanh Quan Street, District 3, Ho Chi Minh City. Tel. (84 8) 8292438. Hours 7 am to 11 am and 2 pm to 5 pm. Sermons delivered at 8 am and 10 am every Sunday.

Christianity

Cha Tam Church, 25 Hoc Lac, District 5, Ho Chi Minh City. This Church located in Chinatown holds regularly scheduled Sunday services.
Notre Dame Cathedral, Dong Khoi Street, District 1, Ho Chi Minh City. Mass is held on Sundays at 5:30 am, 7:30 am, 9:30 am and 5 pm.

Hinduism

Mariamman Temple, 45 Truong Dinh, District 1, Ho Chi Minh City. The temple remains open all day from 7 am to 7 pm.

Islam

Saigon Central Mosque, 66 Dong Du Street, District 1, Ho Chi Minh City. Regular services held.

NIGHTLIFE & ENTERTAINMENT

Bars

The pub crawl goes on every weekend. The bars in Ho Chi Minh City cater to the expatriate crowd, and attract a large number of Vietnamese as well. Standard practice is to hit a few places in one night; since the bars are close to each other, this is no challenge.

APOCALYPSE NOW, *2C Thi Sach Street, District 1, Ho Chi Minh City.*
The jungle-style bar has been enlarged to include pool tables and a dance floor. This is the most popular place for travelers and locals to have a few beers; it was one of the first places to stay open very late. The trendy Vietnamese who come here love to practice English. Make Apocalypse Now the last stop of the evening. The bar starts hopping after midnight.

BAR CATINAT, *4 Nguyen Thiep Street, District 1, Ho Chi Minh City. Tel. (84 8) 8220496. Daily 4 pm to 2 am. Happy hour from 5 pm 7 pm.*
This is a good old European-style bar. The bar tenders here love to serve shots, so be ready to drink some potent potions.

BERNIE'S BAR, *74/A2 Hai Ba Trung Street, District 1, Ho Chi Minh City.*
Bernie's is a jazz bar with an inviting atmosphere. It's a good place to kick back for a few hours. And probably the only place to find Belgian beer on tap.

BUFFALO BLUES, *72A Nguyen Du Street, District 1 Ho Chi Minh City. Tel. (84 8) 8222 874. Daily 11 am to 1 am. Credit cards accepted.*

Buffalo Blues has lively weekend nights featuring jazz bands. The pool room and draft beer complete the pub atmosphere. The restaurant serves barbecue, European and Vietnamese food. All day, every day happy hour runs from 11 am to 8 pm. Live jazz and blues music after 8:30 pm.

THE GECKO, *74 Hai Ba Trung Street, District 1, Ho Chi Minh City. Tel. (84 8) 8242754.*

You can sit at the long bar and take in the satellite television or have appetizers with your drink. The whole place is not much larger than the bar itself, and that gives the Gecko a friendly environment where you will probably meet others.

GUITAR BAR, *62 Hai Ba Trung Street, District 1, Ho Chi Minh City.*

This friendly, informal bar features music spun by a DJ. It is one of the few places to hear funk and hip-hop, among the other selections.

THE JUNGLE BAR, *205 Pham Ngu Lao Street, District 1, Ho Chi Minh City.*

The roof-top bar has great views of the city. This is a good spot to stop for drinks in the backpacker's area.

THE Q BAR, *Under the Municipal Theater, District 1, Ho Chi Minh City.*

The Q Bar was one of the first western bars to open in Ho Chi Minh City just a few years ago. The chic decor feels more like a night club than your standard bar. The animated crowd provides a great atmosphere for late-night socializing.

RED RHINO, *8 Don Dat Street, District 1, Hi Chi Minh City. Tel. (84 8) 8292216.*

The Red Rhino is a cool place with eclectic decor. A good selection of French wine is available here. Many start the night at Red Rhino.

SAXO, *91 Hai Ba Trung, District 1, Ho Chi Minh City. Tel. (84 8) 8228305.*

The small downstairs bar fills with the sounds of live music on weekend nights. The selections ranges from jazz to hard rock. This informal place is very popular with the local business people. You will find a pool table upstairs.

Discos

You can cure your dancing fever at a number of nightclubs.

CHEERS, *Vien Dong Hotel, 275A Pham Ngu Lao Street, District 1, Ho Chi Minh City.*

Young Vietnamese crowd into this loud, brassy nightclub. There is no cover charge, but your first drink of the evening costs 70,000 dong ($6.40). And the standard prices are not much lower.

DOWNUNDER DISCO, *Saigon Floating Hotel, District 1, Ho Chi Minh City. Tel. (84 8) 8556831.*

This club aims at attracting a trendy crowd, and is popular with tourists. You can dance the night away until 2 am on the Saigon River.

MAXIM'S, *15 Ding Khoi Street, District 1, Ho Chi Minh City. Tel. (84 8) 225554.*

At 5 pm the dance floor gets pumped up at this favorite restaurant. If your are not in the mood to dance, give the karaoke a try.

Dinner Shows

THE MONDIAL HOTEL DINNER THEATER, *109 Dong Khoi Street, District 1, Ho Chi Minh City. Tel. (84 8) 8296291; Fax (84 8) 8296273.*

The Au Co Troupe plays traditional music on instruments like bamboo xylophones, bronze gongs and flutes accompanied by folk songs. The troupe performs Tuesday through Friday evenings in the hotel's Skyview Restaurant.

SPORTS & RECREATION
Golf

Golf is a popular pastime among both expatriates and locals. The best courses are found at resorts outside Ho Chi Minh City (in Dalat and Phan Thiet). Most golf courses are private, but allow daily play and equipment rental. The cost of one day of play runs around $100 per person.

• **Song Be Golf Course**, *Thuan Giao Commune, Thuan District, Song Be Province. Tel. (84 8) 855802 or 855803; Fax (84 8) 855804. Office: 254 Nguyen Dinh Chieu Street, District 3, Ho Chi Minh City. Tel. (84 8) 8231218 or 231223.* The resort is 20 kilometers from the city center on Highway 13. The facilities include an 18 hole course, a 56 bay, 2 story driving range, tennis courts and a snack bar. Special package rates available Tuesdays through Fridays.

• **Vietnam International Golf Club**, *Thu Duc District, Ho Chi Minh City. Office: 40-42 Nguyen Trai, District 1, Ho Chi Minh City. Tel. (84 8) 8322084; Fax (84 8) 832093.* Opened in 1993, this Saigon Tourist golf club is backed by Taiwanese interests, and was the first foreign club of its type. The driving range offers a less expensive alternative for practice.

Sailing

You can get information about sailing trips along the Saigon River from the following places:

• **Ben Nghe Sailing**, *Tel. (84 8) 8290855*
• **Samaser Sailing**, *Tel. (84 8) 8225230*

Running
- **Hash House Harriers**, *Floating Hotel, 1a Me Linh Square, District 1, Ho Chi Minh City*. The Hash House Harriers is an infamous group of expatriates who hold serious weekend runs. The group usually takes a bus to the country, then runs and walks along rural roads and country trails. The meeting point is the Floating Hotel at 2:30 on Sundays. Check message boards in area restaurants for more information.

Swimming
- **The Floating Hotel**, *1a Me Linh Square, District 1, Ho Chi Minh City. Tel. (84 8) 8290783*. This boat/hotel on the Saigon river allows use of the hotel pool for a fee of $10 per day.
- **International Club**, *285b Cach Mang Thang Tam, District 10, Ho Chi Minh City*. The club allows non-members to use the pool for a nominal daily fee.
- **Lam Son Pool**, *342 Tran Binh Trong, District 5, Ho Chi Minh City*. This public pool is competition size, and a good place for a serious workout.
- **The Worker's Club**, *55b Nguyen Thi Minh Khai, District 3, Ho Chi Minh City*. For the French this was the Circle Sportif. In the park next to Reunification Hall you can enjoy the outdoor swimming pool, clay tennis courts and volleyball courts at reasonable prices. Day passes for swimming cost 15,000 dong. Or simply stroll along the park's garden-lined pathways.

Tennis & Court Sports
- **The Rex Hotel Tennis Center**, *141 Nguyen Hue, District 1, Ho Chi Minh City. Tel. (84 8) 82892185*. The two cement courts are lit for night play. Reservations made through the Rex Hotel.
- **The Worker's Club**, *55b Nguyen Thi Minh Khai, District 3, Ho Chi Minh City*. Outdoor clay and cement tennis courts and volleyball courts at reasonable prices.
- **Phan Dinh Phung Stadium**, *8 Vo Van Tan, District 3, Ho Chi Minh City. Tel. (84 8) 8224355*. This indoor stadium has adjoining basketball courts and a track.

Working Out
- **World Gym**, *Tel. (84 8) 895950*. The city's first private gym, has fitness equipment, weight machines and saunas. This club has limited membership but allows visitors to use the facilities for a daily fee.

Spectator Sports

• **Phu Tho Horse Racing**, *2 Le Dai Hanh Street, District 11 Tel. (84 8) 8551205.* You can catch the horse races every Sunday afternoon. Admission to the VIP lounge is only $2.

• **Phan Dinh Phung Stadium**, *8 Vo Van Tan, District 3, Ho Chi Minh City. Tel. (84 8) 8224355.* Indoor stadium hosts a variety of sporting events including international volleyball and soccer matches.

SHOPPING

Most travelers are savvy to the Zippo lighters, US Army dog tags and other manufactured memorabilia enterprising Vietnamese are trying to pass off as original relics from the Vietnam War. For the uninitiated, beware: the city is still flooded with these fake items.

Yes, the tortoise shell is real. Eyeglass frames, bracelets, and knick-knacks literally fill display cases. The unnecessary slaughter of these animals is of nearly epidemic proportion in Vietnam. Of course it is illegal to bring any tortoise shell into the United States.

Lacquerware makes an excellent souvenir or gift. You can find lacquerware boxes and plates in a variety of sizes. Not only is it inexpensive and lightweight, but it is a specialty of Vietnamese artisans. The beautiful lacquerware for sale in Ho Chi Minh City is produced in the south of Vietnam. The process involves numerous painted glazes.

ART GALLERIES IN HO CHI MINH CITY

Artexport, 159 Dong Khoi Street, Ho Chi Minh City. This large gallery is in the city center.

Barotex, 30 Dong Khoi, District 1, Ho Chi Minh City. Tel. (84 8) 8292574. The works here are traditional Vietnamese watercolor paintings.

Hoang Hac, 73 Ly Tu Trong, District 1, Ho Chi Minh City. Tel. (84 8) 8223198. This gallery specializes in oil paintings by local artists.

The Rex Hotel has a gallery on the second floor of the Rex Hotel Coffee Shop.

Saigon Tourist Art Gallery, 55 Dong Khoi Street, District 1, Ho Chi Minh City. Tel. (84 8) 8297473 or 8293444; Fax (84 8) 8291206. Features Vietnamese as well as foreign artists.

Thanh Le Lacquer ware, 102A Nguyen Du Street, District 1, Ho Chi Minh City. Tel. (84 8) 8293558.

Tu Do Art Gallery, 142 Dong Khoi, District 1, Ho Chi Minh City. Tel. (84 8) 8231785; Fax (84 8) 8290936. The owner Thu Ha, is the featured painter.

Jewelry is a hot item. The stores on Dong Khoi Street south of Le Loi Street have cases are full of amber necklaces and bracelets from eastern Europe. Cat's eye, lapis and other colorful stone jewelry are plentiful but no great bargain. Sapphires and rubies of various quality are easy to find, and gold jewelry abounds.

The finest quality jewelry can be found in small neighborhood shops. However be cautious—although the deeply yellow gold and fine workmanship may be appealing, the jewelry may not fit your body. Rings are usually small (often 4 is the largest size), since Vietnamese have smaller hands than Westerners, in general. Shops for tourists will happily re-size a ring to your finger. If you buy pierced earrings at a shop that caters to locals note the stems are much thicker than American earrings, and may have to be replaced.

Shops in District 1 offer souvenirs imported from China such as carvings of Buddha.

Books

You can find books in English at **Cuu Long Book Shop**, *41 Ham Nghi, District 1, Ho Chi Minh City.*

Quoc Su, *20 Ho Huan Nghiep Street, District 1, Ho Chi Minh City. Tel. (84 8) 8244388,* resembles an old attic. The shelves are full of old books, most of which are not collectable, but merely interesting. The store also sells photocopies of history books.

Furniture

One of the largest suppliers of rattan furniture operates a showroom in the center of the city. **Duc Thanh Rattan**, *182 Pasteur Street, District 1, Ho Chi Minh City. Tel. (84 8) 8294991 ext. 3389,* made the rattan furniture in the Rex Hotel and the Caravelle Hotel. Special arrangements for international shipping can be made.

Silk

Cuu Long Tailor Shop, *177 Dong Khoi Street, District 1, Ho Chi Minh City. Tel. (84 8) 8296831.* This shop has the reputation of being the place to buy ao dais, the traditional woman's outfit of a flowing shirt over billowy pants. Both ready-made and tailor-cut ao dais available.

Markets

Ben Thanh Market, *at the start of Le Loi Street, District 1, Ho Chi Minh City. Tel. (84 8) 8292096.* It is easy to see why Ben Than Market is popular: it is clean, organized, and indoors. The market was built in 1914. In 1986, the market complex was completely renovated. The streets surrounding the market are lively and as full of local goods as the market itself.

SAIGON'S SOUVENIR SHOPS

Bi's Shop, 12 Pham Ngu Lao Street, District 1, Ho Chi Minh City. Tel. (84 8) 8357707. Weavings and handicrafts from the hill tribes are sold here.

Cultural Shop, 50 Dong Khoi Street, District 1, Ho Chi Minh City. Tel. (84 8) 8292896. This is your basic souvenir shop, with a good selection and reasonable prices.

Fine Art and Ceramic, 28 Nguyen Hue Street, Ho Chi Minh City; Tel. (84 8) 8231434.

The shop is stronger on the ceramics than fine art.

Intershop, 101 Nam Ky Khoi Nghia Street, Ho Chi Minh City. Tel.. (84 8) 8293191.

This international trading center offers a large assortment of high quality merchandise, including silk clothing.

Lam Son Gallery, 106 Nguyen Van Troi Street, Ho Chi Minh City. Tel. (84 8) 8442304. Lam Son has a good selection of lacquerware and other souvenirs.

Les Spices, 25 Dong Khoi Street, District 1, Ho Chi Minh City. Original gifts of spices, jam, coffee or tea in artfully made containers.

Number 1, Nguyen Hue Street, District 1, Ho Chi Minh City. Tel. (84 8) 8291516, extension 8075. This shop has a large selection of inexpensive souvenirs.

Number 47, Vo Thi Sau Street, Ho Chi Minh City. Tel. (84 8) 8225978, has good lacquer ware that is so popular among tourists. This tiny Chinese import store sells primarily to locals, so you'll get better prices on Chinese trinkets for the folks back home.

Trang, 45 Dong Khoi Street, District 1, Ho Chi Minh City. This shop sells traditional musical instruments.

Another market, in District 3, remains untouched by tourists, although it has most of what Ben Thanh offers: silk, produce, toiletries, house ware. Naturally prices are lower here, but the market is more congested and less clean than Ben Thanh. You can get to the market by asking a cyclo driver to take you to the market in District 3.

Binh Tai Market, *Hau Giang Street, District 5, Ho Chi Minh City. Tel. (84 8) 8556130.* The Cholon market, which lines the heart of the district, is a true Chinese marketplace. The entire Cholon market is a piece of China. Colorful stands and exotic aromas fill the senses. While in Cholon walk through the Thuan Kieu Street to see the bird market.

Practical Shopping

Don't despair should you loose your tooth brush, razor, or shampoo. If you must shop out of necessity and not pleasure, you will have no problem finding what you need, although prices may be slightly higher than back home. The Ben Thanh Market has many stands which sell western shampoo, deodorant and even cologne. The unnamed and unnumbered **department store**, *Le Loi Street and Nguyen Hue, District 1, Ho Chi Minh City. Tel. 299973*, carries a toiletries, clothes and other items you made need.

The **Student Mart**, *138 Tran Quang Khai Street, District 1, Ho Chi Minh City. Tel. (84 8) 8444068*, is a convenience store owned by a group of college students. It is well-stocked with many incidental toiletries you may need as well as a variety of snacks and beverages.

Photography & Film

Film, photo processing and even cameras are readily available in many shops along Nguyen Hue Street. The best price on Kodak slide film is at Sinh Cafe.

Some places you can buy cameras and film include:
- **Minilab**, *27F, 56 Nguyen Hue Street, District 1, Ho Chi Minh City. Tel. (84 8) 8292860*.
- **Huong Sen**, *66 Dong Khoi Street, District 1, Ho Chi Minh City*.
- **Sinh Cafe**, *179 Pham Ngu Lao, District 1, Ho Chi Minh City. Tel. (84 8) 8355601*.

DAY TRIPS & EXCURSIONS

The **Cao Dai Temple** in Tay Ninh, lies about 101 kilometers north of Ho Chi Minh City. For years this Holy See was off-limits to tourists. The eclectic temple pays tribute to the Cao Dai pantheon which includes Buddha, Jesus, and French writer Victor Hugo. The Divine Eye is the symbol of unity in the Cao Dai belief. At noon you can stand on the indoor balconies and watch the daily prayers. Either hire a car from your hotel or join a cafe tour to the Cao Dai Temple.

The **Black Lady Mountain** is the site of pilgrimages in February and August and has been used as a place of worship for generations. A path leads visitors along the side of the mountain to the Van Son pagoda at the top of the mountain. The pagoda is dedicated to the Black Lady who is revered as a goddess. This mountain, 884 meters high, is part of a range of low mountains 15 kilometers north of Tay Ninh, and is often included in tours to Cao Dai Temple.

Cu Chi Tunnels are a military tunnel system and offers a strong testimony to the determination of the resistance struggle against the

French. Over 200 kilometers of tunnels, built in the 1940s, held medical centers, houses and military command rooms. They are about 50 kilometers from Ho Chi Minh City. For more information call Cu Chi Tunnels office at *(84 8) 8920384 or 8920244.*

At Cu Chi, there are a handful of cafes that serve standard, inexpensive Vietnamese food and cater to the tour crowds passing through. Among these are the **Bai Dua Restaurant**, *88 Ha Long Street, Cu Chi Central District*; **Huong Bien Restaurant**, *47 Quang Trung Street, Cu Chi District*; and **Thang Muoi Restaurant**, *7-9 Thuy Van Road, Cu Chi Central District.*

PRACTICAL INFORMATION
Banks
• **Nam Do Bank**, *175 Ham Nghi, District 1, Ho Chi Minh City.* This office is close to Ben Thanh Market.
• **The Vietcom Bank**, *17 Ton Duc Than Street, District 1, Ho Chi Minh City. Tel. (84 8) 8299226.* The Vietcom Bank has an exchange office on Dong Khoi Street, across from the Hotel Continental.
• **Vinasiam**, *2 Pho Duc Chinh, District 1, Ho Chi Minh City. Tel. (84 8) 8210557; Fax (84 8) 8210585.* This is a joint venture between Vietnam Agriculture Bank and the Siam Commercial Bank and other Thai interests.

Travel Offices
• **Diethelm Travel**, *1a Me Linh Square, District 1, Ho Chi Minh City. Tel. (84 8) 8294932; Fax (84 8) 8294747.* Diethelm Tours operates branch offices throughout Asia. They can make arrangements for travel in Vietnam and other countries.
• **Dong Nai Tourist Company**, *75 Le Thanh Ton Street, District 1, Ho Chi Minh City. Tel. (84 8) 8296093; Fax (84 8) 8293024.*
• **Minh Chau**, *39/3 Tran Nhat Duat, District 1, Ho Chi Minh City. Tel. (84 8) 8442807; Fax 439471.* Regional Specialists arrange highland treks, veteran tours, and excursions to Laos and Cambodia.
• **Global Holidays**, *106 Nguyen Hue, District 1, Ho Chi Minh City. Tel. (84 8) 8228453; Fax (84 8) 8228454.*
• **Sinh Cafe**, *179 Pham Ngu Lao, District 1, Ho Chi Minh City. Tel. (84 8) 8355601.*

KEY SAIGON PHONE NUMBERS

Emergency Numbers (from pay phones)
Ambulance 115
Fire 114
Police 113

Useful Numbers (from pay phones)
Directory Assistance 116
Information 108
International operator 110

Information Numbers
Airport Information 443179
Tourist Assistance 296983
Train information: (84 8) 8945543
Vietcom Bank Tel. (84 8) 8225705 or 297238

12. MEKONG DELTA & THE SOUTHERN COAST

THE MEKONG DELTA

The sprawling wetlands and stretching waterways of Vietnam's south-ernmost region are part of the country's most fertile area. The **Mekong River** continually deposits silt, adding land mass and rejuvenating the region. One of the world's longest rivers, it runs from the Tibetan highlands, through Myanmar (Burma), China, Laos, Thailand, and Cambodia to the sea. The Mekong is known to the Vietnamese as the *River of Nine Dragons* (Song Cuu Long) because it divides into nine tributaries in the Mekong Delta.

The **Mekong Delta** begins in Phnom Penh, Cambodia. From May to November the area is awash in monsoon rains. The rain not only raises the water level of the Mekong, but reduce its salt content. In September the river is at its highest.

Here is the heart of Vietnamese agriculture, a land that supports two full rice seasons per year and a variety of crops ranging from green vegetables to tropical fruit. Fish farms are found throughout the area.

About 15 million people live in the Mekong Delta, many spend most of their lives directly on the water, in boats or "floating" houses (which are supported by stilts). Village life on the Mekong maintains a unique system of dependence upon the water; the water is a lifeline that provides everything from occupation (agriculture) to recreation. The Khmer and Cham minorities call the Mekong Delta home; their traditions flavor the region.

The Mekong Delta hosts an array of birds, many of which are endangered. Cranes, egrets, herons and migratory ducks are found in the southern Mekong Delta. Conservation measures attempt to protect this rare ecosystem.

PROVINCES OF THE MEKONG DELTA
Long An
Tien Giang
Dong Thap
An Giang
Ben Tre
Kien Giang
Hau Giang
Cuu Long
Cantho
Minh Hai
– and parts of **Tay Ninh, Song Be,**
and **Dong Nai** *Provinces*

Mytho – Tien Giang Province

The town of **Mytho** (population 90,000) is the capital **Tien Giang Province**. Mytho is only 75 kilometers (45 miles) south of Ho Chi Minh City. Many tourists make a day trip to Mytho to get a taste of the Mekong Delta.

Boat trips from Mytho along the Mekong River show you the beauty of life on the Mekong, although the foliage along the river is more lush further south. You can cross the Mekong by ferry. Just a few blocks from the ferry landing is a street that specializes in selling snakes. Live snakes, snakes preserved in jars, and snakes prepared for cooking are all sold at the stands.

ARRIVALS & DEPARTURES

Mytho is on Highway 1 between Ho Chi Minh City and Cantho. The cafes tours run short trips (1 to 3 days) to the Mekong Delta that include Mytho.

ORIENTATION

Mytho is on the river and the ferry crossing is in the center of town. You can hire boats at the ferry crossing for trips to the floating market or nearby islands.

WHERE TO STAY

HUONG DUONG HOTEL, *33 Trung Trac Street, Mytho. Tel. (84 73) 872011. Singles/doubles $20.*

This 20 room hotel has basic rooms and reasonably good service.

SONG TIEN HOTEL, *101 Trung Trac Street, Mytho. Tel. (84 73) 872009 or 873126. Singles/doubles $20 to $40.*

This is the largest hotel in the city and the only one that caters to foreign tourists. All rooms are clean and have air-conditioning. The restaurant serves good regional food for reasonable prices. The hotel has a small nightclub and shops.

WHERE TO EAT

SING TIEN RESTAURANT, *Vietnamese, 1 Lanh Binh Can, Mytho. (84 73) 855441.*

Sing Tien is one of a number of cafes found in the center of town. The food is simple and good.

SEEING THE SIGHTS

The **Catholic Church**, *32 Hung Vuong Street, Mytho*, was constructed just before the turn of the century. Two services are held on Sundays.

You can hire a small motorized boat and driver for excursions along the Mekong River. There are many beautiful islands to visit in the area. One of the most interesting is **Tan Phong Island** where orchids are cultivated.

The sanctuary on the **Island of the Coconut Monk** was home to the Coconut Monk and his followers for years. The pacifist monk allowed this island to be a refuge for those who disagreed with the war. He was persecuted by the South Vietnamese government, then after Reunification, the Vietnamese officials. The Island and its fanciful temple is sometimes not open to visitors.

If you did not see enough snakes in the market, visit the **Snake Farm**, *Tel. (84 73) 8493*. It is a collection of reptiles and exotic regional animals, such as monkeys. And, of course, a farm where snakes are raised to be sold. The Snake Farm is on highway 1, about 10 kilometers (6 miles) north of Mytho.

PRACTICAL INFORMATION

• **Tien Giang Province Bank**, *15B Nam Ky Khoi Nghia Street, Mytho.*
• **Post Office**, *1 Le Loi Street, Mytho. Tel. (84 73) 872347 or 87246.*
• **Tien Giang Province Tourist Office**, *56 Hung Vuong Street. Mytho. Tel. (84 73) 83591.*

Chau Doc – An Giang Province

The variety of religious diversity comes into focus in **An Giang Province**. About 75 percent of the 70,000 Muslims in Vietnam live in the province. **Chau Doc** is one of the towns where you can catch a glimpse of Cham Muslims and Hoa Hoa and Hindu communities.

In the decoration of the houses you will find interesting details. The Muslim houses have cut-out carvings of crescent moons; light blue paint accents the trim. Many people raise fish in cages under their floating houses. Rice and other crops are grown in the area.

ARRIVALS & DEPARTURES

Chau Doc is on the Vietnam-Cambodia border. The 250 kilometer (156 miles) drive from Ho Chi Minh City on Highway 91 takes almost seven hours. Buses make the trip daily.

WHERE TO STAY

HANG CHAU HOTEL, *Le Loi Street, Chau Doc. Tel. (84 76) 866196 or 866197 to 866198, Fax (84 76) 866599. Singles/doubles $23 to $35.*

This 34 room hotel is the only tourist hotel in the area. The hotel offers standard amenities and has a good restaurant.

WHERE TO EAT

The restaurant at the **Hang Chau Hotel** is the best in town. You will find a number of cafes along **Chi Lang Street**.

SEEING THE SIGHTS

The Chau Doc Catholic Church, *450 Le Loi Street, Chau Doc*, was built in 1922. Services are still held here.

A visit to the **Temple of Lady Chau Xe** is a rich experience that fills the senses. In the center of the courtyard a large urn stands. Here brightly colored paper and tinsel offerings are burnt.

Inside the temple, incense hangs from the ceiling and giant columns of incense burn at the altars. Families sit on blankets on the floor, mingle outside and slowly move around the altars holding incense and bowing in prayer. Offerings of food are brought to Lady Chau Xe so she will grant prosperity to families. People bring what they can: the rich bring whole, roasted pigs, the poor bring fruit. Food fills the altar. The temple is outside the city center on Lady Chau Xe Temple Street.

Sam Mountain has a view of Cambodia. The walk up the winding staircases takes about one-half hour. At the top of the mountain a refreshment stand sells cold drinks. The mountain is about 2 kilometers (1.25 miles) from Chau Doc.

Long Xuyen – An Giang Province

Long Xuyen is a small Mekong town which has a Khmer population. The small city has churches and temples, but the most notable attraction is the Tong Duc Thang Museum, which holds ancient artifacts found in the area.

ARRIVALS & DEPARTURES

Long Xuyen lies near the mid-point of Highway 91 that runs between Chau Doc and Cantho. Regular buses serve the city.

WHERE TO STAY

LONG XUYEN HOTEL, *17 Nguyen Van Cung Street, Long Xuyen. Tel. (84 76) 852927 or 852659. Singles/doubles $16 to $26.*

The Long Xuyen Hotel has comfortable rooms with air-conditioning and amenities.

WHERE TO EAT

Many small cafes in the city center serve good Vietnamese food.

SEEING THE SIGHTS

The **Tong Duc Thang Museum** holds artifacts from the ancient civilization of the area. The Oc-Eo civilization flourished in the first half of this millennium, but very little is know about their history. Archaeological excavations have yielded the only clues to this mysterious civilization, and includes coins, ceramic ware and some metalwork. Most of the artifacts date from the 3rd and 4th centuries. This museum is the only repository that preserves what remains of the Oc-Eo civilization.

PRACTICAL INFORMATION

• **Provincial Bank**, *17 Nguyen Van Cung Street, Long Xuyen. Tel. (84 76) 852184 or 852345.*
• **An Giang Tourist**, *83/55 Nguyen Hue Street, Long Xuyen. Tel. (84 76) 852635 or 852554.*

Cantho – Hau Giang Province

The largest town in the Mekong Delta, **Cantho** (population 300,000) is the capital of **Hau Giang Province**. Rice husking mills, mango, durian and orange orchards, and river transportation make the town the economic center of the Mekong Delta. Cantho has a Khmer population of significant size. During the Vietnam War, Cantho was a large military base.

ARRIVALS & DEPARTURES

The Cantho airport lies outside the city. A tax of 15,000 dong ($1.37) is charged to passengers. A taxi to the city center costs $3.

Most tourists arrive by car or bus on Highway 1. Cantho is 170 kilometers from Ho Chi Minh City. The cafes in Ho Chi Minh City operate tours that include Cantho. You may leave the tour at any point to explore the Mekong on your own.

ORIENTATION

The city sits on the water. The main pier is near the central market. A large park runs along the water. The bus station is about two kilometers from the city center.

GETTING AROUND TOWN

You can easily walk around Cantho, and in one afternoon see the interesting parts of the city. Taxis are available.

Cantho is a hub of trade, so the tributaries of the Mekong that flow into the city are crowded and busy waterways. The intense beauty of life on the Mekong River can be seen by taking a boat ride to the nearby hamlets. Hire the boat at the dock near the central market. Some of the drivers speak some English and have written testimonials from and photographs of their previous passengers. You should be able to negotiate the price down from the hourly rate for half and full day trips.

WHERE TO STAY

CANTHO HOTEL, *16 Hai Ba Trung Street, Cantho. Tel. (84 71) 822218. Singles/doubles $16.*

The Cantho Hotel is a good bet for budget travelers. The rooms are clean and adequate. If you opt for no air-conditioning, the price is reduced to $10.

INTERNATIONAL HOTEL (Quoc Te Hotel), *12 Hai Ba Trung Street, Cantho. Tel. (84 71) 822079 or 822080, Fax (84 71) 821039. Singles/doubles $30 to $55. Credit cards accepted.*

The 40 room International Hotel is the most noticeable building on the skyline. At night a green strip of lights outlines the hotel. This is a reasonable tourist hotel with little personality. The restaurant serves good regional dishes.

NINH KIEU HOTEL, *2 Hai Ba Trung Street, Cantho. Tel. (84 71) 821171 or 825285 or 824583, Fax (84 71) 821101. Singles/doubles $40 to $60. Credit cards accepted.*

This is the best hotel in the city. The white hotel looks like a large house. It sits at the end of the waterfront, isolated from the city noise, and the grounds are surrounded by water on two sides. The rooms are comfortable with modern amenities. The waterfront restaurant serves excellent seafood.

WHERE TO EAT

NINH KIEU HOTEL RESTAURANT, *Vietnamese/moderate, 2 Hai Ba Trung Street, Cantho. Tel. (84 71) 821171 or 825285 or 824583, Fax (84 71) 821101.*

This elegant restaurant on the waterfront specializes in regional seafood. The service is excellent, and the atmosphere is the most inviting in the city. This is the perfect place for an evening meal. Large windows overlook the river and sparkling city.

VINH LOI RESTAURANT, *Vietnamese/inexpensive, 42 Hai Ba Trung Street, Cantho. Tel. (84 71) 821124.*

This small restaurant across from the waterfront serves good seafood and vegetarian dishes. The tables upstairs give you a nice view with your meal.

SEEING THE SIGHTS

The provincial seat of higher learning, **Cantho University**, *30 Thang 4 Street*, is not open for visits from foreign tourists. Founded in 1966, the university has 14 departments and specializes in agricultural studies.

You can hire a boat from the dock at the main market to visit the **floating markets at Phung Hiep and Phong Dien**. A motorized boat that holds eight should cost no more than $5 per hour. These markets are fascinating. At the markets groups of boats come together, some selling produce, others with household goods or clothes. Visiting the market gives you a sense of life on the river. Go ahead and buy something if it catches your eye. Prices on the water are better than in town.

The **Museum of Ho Chi Minh**, *Hoa Binh Street, Cantho*, a standard utilitarian-style concrete building, is in the center of town. It contains items pertaining to Ho Chi Minh and traces his life and rise to power.

The Khmer community attends services at **Munirangsyaram Pagoda**, *32 Hoa Binh Street, Cantho*. The Buddhist sanctuary has decoration unique to the Khmer traditions. Visitors are welcome to witness evening prayer everyday at 5 pm .

NIGHTLIFE & ENTERTAINMENT

The most superb view of Cantho is from the water at night. As boats slowly paddle across the Mekong in the glow of the few neon signs, the perspective of timelessness and change that characterizes the entire country comes into focus. Boats hired from the dock by the central market are less expensive in the evening.

SHOPPING

The **central market** is one of the most colorful and interesting that you will find in Vietnam. The food available here is a good sampling of the region's tropical fruit and noodle specialties.

You can see the catch of the day en route to local restaurants as vendors clean the fish and sell seafood in the center of the market.

PRACTICAL INFORMATION

- **Vietcom Bank**, *2 Ngo Gia Tu Street, Cantho. Tel. (84 71) 820445.*
- **Post Office**, *2 Hoa Binh Street, Cantho. Tel. 84 71) 820445.* This is the largest post office in the Mekong Delta.
- **Cantho Tourist**, *27 Chau Van Liem, Cantho. Tel. (84 71) 821853 or 821804 or 821852, Fax (84 71) 822719.* This branch of the government tourist organization operates nine hotels in the region.
- **Cantho Tourist and Vietnam Airlines Office**, *20 Hai Ba Trung, Cantho. Tel. (84 71) 822854 or 821853, Fax (84 71) 822719.*
- **Hospital** at the corner of Hoa Binh Street and Chau Van Liem Street for medical emergencies.

Rach Gia – Kien Giang Province

Rach Gia is a small town in the southern part of the Mekong Delta, and is the capital of **Kien Giang Province**. Rach Gia is close to the Cambodian border, and many Khmer live here. The mountains which form a natural border with Cambodia and the Gulf of Thailand make Rach Gia a picturesque and tranquil city. Most foreign tourists come to Rach Gia on their way to Phu Quoc Island.

ARRIVALS & DEPARTURES

Vietnam Airlines has flights from Rach Gia to Ho Chi Minh City and Phu Quoc Island. These flights are scheduled for Tuesdays, Thursdays and Saturdays. Buses connect Rach Gia to Cantho and Ho Chi Minh City. Ferries make the twelve hour trip to Phu Quoc Island.

ORIENTATION

Rach Gia is a small town, with its center on an island which is surrounded by The Cai Lon River on two sides and the Gulf of Thailand on the third. The town is often used as a gateway to Phu Quoc Island.

WHERE TO STAY

MAY FIRST HOTEL, *38 Nguyen Hung Son Street, Rach Gia. Tel. (84 77) 862103. Singles $20; doubles $25.*
The May First Hotel is run by the regional tourist authority. It is the newest hotel in the city and probably the best run. All rooms have air-conditioning and standard amenities.

WHERE TO EAT

SUNFLOWER RESTAURANT, *Vietnamese/inexpensive, 680 Nguyen Van Cu, Rach Gia. Tel. (84 77) 863350.*
Seafood is the specialty of the house here. The restaurant serves tasty Vietnamese dishes which are typical to the Mekong Delta.

SEEING THE SIGHTS

The **Ong Bac Pagoda**, *14 Nguyen Du Street*, is a Chinese temple which holds a statue of a reincarnation of the Jade Emperor.
One of the oldest pagodas in the region is **Phat Lon**, *Quang Trung Street, near Mac Dinh Chi Street*, which was constructed over 200 years ago. The Phat Lon Pagoda is a center of worship for the region's Khmer population.
The **Rach Gia Museum**, *21 Nguyen Van Troi Street, Rach Gia*, offers insight to the history of the area.

PRACTICAL INFORMATION

• **Bank**, *1 Nguyen Cong Tru Street. Tel. (84 77) 863578.*
• **Kien Giang Province Tourist Office**, *12 Ly Tu Trong Street, Rach Gia. Tel. (84 77) 862001, Fax (84 77) 86221.*

Phu Quoc Islands – Kien Giang Province

The island of **Phu Quoc** offers some of the best beaches and most beautiful undisturbed natural landscape in the country. It lies only 15 kilometers from Cambodia and 45 kilometers (28 miles) from mainland Vietnam. The sleepy town of 50,000 inhabitants, once known for growing peppers and making fish sauce (nuoc mam), is striving to become a major tourist destination. With over 40 (25 miles) kilometers of empty beaches, the island attracts tourists and expatriates alike.
A trip to Phu Quoc means getting away from it all. The only town is Duong Dong fishing village, a community warm and welcoming to foreigners. The most popular sport for vacationers here is reading. At 10 pm every night electricity on the entire island shuts down, so there are no noisy bars or discos.

ARRIVALS & DEPARTURES

Vietnam Airlines has regular flights from Ho Chi Minh City to Phu Quoc Island. You can hire a boats to Phu Quoc from Ha Tien town in the Mekong Delta.

ORIENTATION

When you arrive at the airport, a half-hour trip by motorbike will take you to the island's only hotel.

GETTING AROUND TOWN

The best means of transportation is by foot. You can catch a ride on a motor bike if necessary.

WHERE TO STAY

HUONG BIEN GUEST HOUSE, *Duong Dong Town, Phu Quoc Island. Tel. (84 77) 846050 or 846082. Singles/doubles $15 to $20.*

This simple 12 room guest house is the only place for tourists to stay on Phu Quoc Island. The electricity on the entire island shuts off at 10 pm every night, leaving you alone with the sea-breeze and moonlight.

SEEING THE SIGHTS

Most visitors to Phu Quoc come here for solitude in the gorgeous natural surroundings. The guest house is on Truong Khoe beach, where there is never more than a handful of tourists. The northern part of the island has primeval forests that you can explore.

This is the most intense slice of fishing village life you will find. Colorful marine blue and red fishing boats fill the docks on Phu Quoc. When you get your fill of the subtleties and aromas of fishing village life, you can visit one of the many factories that make fish sauce (nuoc mam).

PRACTICAL INFORMATION

- **Post Office** *is across the street from the hospital on the main street of Duong Dong town.*
- **Tourist Office** is the Huong Bien Guest house, *Tel. (84 77) 846050.*

Bac Lieu – Minh Hai Province

Bac Lieu is an interesting place for a quick visit. Area conservation efforts attempt to maintain the gentle balance that preserves the regional wildlife. Much of the low-lying coastal plains of Minh Hai are protected areas.

ARRIVALS & DEPARTURES

Highway 1 runs south from Cantho to Bac Lieu; buses serve the city regularly.

WHERE TO STAY

BAC LIEU HOTEL, *4 Hoang Van Thu, Bac Lieu. Tel. (84 78) 822621 or 822623. Singles/doubles $20.*

This decent establishment offers air-conditioned rooms; it is the only reasonable tourist hotel in the city.

SEEING THE SIGHTS

The southern Mekong province of Minh Hai is a vast wetland that is home to migratory birds. The largest bird colonies are found near Bac Lieu. This province has a concentration of coastal marshes and hundreds of types of birds. Preservation of the wetlands offer protection for the many rare species in the area.

Visitor centers are being built with the assistance of foreign aid. Just outside Bac Lieu town two preserved areas; the **Bac Lieu Bird Colony** is only 5 kilometers (3 miles) from the town, and the **Ngoc Hien Bird Colony** is 70 kilometers (43 miles) to the south.

PRACTICAL INFORMATION

• **Post Office**, *Tran Phu Road, Bac Lieu.*
• **Minh Hai Tourist**, *2 Hoang Van Thu Street, Bac Lieu. Tel. (84 78) 822623.*

THE SOUTHERN COAST

Vung Tau

Vung Tau is spread out over a peninsula; all three sides on the water are lined with beaches. Known as Cape Saint Jacques during French colonial period, Vung Tau sits on a peninsula at the base of low mountains. The long beaches and budding nightlife provide a welcome change of scenery from Ho Chi Minh City.

It is the country's most visited seaside resort, in part due to its proximity to Ho Chi Minh City, and the warm, mild climate which allows year-round swimming. Like other hosts of a constant tourist season, Vung Tau is not without its urban problems, such as crowding and pollution.

Vung Tau often gets booked-up during holidays (especially Christmas and Thanksgiving), since many locals and expatriates flood the beaches during time-off. The many new hotels have helped to curbed this problem and more resorts are in the works. The area is also being expanded as a base for oil exploration and drilling.

Temperatures range from a low of 15°C (59°F) in December to 31°C (88°F) in May. Humidity rarely drops below 80 percent, and rainy season hits between July and September.

ARRIVALS & DEPARTURES

By Air

The city has an airport, located just off Pham Hong Street, about eight kilometers from the city center. However, Vietnam Airlines does not currently fly to Vung Tau, although there are plans to begin service. Helicopter flights connect Ho Chi Minh City with Vung Tau.

By Bus

The Vung Tau **Bus Station**, *52 Nam Ky Khoi Nghia Street*, lies between the city center, to the east and Back (Bai Sau) Beach, to the west, about 1.5 kilometers from either. You can catch buses to Ho Chi Minh City at the Ha Long Hotel and the Hanh Phuoc Hotel.

By Cafe Tour

Cafe tours run vans to Vung Tau about once per week.

By Car

Highway 51, a road in good repair, connects Ho Chi Minh City to Vung Tau. The 128 kilometer (80 mile) drive takes about two hours.

By Hydrofoil

The best way to go to Vung Tau is by **hydrofoil** from Bach Dang Quay in Ho Chi Minh City. The one-hour and fifteen-minute ride costs $12 each way. The hydrofoils travel four times daily from 7 am to 6 pm.

For more information contact **Vina Express**, *6A Nguyen Tat Thanh Street, District 4, Ho Chi Minh City. Tel. (84 8) 8253888 or 8224621; Fax (84 8) 825333.*

By Mini-Bus

You can catch a mini-van from the Van Thanh Bus Station in Ho Chi Minh City. A one-way trip costs $3.

ORIENTATION

The city is surrounded by sand and surf, but the best beaches are a few kilometers out of the city. From the city center, the Big Mountain (Nui Lon) lies to the northwest, and Little Mountain (Nui Nho) to the south. Hoang Hoa Tham Street is the center for restaurants. On the northern Cape you'll find Ben Da fishing village which supplies the restaurants with fresh seafood and provides photo opportunities for tourists.

GETTING AROUND TOWN

The easiest way to get around the peninsula is by motor bike. Most of the sights and the better spots of beach are away from the city center. The walk from one side of the peninsula to the other may be long, but is by no means difficult.

WHERE TO STAY

CANADIAN HOTEL, *48 Quang Trung Street. Tel. (84 64) 8459852 or 853321 or 852523, Fax (84 64) 859851. Singles/doubles $50 to $100. Credit cards accepted.*

This hotel with new rooms is popular with expatriates who escape Ho Chi Minh City on the weekends. The fresh, clean rooms are pleasant to come back to after spending a few hours in the sun.

PALACE HOTEL (Hoa Binh Hotel), *11 Nguyen Trai, Vung Tau. Tel. (84 64) 852411 or 852265, Fax (84 64) 859878. Singles $28 to $32; doubles $30 to $53. Credit cards accepted.*

This pleasant hotel in the city center has only twenty rooms and a friendly atmosphere. The 20 room hotel has a restaurant, cafe and beauty salon. After a harrowing day at the beach you can get a massage at the Palace.

PETRO HOUSE HOTEL, *89 Tran Hung Dao Street. Tel. (84 64) 852014, Fax (84 64) 852015. Singles/doubles $50 to $100. Credit cards accepted.*

Another expatriate weekend retreat, and the most comfortable place in the city. The 60 room hotel is built in the French colonial style. The decor does not take the theme too far. Inside you will find comfortable rooms with modern amenities. The French restaurant, Ma Maison, has tasty dinner specials.

PHUONG DONG HOTEL, *2 Thuy Van Street, Vung Tau. Tel. (84 64) 852185 or 852593, Fax 859336. Rates: single $20 to $40, double $25 to $45.*

This small hotel on Back (Bai Sau) Beach caters to Asian travelers. Consequently, the facilities are large and comfortable. The hotel is a rather good deal, considering prices in Vung Tau are higher than in other parts of the county.

REX HOTEL (Thang Loi Hotel), *1 Duy Tan Street, Vung Tau. Tel. (84 64) 852135 or 852612, Fax (84 64) 859862. Singles $28 to $42; doubles $30 to $45.*

The large tourist hotel is completely unremarkable. It is not affiliated with the Rex Hotel in Ho Chi Minh City. The only reason to stay here is to play tennis on the hotel's courts.

THANG MUOI HOTEL, *4 Thuy Van Street, Vung Tau. Tel. (84 64) 852665 or 852313 Singles/doubles $30 to $65. Credit cards accepted.*

These bungalows are on Back Beach away from the center of town. The Thang Muoi lets you thoroughly enjoy the beach. This is a reasonably secluded place to stay.

WHERE TO EAT/NIGHTLIFE

Moderate

FRENCHIE'S RESTAURANT, *French/moderate, The Grand Hotel, 26 Quang Trung Street. Tel. (84 64) 856164, Fax (84 64) 856088.*

This restaurant serves real French food prepared by a real Frenchman. The wine selection, all French, is good. The tables in the garden are a good place to have a reclusive meal.

MA MAISON RESTAURANT AND BAR, *French/moderate, Petro House Hotel, Tran Hung Dao Street, next to Petro House Hotel. Tel. (84 64) 852014.*

This eatery is the nicest place in town. And it strives for elegance as part of the colonial-style surroundings of the Petro house. This is a good place to come if you seek wine to complement your French food.

MY PLACE, *Western/moderate, 14 Nguyen Trai Street. Tel. (84 64) 856028.*

The restaurant features a salad bar and table cooking. Good bar-be-cue and sedate atmosphere. The bar upstairs is air-conditioned and the beer garden is open air. My Place is the place for hamburgers in Vung Tau.

WHISPER'S CAFE AND FUN BAR, *Western/moderate, 438 Truong Cong Dinh Street, Vung Tau. Tel. (84 64) 856762. Open daily 11 am to 2 pm lunch, 5 pm to 9:30 pm dinner and disco from 10 pm to late.*

Lunch and dinner served, then the discotheque lights come up and the "fun bar" begins. The place has the reputation as the spot where oil field workers hang.

Inexpensive

HOP THANH RESTAURANT, *Vietnamese/inexpensive, 209 Ba Cu Street, Vung Tau.*

Fried calamari is the best dish in the house. All the other selections will not leave you disappointed.

THUY RESTAURANT, *Vietnamese/inexpensive, 63/1 Hoang Hoa Tham Bai Sau, Vung Tau. Tel. (84 64) 859565.*

If you just want to get away from all the tourist hub-bub, have a meal at Thuy Restaurant for good food and standard noodle-house atmosphere.

NIGHTLIFE & ENTERTAINMENT

APOCALYPSE NOW, *438 Truong Cong Dinh Street.*

In the style of the Apocalypse Now Bar in Ho Chi Minh City, this bar plays classic rock, serves cold beer and has a late night crowd.

CHI-CHI'S BAR, *236 Ba Cu, Vung Tau. Tel. (84 64) 853498.*

The self-proclaimed "sportsman's bar in Vung Tau" has a great atmosphere and the standard pool table. Happy hour runs from 5 pm to 7 pm every day. The bar gets lively after happy hour on weekends.

SEEING THE SIGHTS

Chua Son Buu Pagoda offers the best view of the city and harbor. This peaceful, old pagoda inspires mediation and relaxation. To reach the pagoda, take the steps from Front Beach, just past the Hai Au Hotel.

The French left a lasting legacy: their military fortification. **The French Lighthouse**, dating from 1907, is a working lighthouse 80 meters tall and open to the public. It sits atop Nui Nho Mountain at the southern end of the peninsula. **The French Fort** is now in ruins. This nineteenth century fortification can be seen from the surrounding hillside. A few trek up to take a look at what remains.

Niet Ban Tinh Xa or more simply put, the Reclining Buddha, took five years to construct and was completed in 1971. The concrete statue is 15 metes high, and the marble in the pagoda is from Danang. To reach Niet Ban Tinh Xa, go south along Qung Trung Street, the main avenue that runs along the waterfront in downtown Vung Tau.

You don't have to go to Rio de Janeiro to take in an immense **statue of Jesus**. The Vung Tau version stands nearly 40 meters tall, and has observation balconies at the shoulders. The statue stands on the southern tip of the peninsula. There is a trail that leads from Back Beach to the statue.

Thich Ca Phat Dai Pagoda, *Tran Phu Street*, was built into the side of Lon Mountain in 1941. The white cement Buddha is 10 meters tall and 6 meters across. Due to the size, thankfully the view is better from a distance. The pagoda is located on the northwestern tip of the peninsula and can be reached by heading north on Le Loi Street and turning left on Tran Phu Street.

The **White Palace**, *Quang Trung Street*, was built at the turn of the twentieth century as a vacation residence for the Governor of Indochina. Although it is known as a "royal residence," the only royalty to inhabit the house was King Thanh Thai, who was being kept prisoner here by the French. It later served as residence for Vietnamese President The. Beautiful gardens and grandiose French style give visitors a taste of the bygone colonial lifestyle. A collection of porcelain from the Qing Dynasty is on display. White Palace is located just north of downtown.

BEACHES IN VUNG TAU

Back (Bau Sau) Beach stretches eight kilometers on the eastern edge of the peninsula, from the French Fort at the tip, north to a group of hotels. This is the best beach in Vung Tau proper. Locals call this beach Thu Van.

Bai Dau Beach is a small stretch of sand with calm surf that lies at the base of Lon Mountain.

Bai Dua Beach is parallel to Tran Phu Street, which runs along the northern tip of the peninsula. This beach is relatively quiet compared to the others, left alone by tourists, with the exception of those who stay in its moderately-priced guest houses.

Front (Bai Truoc) Beach is the closest to the city center. Calm water, restaurants and souvenir shops are the earmark of this beach, which is the perfect place for a quiet evening stroll. However, its not much of a beach during the daytime since the silty sand feels like mud.

O Quan Beach has clear water and lively surf, which are its trademarks. An island in miniature, Bong Dao, lies just off the coast.

SHOPPING

Since Vung Tau is a tourist town, you'll have no trouble finding souvenir shops. Shells and other booty from the sea are the most popular items for sale.

DAY TRIPS & EXCURSIONS

Binh Chau Hot Spring and Resort, *Xuyen Moc District, Binh Chau*, is fed by dozens of underground waterways and the hot water springs are reputed to have curative powers. There are plenty of hiking trails through the countryside, after which you can relieve your muscles with a massage and mineral water treatment in the resort. The resort has decent rooms for $10 per night. On the way to Binh Chau you will pass the superb **Ho Hoc Beach**, where you can stay in a spartan bungalow for $6 per night.

To get to the Hot Springs, take Highway 51 northeast from Vung Tau to Binh Chau, about 55 kilometers (25 miles). Ho Hoc Beach is about 20 kilometers (9 miles) from Vung Tau. Take the second turn off on Highway 51 from Vung Tau to get to the beach.

A few pagodas in the area are popular with Vietnamese tourists. **Chua Phap Hoa Pagoda**, is home to 200 monks and is a tranquil pagoda in a beautiful area. It is located off Highway 51. **Thien Vien Chuoy Chiey Pagoda** is 50 kilometers north of Vung Tau on Highway 51 heading towards Ho Chi Minh City.

Thuy Duong Beach is 24 kilometers from Vung Tau and makes for a nice excursion from Vung Tau. There is a restaurant on the beach and facilities to change clothes, and lifeguards on crowded days. See section in this chapter on South Coast Beaches for more information.

Con Dao Islands is a group of 14 islands 180 kilometers south of Vung Tau, in the South China Sea and can be reached by boat from Vung Tau. See the section in this chapter on South Coast Beaches for more information.

PRACTICAL INFORMATION

- **Currency Exchange**: Most hotels will change money. But if you seek a bank, the local branches of the Vietcom bank, *27 Le Loi, Vung Tau or 27-29 Tran Hung Dao Street, Vung Tau, Tel. (84 64) 852309, Fax (84 64) 859859*, has a full-service exchange office.
- **Post Office**, *4 Ha Long Street, Tel. (84 64) 852377 or 858500.*
- **National Oil Services Company**, *2 Le Loi, Vung Tau. Tel. (84 64) 852012 or 852603 or 852405, Fax (84 64) 852834*, operates fourteen hotels in Vung Tau.
- **Tourism and Service Industry Development Company**, *18 Thuy van, Vung Tau, Tel. (84 64) 852314 or 852138.*
- **Vietnam Youth Tourist Center**, *46A Thuy Van Street, Vung Tau, Tel. (84 64) 852275 or 852607*, is a full-service travel agency,
- **Vung Tau International Tourist Company**, *40/5 Thu Khoa Huan, Vung Tau, Tel. (84 64) 852385, Fax (84 64) 853860.* The agency can help arrange tours to local sites or other travel arrangements you might require.
- **Veteran's Clinic**, 1.5 kilometers north of the city center, provides medical assistance to travelers.

Phan Thiet

The most beautiful stretch of coast in Vietnam runs from **Phan Thiet** north to Mui Ne. Here the sloping countryside meets the white sand and clear water. The dunes at Mui Ne are large enough to be graceful hills of sand. Tall palm trees canopy the road and the only sound is the gentle breaking of the surf. Miles of beach are yours for the asking.

Phan Thiet is best known as the home of fish sauce, *nuoc mam*, the condiment which accompanies every meal. The town has little more than a few simple restaurants and hotels. You can visit the a factory where fish sauce is made, as well as the fishing village at the end of Mui Ne Peninsula. Mui Ne means "nose" in Vietnamese. So it comes as no surprise that the peninsula resembles a nose.

ARRIVALS & DEPARTURES

Highway 1 runs from Ho Chi Minh City to Phan Thiet. You can hire a car to make the three hour journey.

Trains run along the coast from Ho Chi Minh City to Muong Man, 12 miles from Phan Thiet.

Mini-vans from the **Sinh Cafe**, *179 Pham Ngo Lao Street, District 1, Ho Chi Minh City, Tel. (84 8) 8355601*, charge $10 for the 200 kilometer ride.

ORIENTATION

Phat Thiet is a small town on Highway 1. The beach that makes the town famous is Mui Ne Beach, which is on Mui Ne Beach Road. To get to the beach, turn at the large war memorial in town; this is the major road that leads away from the town. The road to Mui Ne Beach is lined with a canopy of palm trees.

You can stop at one of the beach-side restaurants for a meal of fresh seafood or coconut juice.

GETTING AROUND TOWN

If you stay in town, the best way to explore the area is by motor bike and it's the easiest way to get to the beach.

WHERE TO STAY

HAI DUONG RESORT, *Coco Beach, Mui Ne Peninsula, Phan Thiet. Tel. (84 62) 823591 or 848401 or 848402, Fax (84 62) 823590. Singles/ doubles $60.*

You can stay in the town of Phan Thiet, but why? The Mui Ne beach is only a few kilometers from town. The Hai Duong Resort is a group of new bungalows built and run by a European couple. The rooms are large and comfortable, with air-conditioning, rattan furniture and patios that look onto the beach.

The beautiful restaurant, which is decorated in carved Vietnamese furniture, serves European and Vietnamese gourmet food. Sail-boards, jetskis and bicycles can be rented.

HOTEL 19/4 (aka **KATCH SAN 19/4**), *1 Tu Van Tu Street, Phan Thiet. Tel. (84 62) 821794 or 822194 or 25216, Fax (84 62) 825184. Singles/doubles $12 to $25. Credit cards accepted.*

The only tourist hotel in the city, this large white building has budget and standard rooms. The low-end rooms do not have air-conditioning and can accommodate three people. The first and second tier rooms have air-conditioning and television. All rooms have private modern bath facilities.

The hotel restaurant serves local seafood specialties including crab, sea snails and whole, large squid. You can rent transportation at the front desk.

THE OCEAN DUNES RESORT, *Phan Thiet.*

This soon-to-open golf resort will take the lead as the premier place to stay in the area. The 18 hole golf course is nearly ready for players, and the luxury hotel is under construction. No address or phone number as of this writing, but ask the folks at Sinh Cafe in Ho Chi Minh City, *Tel. (84 8) 8355601* and they should be able to help you out when it opens.

WHERE TO EAT

There are a number of small restaurants on the main road, Tu Van Tu Street. On the way to Mui Ne you will find a few thatched-roof restaurants right on the beach that serve fresh fish to eat and coconuts to drink.

SPORTS & RECREATION

The Ocean Dunes Resort and Golf Club is under construction. The spectacular golf course, with its many sand dunes, has ocean views from many of the holes.

The best recreation at the beaches is relaxation. For those who need activity, snorkeling and sailing equipment is available at Hai Duong Resort.

DAY TRIPS & EXCURSIONS

Isolated **Pho Hai** is the country's oldest Cham site. It is believed the towers were constructed during the ninth century AD; they are still used for rituals. The site consists of two main towers, both in disrepair. Strong Cham and Khmer influences are evident. Although detail has worn off, the glory of ancient Champa makes a strong statement in the architecture.

The coastal setting and lack of tourists adds to the atmosphere. To reach Pho Hai, take Highway 1 north from Phan Thiet. About 2 kilometers (1.25 miles) from the city turn onto the small, paved road which runs east. Follow this road about 5 kilometers (3.1 miles).

Phan Rang

The lands south of **Phan Rang** were the last strongholds of the Cham empire. In the sixteenth century the Vietnamese kingdom attacked and defeated the Cham. Today, Cham temples remain as the lasting symbols of the once powerful nation. Visitors come to Phan Rang to see Po Klung Gari, a Cham site dating from the 1200s, and other Cham temples.

The story of the defeat of the Cham is the type of intrigue that would make a juicy romance novel. The daughter of the Vietnamese king married the son of the Cham king to solidify political ties. Soon after the wedding the Vietnamese king demanded Cham lands in exchange for his daughter's hand. When the Cham king refused to succumb to the demands, the Vietnamese king launched a war against the Cham. Although one would imagine that this would devastate the newlyweds, only the son of the Cham king truly suffered. The daughter of the Vietnamese king had been a spy and carrying on an elaborate ruse the whole time.

The region's dry, rocky land is virtually uncultivated, save for small grape farms in the countryside. Sea salt is mined on the coast. The Van Hao spring has the country's best mineral water. The small, square houses along the highway are painted in cheerful hues of purple and yellow.

ARRIVALS & DEPARTURES

Phan Rang is at the intersection of Highways 20 and 1. Highway 20 extends southeast from Dalat and ends at Phan Rang. The 100 kilometer (62 mile) road curves down through the mountains. Phan Rang is 350 kilometers (218 miles) north of Ho Chi Minh City on Highway 1.

The train stops at the Thap Cham Station, about 10 kilometers (6 miles) from Phan Rang.

ORIENTATION

Phan Rang sits on Highway 1, also called Thong Nhat Street, which is the main street of the town.

GETTING AROUND TOWN

You should bring your own transportation—car, motor bike or feet—and plan to use it since the Cham sites are some kilometers out of town.

WHERE TO STAY

HAI SON HOTEL, *Highway 1, Phan Rang. Singles/doubles $15.*

Phan Rang offers no choice of where to hang your hat for the night This dirty hotel without air-conditioning is the only one in town. You would do better to plan your trip so you stay in another town.

WHERE TO EAT

A few small restaurants can be found near the center of town.

SEEING THE SIGHTS

The small town of Phan Rang has a pink-walled temple close to the central market. The only attraction to visitors is the Cham site, Po Klun Gari.

When you arrive at **Po Klun Gari**, you will come to stairs that lead through the free-standing arch at the base of the temple complex. The three temple towers of Po Klun Gari are excellent examples of the architecture of Champa. Nine years of restoration on the group ended in 1990. The walls and doorways are reinforced, and parts of the walls have been patched. Elements on these towers are in far better conditions than others you may see.

The central tower has a four-tiered roof and stands nearly 45 feet tall. On the corners of the roof tiers are well-preserved flame ornaments. The sanctuary for offerings and a gate tower stand with the central tower. As is typical of Cham towers, they have an eastward orientation.

The site is known for friezes, many of which have been destroyed. Some survive on the outer walls of the towers. Engraved lotus flowers and dancing Shivas can be seen on the main tower.

Ceremonies marking the Cham new year (around the beginning of the tenth lunar month or late October, early November) are celebrated at Po Klun Gari.

To reach Po Klun Gari take highway 27 north to the 288 kilometer (180 mile) marker. Take this road west to the towers.

Ba Toc, also called Hoa Lai, is a group of three Cham towers located just off Highway 1, to the north of Phan Rang. Much of the tiered roofs are crumbling away, and one structure is completely destroyed. This makes the date of construction difficult to determine. Carvings are still evident on the temples. To reach Ba Toc take Highway 1 north from Phan Rang for 15 kilometers (9 miles). The temple stands on the south side of the road.

The temples of **Po Rome** are difficult to reach. They stand on a hill overlooking small villages. These are late towers, dating from after the sixteenth century, which marks the end of such construction. The main temple is dedicated to the worship of the Cham King Po Rome. To reach Po Rome take Highway 1 north from Phan Rang. Turn west at Ninh Phuoc town. The temples stand near Hau Sanh Hamlet.

DAY TRIPS & EXCURSIONS

South of Phan Rang about 50 kilometers (31 miles) is **Ca Na Beach**. It's located between Phan Rang and Phan Thiet. For more information see South Coast Beaches.

Cam Ranh Bay is a beautiful bay where the main industry is seafood. And as many Americans may recall, it has a long history of military importance. Russian ships docked at Cam Ranh in 1905 seeking refuge from the weather and the Japanese (with whom the Russians were at war) and the French hoped to develop a port at Cam Ranh. But it was not until the 1960s that the United States built a naval base with a deep-water harbor in Cam Ranh Bay.

After the war, this was used extensively by the Russians until 1990. Today only a handful of Russian soldiers keep the base active. Cam Ranh Bay lies on Highway 1, about 60 kilometers (37 miles) from Phan Rang.

PRACTICAL INFORMATION

- **Bank of Ninh Thuan Province**, *17 Nguyen Trai Street, Phan Rang. Tel. (84 68) 822704 or 822741.*
- **Post Office**, *4 Le Hong Phong Street, Phan Rang. Tel. (84 68) 823407 or 823408.*
- **Ninh Thuan Province Tourism**, *233 Thong Nhat Street, Phan Rang. Tel. (84 68) 822719 or 822720, Fax (84 68) 822600.*

Ca Na Beach

Marked by a lovely rocky shore, **Ca Na Beach** sits at the base of steep mountains. The calm blue waters are refreshing. The single other attraction is a Buddhist shrine just across from the hotel. At sunset you can sit on the large rocks and watch fishermen return home.

The only hotel around, the Ca Na Hotel, is an adequate rest-stop during the Phan Rang–Phan Thiet journey. The beach is located on Highway 1, about 110 kilometers north of Phan Thiet and about 50 kilometers south of Phan Rang.

WHERE TO STAY

CA NA HOTEL, *Highway 1, Ca Na. Singles/doubles $12 to $15. Breakfast included.*

The hotel sits right on the coast, and the rooms overlook the water. The rooms are a bit rough. The algae green formica bathroom vanities are the fanciest part of the rooms. Plywood floors don't keep the geckos out; but that is good, because the little lizards eat bugs that fly in through the open window. The shower is cold-water only, which will combat the heat in rooms without air-conditioning.

Thuy Dong Beach

Long Hai town is the gateway to **Thuy Dong Beach**, which is by far the best beach in the Vung Tau area. There is a restaurant on the beach, facilities to change clothes, and lifeguards on crowded days.

You can reach Long Hai by car from Ho Chi Minh city; the ride takes two hours. You can also reach Long Hai from Vang Tau: it is twenty kilometers north of Vung Tau and Thuy Dong Beach is another four kilometers. There is no scheduled tourist transport.

WHERE TO STAY

There is only one hotel in Long Hai:

LONG HAI HOTEL, *Long Hai. Tel. (84 64) 868010. Singles/doubles $20*. The rooms are a little shabby with no amenities.

Con Dao Islands

This group of 14 islands lie 180 kilometers south of Vung Tau, in the South China Sea. **Con Son**, the largest island in the archipelago, is only 20 square miles and has a population of 2,000. This is the only island that has tourist facilities.

Forests, cliffs and coral reefs are among the natural splendors found on Con Son. Rugged mountains rise seemingly straight out of the sea. The prime attraction is the calm, clear, blue-green water and the natural tranquillity of the islands.

ARRIVALS & DEPARTURES

Boats connect Con Dao Islands to Ho Chi Minh City and Vung Tau. These islands don't get many visitors, so the price for a boat ride is completely negotiable. The largest island, Con Son, has only one pier, which will be your point of arrival and departure. Just ask how to get to the hotel, or go by motorbike.

WHERE TO STAY

PHI YEN HOTEL, *on Con Son Island of the Con Dao Islands. Tel. (84 64) 30168. Singles/doubles $20.*

The hotel is as remote as the island itself. If offers no amenities, but is adequate. Rent a bicycle or motor bike to explore the island.

SEEING THE SIGHTS

The **Paulo Condor Prison**, dating from the French colonial era, is open to tourists. It was built to hold 10,000 prisoners, including Vietnamese who favored independence from French rule. Later, the South

Vietnamese government used this as a torture chamber for dissidents. There is a small museum which provides background information.

The other main attraction is renting a boat to take you around the beautiful islands of the archipelago.

PRACTICAL INFORMATION

• **Post Office**: the address of the post office is simply Con Dao Post Office, *Con Dao Island.*

Phu Quy Island

The windy retreat of **Phu Quy Island** invigorates the senses with its pristine coastline and muscular breezes. If you want to get in touch with the life and people of Vietnam, this trip will be your most valuable.

Phu Quy is a small island 80 kilometers from mainland Vietnam. The island supports a fishing village that is a gem of untouched culture. The people here are charmed by foreign visitors. You can fill your hours with relaxing walks along the coastline

ARRIVALS & DEPARTURES

The only way to reach Phu Quy is to hire a boat from Vung Tau, Phan Thiet or Nha Trang. Since there are no tourist boats that serve the island, be certain to allot ample time for your journey, it takes about 10 hours to get there. You have to catch a ride on a fishing boat, or some other trade boat, and negotiate your fare with the boat owner.

WHERE TO STAY

The challenge of your trip will be accommodations. There are not yet hotels on the island. Visitors have been able to rent a rooms with local families. If you bring your own camping gear, you can try to find a sheltered area on the beach.

13. DALAT
&
THE CENTRAL HIGHLANDS

Dalat

At the turn of the century, the French doctor Alexander Yersin, who studied under Louis Pasteur, came ashore at Nha Trang to explore the mainland. When he reached the **Dalat** area he realized that he found an extraordinary place. The cool climate, pine covered mountains and lovely lakes felt more like Europe than Asia.

Dr. Yersin recognized the health benefits of the mild weather and crisp air. In 1912, he founded a retreat in Dalat for the French living in the hot, humid south. Today, 116,000 Vietnamese call Dalat, the capital of **Lam Dong Province**, home.

Downtown Dalat is busy and unremarkable. The large market is at the heart of the city, and is full of consumer goods, local treats such as strawberry candy. Nearly all of the city's restaurants are downtown, close to the Hoa Binh Square. The beauty of Dalat is found in French villas and chateaux, away from downtown.

"When you stand in front of the chateaux," one visitor noted, "if you close your eyes and take a deep breath, you are transported back in time, to another place."

Nestled in the beauty of three lakes and seven waterfalls, Dalat is the city of romance and honeymooners. Getting married close to the time of Tet (lunar New Year) is believed to be lucky. So from late January through February newlyweds flock to Dalat. The fresh, crisp air and tall evergreen trees compose a unique atmosphere which allows young couples to feel as if they are visiting another country.

Dalat is famous for flower cultivation; orchards and roses are the specialties of the area. The botanical gardens cultivate examples of all the varieties of plants grown in Dalat. Regional strawberries are used to make sweet, tasty wine and candies. And persimmons are a prized crop.

The temperature maintains a year-round average of about 22°C. The dry season runs from December to March, but even during these months cool mist and light morning drizzle is common. Rain marks the months from May to October.

ARRIVALS & DEPARTURES
By Air
Vietnam Airlines, *Tel. (84 63) 822895*, has direct flights between Dalat and Hanoi or Ho Chi Minh City on Wednesday, Friday and Sunday. Lien Khuong Airport is a 30 kilometer drive from Dalat. A taxi ride between the airport and Dalat is about $3. The airport levies a tax of 15,000 dong ($1.37) on all passengers.

By Bus
The local bus station is on the southern edge of the city by the intersection of Pham Ngu Lao and Le Dai Hanh Streets. The **open ticket buses** stop is in the city center of Dalat.

By Train
There is no train service to Dalat.

ORIENTATION
Dalat is on the shore of Xuan Huong Lake, a man-made lake created by the French. The name means Cherry Blossoms of Spring, and each spring the Cherry Blossom trees burst into bloom. Trails and roads lead around the lake. The large indoor/outdoor market is the center of town. Hotels and restaurants are downtown, close to the Hoa Binh Square. The interesting sights in Dalat are a few kilometers away from the city.

GETTING AROUND TOWN
Since Dalat is a small town, taxis are not a common sight yet. Your hotel can call a taxi when you need one. It is a good idea to rent a motor bike or car. Either your hotel or tourist office can arrange this. The hilly terrain makes bicycle riding difficult, unless you are in great shape.

WHERE TO STAY
DALAT PALACE (**Hotel Sofitel**), *12 Tran Phu Street, Dalat. Tel. (84 63) 825444 or 800/221-4542 in the US. Singles/doubles $120 to $350.*

If you allow yourself only one indulgence on your entire trip this should be it. The Dalat Palace was the grande dame of accommodations when it was built in 1922. For a brief period during World War II, Japanese troops occupied the hotel. Today it has regained its status as the foremost luxury resort of the country. The Palace offers the most tranquil surroundings in Dalat, on a hill which overlooks the city.

The interior is nothing short of extraordinary. Entering the hotel, warmth and beauty floods the eye. You walk into a grand sitting room, with a grand fireplace and elegant sofas. The painstaking renovation took four years. Decoration from all over the world went into the 43 gracious rooms. Right down to the large, antique bathtubs, the comfort is an indulgence.

Le Rabelais, the hotel's French restaurant, serves masterfully created French meals. Perhaps the most remarkable aspect of the hotel is that the standard of service lives up to the hotel. The staff truly knows how to make guests feel comfortable and content.

The Dalat Palace has the best night spot to be found. Larry's Bar is a most pleasant evening spot for a drink and conversation. Depending on how many guests are at the hotel the bar will either be full and lively or quiet. The warm, rustic atmosphere is reminiscent of a French wine cellar.

The hotel has an English-speaking doctor. A shuttle runs from the hotel to the near-by golf course. The $120 rooms are a bargain by Asian standards of luxury prices.

NOVOTEL DALAT (The Dalat Hotel), *7 Tran Phu, Dalat. Tel. 800/ 221-4542 in the US. Singles/doubles $70 to $140.*

Formerly a favorite destination for honeymooners, the Dalat Hotel is being renovated by the Sofitel group. The hotel is due to open in early 1997 as a Novotel Hotel. Novotels are luxury accommodations priced lower than the Sofitel resorts. The 144 room hotel will offer a gourmet restaurant, baby sitting and a health club in addition to the standard amenities.

GOLF HOTEL, *11 Dinh Tien Hoang Street, Dalat. Tel. (84 63) 824082 or 821281, Fax (84 63) 824945. Singles/doubles $55 to $60. Credit cards accepted.*

The closest hotel to the golf course, the Golf Hotel, used to be the city's sporting resort. Although it is now overshadowed by the Dalat Palace, this hotel still offers 36 very comfortable and desirable rooms. The tourist-class rooms are pleasant and clean and only a stone's throw from the green. The restaurant serves good food, with both European and Vietnamese dishes. The hotel has a sauna and offers massages, so you can unwind after a grueling 18 holes. The hotel is north of Xuan Huong Lake and 1 kilometer east of the city center. The Golf Hotel has a unique pricing policy: the rate goes down for each room you take. For example, one room costs $55, if you take two rooms the second is $45; for three, the third is $35.

ANH DAO HOTEL, *50-52 Hoa Binh Square, Dalat. Tel. (84 63) 822384. Singles/doubles $29 to $55. Breakfast included. Credit cards accepted.*

This 27-room tourist class hotel stands in front of the market. The location is noisy, but convenient since you can walk to the market and nearby restaurants. The rooms are comfortable. If the Anh Dao is full or you prefer more quiet surroundings you can stay at its sister hotel, the **ANH DAO II**. It is run by the same staff and has similar quality and price.

BIET THU HOTEL, *28 Tran Hung Dao, Dalat. Singles $25/doubles $50.*

Biet Thu is Vietnamese for "villa." This pink villa dates from the colonial era and was probably the private vacation home of a French family. A stay here will truly take you back in time. Today it is run as a mini-hotel. The rustic feeling is charming. The rooms are very large and comfortable, with simple and clean bathrooms. Beds are low to the ground and the wooden floors are the original. The reception desk sells snacks, but there is no food available. Of the French villas that line Tran Hung Dao Street, this is the only one currently open. Most are in the process of being renovated into mini hotels.

HOME OF DR. DANG VIET NGA, *3 Huynh Thuc Khang Street. Tel. (84 63) 822070.*

The proprietor, Dr. Dang Viet Nga rents what is best described as a conglomeration of rooms in her house. The surrealistic structure has been dubbed Art House, Crazy House and Dali Villa. Inside the house/gallery statuary meshes human and plant forms, rooms emerge from tree roots. The location, next to a cemetery, adds to the mystique. Dr. Nga, the daughter of President Truong Chinh, is an architect and artist. She created and lives in the house and often hangs out in the cafe to talk with guests and share her fascinating stories. The rooms have various themes. One traveler who stayed in the cave room described the house as "the strangest experience of my whole trip." Single travelers may be paired with a room-mate.

HAI SON HOTEL, *1 Nguyen Thi Minh Khai Street, Dalat. Tel. (84 63) 822379. Singles/doubles $25 to $50. Credit cards accepted.*

The hotel is situated in the busiest part of town, just around the corner from the market. The location may account for the unfortunate problem of guests being hassled by beggars when they leave and enter the hotel. This large, noisy place handles many tour groups. The rooms have undergone renovation, but the overall atmosphere is far from comfortable in part because the bar on the first floor has sleazy overtones.

MIMOSA HOTEL, *170 Phan Dinh Phung Street, Dalat. Tel. (84 63) 822656 or 822180. Singles $6 to $8/doubles $12 to $20.*

The kindest way to describe this hotel is as a bargain basement accommodation for rugged travelers. Often one of the hotel's 55 dirty rooms can be bargained down to $8 per night. Considering hot water is included, its not a bad deal, but do not expect more than you pay for.

MINH TAM HOTEL, *20A Khe Sanh Street, Dalat. Tel. (84 63) 822447. Singles $27/doubles $50.*

The quaint Minh Tam Hotel is called Dalat's "second flower garden" because of the beautiful grounds. Most guests here are Vietnamese honeymooners. Bungalows by the garden are especially romantic. The hotel is reported to get quite cold in the winter.

NGOC LAN HOTEL, *54 Nguyen Tri Phuong Street, Dalat. Tel. (84 63) 822136 or 822817, Fax (84 63) 824032. Singles/ doubles $20 to $30.*

A 30-room tourist hotel, many of the rooms have lovely lake views. Standard amenities are included in each room. Despite the renovation, the hotel is lackluster. Downstairs you will find a karaoke lounge, a disco and a bar.

WHERE TO EAT

While here, treat yourself to one of Dalat's terrific **bakeries**, where the French influence is alive and well. You will find delectable pastries at *1 Ngu Van Trou* and *2 Khu Hoa Binh*, close to each other on the small streets that lead off the Hoa Binh Square.

Expensive

THUY TA RESTAURANT, *Vietnamese and European, Xuan Houng Lake, Dalat. Tel. (84 63) 822288.*

The Thuy Ta serves exquisite Vietnamese dishes such as braised prawns in fish sauce and lemon grass chicken. Live music every Tuesday, Thursday and Saturday evening ads to the stark black lacquer decor. From any table in the dining room you will have a candle-lit view of the entire lake.

This is one of the few restaurants that serve English breakfast; it costs a mere 23,000 dong. If you are simply not hungry, you can still enjoy an evening coffee on the patio overlooking the lake.

Moderate

DO YEN RESTAURANT, *Chinese, 7 Khu Hoa Binh Street, Dalat. Tel. (84 63) 822133.*

The restaurant is located across from the market. The chef makes good, authentic Chinese food, and will make it extra-spicy on request. The French-influenced Vietnamese cuisine unique to Dalat is also served here. The chicken dishes are excellent. The restaurant is open for breakfast.

Inexpensive
CENTRAL MARKET, *center of town*.

Excellent and cheap meals can be found in the central market. For about 25 cents per plate, you can feast on rice noodles with vegetables, won ton soup, spring rolls and a cornucopia of other treats. The stands are at the far end of the market complex.

MAISON LONG HOA, *Vietnamese and European, 6 Duy Tan Street, Dalat, Tel. (84 63) 822934.*

A visit to Dalat is incomplete without at least one meal here. This family restaurant truly is just that; the lady of the house cooks, and the proprietor greets his guests and strikes up friendships in English, French or Vietnamese. The European dishes are known as the best in the city, and certainly the atmosphere is unsurpassable. End the meal with a small jar of sweet, fresh yogurt. Strawberry wine on the couch in the back room will make you feel that you are at home. The restaurant is located near the corner of Khoi Nghia Nam Ky Street.

NHU Y 143B, *Vietnamese, 143B Nhu Y Street, Dalat.*

You might mistake this place for a gas station, since the dining room is little more than a picnic area. But you do not come here for the ambiance, you come here for the food. The Vietnamese dishes are excellent and cheap, which is what make this a favorite of locals. While downing a bowl of noodles you will probably befriend a few residents of Dalat.

VEGETARIAN RESTAURANT, *Vegetarian, 15 Phan Dinh Phuong Street, Dalat. Tel. (84 63) 825054.*

The interior is simple, with long cafeteria-style tables, but the food is superior. Here you will find the best and cheapest vegetarian food in Dalat. Go ahead and sample a variety of dishes, each plate costs about $1. The delicate flavors of Dalat's regional cooking come to life in dishes such as the marinated tofu. The salad rolls are not to be missed. Buddhist monks, who are strict vegetarians, frequent this restaurant.

SEEING THE SIGHTS

The **Governor's Residence** (DINH II or Hotel Decoux), *12 Tran Hung Dao Street, Dalat, Tel. (84 63) 822092*, has been run as a hotel but is preserved as a museum. This is the private hunting lodge of the former French Governor, Paul Doumer. The legacy of his hunting skill — the heads of his trophies — decorate the walls. Some of the furnishings are original.

Bao Dai's Summer Villa (DINH III Museum), *1 Trieu Viet Vuong Street, Tel. (84 63) 822093*, is one of three official residences of the country's last emperor. This is the only one operating as a museum. Bao

Dai's Villa was built in Art Deco style in 1933. The museum shows the furnishings which betray Bao Dai's thirst for things foreign, particularly the strong French influence that permeated the Vietnamese monarchy in its final days. Take a stroll around the villa's lush grounds.

The **Cam Ly waterfalls**, *on Hoang Van Thu Street*, is smaller than other falls in the area. Take Tran Phu Street west, out of town. After about 1 kilometer, the road turns into Hoang Van Thu Street. You will find the falls after about another kilometer. There is a campy carnival atmosphere here, but the reason to visit the falls is to see the intriguing **Cam Ly Church**. The chalet-style church was built in the 1960s by a French missionary. Its construction is unusual and gives insight to the merging of highland traditions and the Christian faith. Murals on the walls depict animals that are part of local mythology. The tribes people believe the tiger and phoenix give man special protection and connect the earth to the heavens. Buffalo heads mounted under the cross at the altar symbolize the traditional sacrifice offered to god. The rustic interior is beautifully unique. There is a small entrance fee to the falls.

Dalat is famous for its flowers. **The Dalat Flower Garden**, *Vuon Hoa Street,* was built is 1966. The city garden's neatly arranged flower beds show off some of the flora of the area. A cage of monkeys stands amid the flower beds, ironically holding the little creatures captive in a plantless jail. The entrance fee is 8,000 dong ($.73).

Dalat Cathedral is found on *Tran Phu Street.* The unmistakably European cathedral was built by the French in the 1930's. The European materials, such as the stained glass, used in the construction of the cathedral made the building process a long one. The cathedral was the center of French life in Dalat. Regular services are held every Sunday at 7 am and 4 pm.

The **Linh Son Pagoda**, *Nguyen Van Troi Street*, has a beautiful view of the city since it is located on a hill about 3/4 mile north of the town center. The yellow tower on the right (facing the pagoda) is the tomb of the former resident monk (Thay Chua). The yellow building behind the pagoda is a monastery for high school students. Bui Thi Xuan, the largest grade-school in the city, is next door. At 11:30 am children in their blue uniforms flood the street in front of the pagoda as they leave school.

The Chinese Pagoda (Thien Vuong Co Sat), *Khe San Street*, consists of three temple buildings that were constructed by local Chinese Buddhists in 1958. Pathways lined with souvenir kiosks lead visitors through the sprawling grounds. The first temple is ornately decorated with gold relief dragons spiraling down red pillars. Three large wooden statues covered in gold leaf are the centerpiece of the pagoda. A large, white Buddha peacefully sits under murals depicting the life of the Buddha in the third building.

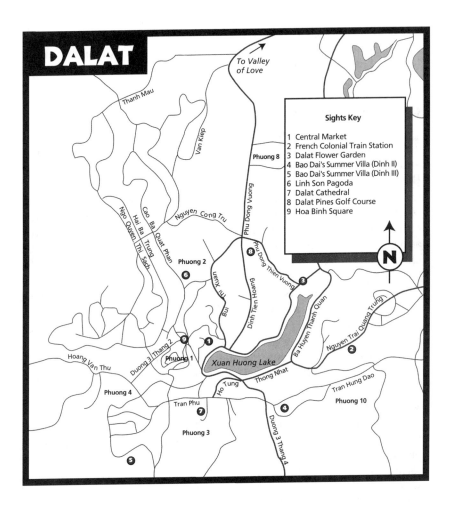

DALAT

To Valley
of Love

Thanh Mau

Van Kiep

Phuong 8

Phu Dong Vuong

Nguyen Cong Tru

Cao Ba Quat Phan

Hai Ba Trung

Ngo Quyen Thi Sach

Phuong 2

6

Sights Key

1 Central Market
2 French Colonial Train Station
3 Dalat Flower Garden
4 Bao Dai's Summer Villa (Dinh II)
5 Bao Dai's Summer Villa (Dinh III)
6 Linh Son Pagoda
7 Dalat Cathedral
8 Dalat Pines Golf Course
9 Hoa Binh Square

N

8

Phu Dong Thien Vuong

3

Bui Thi Xuan

Dinh Tien Hoang

Ba Huyen Thanh Quan

Nguyen Trai Quang Trung

2

9 1

Hoang Van Thu

Duong 3 Thang 2

Phuong 1

Xuan Huong Lake

Thong Nhat

Phuong 4

Ho Tung

Tran Hung Dao

Phuong 10

Tran Phu

7

4

Duong 3 Thang 4

Phuong 3

5

NIGHTLIFE & ENTERTAINMENT

LARRY'S BAR, *Dalat Palace (Sofitel) Hotel*, is a most enjoyable evening spot for a drink and conversation. Depending on how many guests are at the hotel the bar will either be full and lively or quiet. The warm, rustic atmosphere is reminiscent of a French wine cellar.

COFFEE THAN THUY, *Xuan Huong Lake, Dalat, Tel. (84 63) 822262*, is a simple cafe that serves light snacks on a deck overlooking the lake. It is a good place to have a cup of coffee in the evening and watch twilight descend on the lake.

SPORTS & RECREATION

The eighteen-hole **Dalat Golf Course**, *Phu Dong Thien Vuong Street, Tel. (84 63) 821201, Fax (84 63) 824325*, is a paradise for the avid golfer and novice alike. First laid out by the French as a nine hole course, the IMG Group revamped the greens and expanded it to a full 18 holes.

Standing on the bent grass fairway under misty pines, it seems you are playing golf at the top of the world. Dalat's cool, moist climate allows the entire course to maintain perfectly manicured bent grass tees, fairways, and greens. The course spans 7,009 yards and rates a par 72. You will be challenged by lakes that weave through ten holes, then indulge in wide, sprawling greens.

The original club house from the 1920s was renovated into a modern pro-shop and cafe. A new resort club facility is under construction.

Weekday green's fees are $65 per player and weekend fees are $85. You do not need to bring your equipment, club rental runs $20 and shoes $8. Golf carts are not permitted on the fairways; a mere $8 is the fee for a smiling, enthusiastic caddie. The driving range fee is $5.

SHOPPING

Right in the center of town you will find the large **central market**. It is a multistory indoor-outdoor complex. You can spend hours wandering among the stands of local produce, clothes and handicrafts. As with most local markets you will find mostly household supplies. However, if you search carefully you may come across locally made baskets and knitted items, like hats and handbags. The food stalls cook up good and cheap soup and noodle dishes.

The finest **tea** in the country is grown in the mountains surrounding Dalat. You can get fragrant green tea with jasmine flowers. The Do Hau Restaurant on Highway 20 outside Dalat packages and sells freshly dried tea. The red bags are green tea; the bright pink and purple bags contain tea scented with flowers.

About 20 kilometers from Dalat, just off the highway that leads to Pham Rang, you will find the "Chicken Village." A giant chicken pays tribute to a legendary bird who, during a famine, gave the secret of planting seeds to a local man.

Just next to the chicken you can buy **silk and cotton weavings**. The brightly colored, beautiful cloth is made by the women of the village, and is some of the finest handiwork in the Central Highlands.

DAY TRIPS & EXCURSIONS

Dam Bri Waterfall named for the local Dam Bri tribes people, is an ostentatious theme park. Despite the miniature fantasy-land decorations, the waterfall is impressive. The Dam Bri Falls are nearly 100 meters high. To reach the falls, travel down the Dam Bri Road off Highway 20.

The **Lake of the Sighs** is the sight of a legendary Vietnamese "Romeo and Juliet" story. The story takes place in ancient times. Two lovers of royal birth came to the lake as a rendezvous spot. The young man was called to battle one day. When word of his death came his beloved drowned herself in the Lake of Sighs. The rumor was a false one, and he returned only to kill himself with his grief. The lake is about 7 kilometers north of Dalat. The lake is tranquil and you can walk along the shore and through the surrounding forest on trails.

Outside **Linh Phuoc Pagoda** (Lucky Dragon) is an extraordinary 47 meter long dragon made from 13,000 beer bottles. It took the townspeople two years to make the dragon. Inside the pagoda, over the golden Buddha, note the mural along the ceiling which depicts the birth of the Buddha. Ceremonies are held on the 15th or the 30th of each month.

If you have time for only one excursion, make it the train ride to Linh Phuoc Pagoda; it is the most enjoyable trip from Dalat. The small train weaves through terraced farms on rolling hills in the Trai Mat region, scenery that is not to be missed. The farms produce fruit and vegetables that are shipped throughout the country.

You catch the train at the Xuan Hoang railway station. The only train that runs from this station is a small car that travels to Trai Mat town. The station was built by the French and resembles a building you might find in a small European town. If you arrive by 8 am, buy a regular ticket (44,000 dong) for the special single car train to Trai Mat. Otherwise, you must rent the train for a special run for 200,000 dong ($20).

The **Prenn Falls** drops to the base of the Prenn Pass, a 100 meter fall. Paths lead down to the base of the falls, through foliage and rock overhangs, to a suspended bridge that leads across the natural pool. The beautiful cascading water is included in local folklore which attribute magical powers to it. Prenn Falls are located 15 kilometers from Dalat on the Phan Rang road.

Valley of Love (Thung Lung Tinh Yeu), is the honeymooners retreat of Vietnam. Couples stroll on trails around Lac Thien Lake, or rent paddle boats to enjoy the water. Unless you just stepped out of a wedding taxi, you come here for the spectacle, not the romance. Stuffed dear, big decorative hearts and campy statues provide a backdrop more intriguing than the nature. You can have your picture taken with a miniature horse wearing a cowboy hat for a nominal fee. Located about 6 kilometers from Dalat, you can reach the Valley of Love by rented car or motorbike. Bicycles are not rented in Dalat because it's so hilly, but experienced cyclists bring their own bikes and love to bike this area.

Langbiang (Lady) Mountain overlooks Dan Kia Lake 15 kilometers north of Dalat. Conquering the mountain involves a strenuous walk, but you need no rugged mountaineering skill. Here you will find the full variety of indigenous flora and fauna, without the kitsch of the honeymooners' parks. To reach Langbiang Mountain take Phu Dong Thien Vuong Street north, away from the city, until you reach Lat village. The village is at the base of Langbiang mountain, and trails lead to the top.

PRACTICAL INFORMATION

- **Industrial & Commerce Bank,** *Hoa Binh Street, Dalat. Tel. (84 63) 822495.*
- **Post Office**, *14 Tran Phu Street, Dalat. Tel. (84 63) 822777.*
- **Dalat Tourist**, *9 Le Dai Hanh Street, Dalat. Tel. (84 63) 822479.* This office can arrange cars, drivers, tours and plane or bus tickets. Special trips to hunt buffalo can be arranged thorough this office.
- **Lam Dong Province Tourism Office**, *4 Tran Quoc Toan Street, Dalat, Tel. (84 63) 822125 or 822304 or 822520, Fax (84 63) 822661.* This company arranges motorcycle tours through the mountains of Vietnam. In the Central Highlands trip from Dalat to Kontum, you visit and sleep in minority villages. Other itineraries include Danang Truong Son mountains.
- **Lam Dong Youth Tourism Company**, *Lang Bian Youth Hostel, 2nd Floor, 6B Nguyen Thi Minh Khai Street, Dalat. Tel. (84 63) 822316 or 822318.* You can get budget accommodations at a variety of youth hostel-type places through this office.
- **Sinh Cafe Representative Office**, *Huong Tra Hotel, 1 Nguyen Thai Hoc Street, Dalat. Tel. (84 63) 822211 or 823970, Fax (84 63) 821075.* Budget tours, transportation and tourist "open ticket" bus service are available here.
- **Vietnam Airlines Office**, *5 Truong Cong Dinh Street, Dalat. Tel. (84 63) 822895.*
- **Dalat Hospital**, *4 Pham Ngoc Thach Street, Dalat, Tel. (84 63) 822154,* in case of a medical emergency.

CENTRAL HIGHLAND CITIES

As you travel west though the mountains to the Central Highlands plateau, pine trees and rolling countryside give way to rubber and coffee plantations. The major cities of the Central Highlands, **Buon Ma Thuot**, **Pleiku**, and **Kontum**, sit atop a long plateau. Highway 14 runs north to south and connects the cities in a virtually straight line. It extends north of Kontum to the Laotian border.

During the dry season the climate is hot and arid. The summer brings the rainy season, spanning from June through September. Some of the oldest plantations in the country still thrive in this area. Tea, coffee and rubber plants stretch as far as you can see.

Thirty-six different minority groups live on the Central Highlands plateau, including the Ede, Lak, Yali, Bani and Mnong. Most of the tribes are believed to have migrated through China from India or Malaysia in the first millennium AD. Many societies are matriarchal, and women have rights to inheritance and land. The characteristic house is a long-house with a tall, thatched roof. For some tribes long-houses are inhabited by extended families; others use them only for religious ceremonies.

The tourist trade is highly regulated in the Central Highlands. Most of the tourism offices are part of the government. All travelers in the area are required to have guides and permits. These visits to the villages often seem staged, and activities like riding elephants come off as contrived. The restrictive environment makes it difficult to rent transportation other than a car with a driver and guides. Hotels are not as new or well-equipped as those in other, more touristed regions. And restaurants are few and far between.

Buon Ma Thuot

The dusty city of **Buon Ma Thuot**, with more than 150,000 residents, lies in the heart of some of the oldest rubber and coffee plantations in the county. It is the capital of Daklak Province and the southernmost city on the country's central plateau.

Buon Ma Thuot was founded by the French in 1904. It is a major center of commerce. On tranquil Lak Lake, 60 kilometers from Buon Ma Thuot, locals use hollowed-out log canoes. Many waterfalls and villages dot the countryside.

Of the province's 1.3 million inhabitants, ten percent are Ede and five percent are Mnong people. Many tourists choose Buon Ma Thuot as a base for visiting the ethnic minority tribes. The tourist authority requires that permits and guides accompany every tour group in the region.

ARRIVALS & DEPARTURES

By Plane

Vietnam Airlines, *Tel. (84 50) 853850,* has flights between Ban Me Thuot and Danang, Hanoi (Monday, Wednesday, Friday), Ho Chi Minh City (daily), Phu Quoc Island, Rach Gia (Tuesday and Thursday) and Vinh (Monday and Wednesday).

By Bus

Buses connect Buon Ma Thuot to Ho Chi Minh City. The **bus station** is located north of the center of town.

By Tour Group

Private tours can be arranged in Ho Chi Minh City at most tourist offices.

ORIENTATION

The center of Buon Ma Thuot is a traffic circle, south of which streets are laid out on a gird, and to the north is a main street leading to Highway 14.

WHERE TO STAY

There are no luxury accommodations in Ban Me Thuot, although a new hotel is being constructed on the main traffic circle, at the former site of the Thang Loi Hotel.

HOANG GIA HOTEL, *62 Le Hong Phuong Street, Buon Ma Thuot. Tel. (84 50) 852161. Singles/doubles $12 to $15.*

The Hoang Gia is right downtown near the market in a noisy area. The funky floor plan has narrow staircases straight from an Escher drawing. The hotel is unquestionably rundown, but also the only place not charging significantly more than it is worth.

HONG KONG HOTEL, *30 Hai Ba Trung Street, Buon Ma Thuot. Tel. (84 50) 852630. Singles/doubles $30.*

This filthy establishment near the city center is frequented by backpackers. The rate of $30 for a room pushes the level of tolerance for economy-minded travelers, since the place is not worth half of this price.

KHACH SAN HOTEL, *57 Hai Ba Trung, Buon Ma Thuot. Tel. (84 50) 852407. Singles/doubles $12 to $50.*

This dirty excuse for a hotel charges $12 for a room without hot water and $50 for an equally nasty room with hot water. The staff appears as shifty as the men hanging around the pool table on the front patio.

NA KHACH, *18A Nguyen Chi Thanh, Ban Me Thuot. Tel. (84 50) 869211. Singles/doubles $25.*

From the outside this guest house looks clean and new, although the rooms are rather shabby and the bathrooms are a bit dirty. The lobby has the feel of a large, outdoor patio; and so do the rooms with their high ceilings and glass and metal doors. Traffic noise from the street in front of the hotel sounds like a highway, which may be preferable to the city racket downtown. The staff is friendly and helpful; some speak English. The location makes it reasonably safe. Currently this hotel is the most decent the city has to offer.

TAY NGUYEN HOTEL, *106 Ly Thuong Kiet Street, Buon Ma Thuot. Tel. (84 50) 851009 or 851011 or 851012, Fax (84 50) 852250. Singles/ doubles $25 to $30.*

The 21 room hotel is very noisy but otherwise decent.

THANG LOI HOTEL, *1 Phan Chu Trinh Street, Buon Ma Thuot. Tel. (84 50) 852322 or 852865.*

The main hotel located on the city's traffic circle is currently undergoing major renovation. No doubt, this will be the most comfortable place to stay once it is finished. And it will provide the best view for the annual festival in which a parade of elephants parade goes through the town, right around the traffic circle.

WHERE TO EAT

MY CANH, *Vietnamese/inexpensive, 39 Trang Long Street, Buon Ma Thuot.*

There is a notable lack of places to have a meal in Buon Ma Thuot, which makes My Canh a pleasant surprise, and practically a lifesaver. Despite annoyances such as the curious passers-by and beggars that will probably wander in to watch you eat, the food is good and the place is clean. The menu is in English. If you're yearning for Szechuan-style spicy food, try the shrimp with vegetables. Soups are very good also.

SEEING THE SIGHTS

Buon Ma Thuot Prison, *18 Tan Thuat Street, Buon Ma Thuot*, was used by the French for political prisoners in the first few decades of this century. Today it is open for visitors.

Ethnic Minority Museum, *1 Doc Lap Traffic Circle, Buon Ma Thuot, Open 7 am to 10 am, 1:30 pm to 4:30 pm*, displays elements of daily life from the Ede and Mnong tribes. This is the most complete collection about the culture of the area. Also documented is the history of the villagers' participation in the communist path to power.

Lac Giao Family (Communal) House, *47 Phan Boi Chau Street, Buon Ma Thuot*, is open to the public as an example of the traditional lifestyle in the region.

DAY TRIPS & EXCURSIONS

Yang Prong Cham Ruins are about seven centuries old, and located in the Rung Xanh Forest. The single temple is well preserved. You must hire a guide from the local tourist authority to visit the temple.

Many **minority villages** surround Lak Lake, which is 60 kilometers southeast of Buon Ma Thuot.

PRACTICAL INFORMATION

• **Daklak Tourist Company**, *3 Phan Chu Trinh Street, Buon Ma Thuot. Tel. (84 50) 852108 or 852324; Fax (84 50) 852865.* The regional tourist authority arranges tours which last from one to four days, with elephant rides and overnights at villages. The branch office of Daklak Tourist Company, *122 Le Lai Street, District 1, Ho Chi Minh City. Tel. (84 8) 8397486,* offers a convenient way to book tours in south Vietnam.

Pleiku

The town of **Pleiku** (about 35,000) is far more hospitable than its southern neighbor, Ban Ma Thuot. There is a notable lack of orange dust in the streets. The city is growing rapidly, with new buildings and new signs on the streets.

Still, there is little to do here other than visit minority villages. The main tourist office is in Pleiku Hotel, the city's largest.

ARRIVALS & DEPARTURES

By Plane

Vietnam Airlines, *Tel. (84 59) 823834,* has non-stop flights between Pleiku and Ho Chi Minh City or Danang.

ORIENTATION

Pleiku is a tiny city that tourists visit only to travel to nearby minority villages.

WHERE TO STAY

HUNG VUONG HOTEL, *215 Hung Vuong Street, Pleiku. Tel. (84 59) 824270 or 821010, Fax (84 59) 824891. Singles/doubles $25.*

The Hung Vuong is an older hotel, which is run down. Two advantages of staying here are that there is ample parking in back and a good noodle house around the corner. This hotel is adequate and rooms have television.

PLEIKU HOTEL, *124 Le Loi Street, Pleiku. Tel. (84 59) 824628 or 823758. Singles/doubles from $12 to $37.*

This decent tourist hotel has a large lobby, and ample parking. You must pay more for rooms on the second floor. The food in the restaurant is the best you will find in the city. Gialai Travel Service Center is located here.

THANH LICH HOTEL, *86 Nguyen Van Troi Street, Pleiku. Tel. (84 59) 824674, Fax (84 59) 824891. Singles $7 to $10/doubles $20.*

The tiny hotel is a good pick for the budget-minded traveler. The staff has a friendlier disposition than you will generally find in this part of the country.

YALY HOTEL, *89 Hung Vuong Street, Pleiku. Tel. (84 59) 824843 or 824858. Singles/doubles $15 to $35.*

The Yaly hotel is a 54 room place that is run-down. All of the rooms have hot water and air-conditioning. The large restaurant has decent food. The Vietnam Airlines booking office and a tour office are located in the lobby.

WHERE TO EAT

Try the hotel restaurants and the cafe around the corner from Hung Vuong Hotel.

SEEING THE SIGHTS

Bien Ho Lake sits amid rolling hills, in the craters of inactive volcanoes. Nearby villages use Bien Ho Lake for fishing and transportation. You will find Bien Ho Lake about 10 kilometers north of Pleiku on the main highway. There will be signs leading you to the lake.

SPORTS & RECREATION

Trekking tours of the area can be arranged through Gialai Travel Service Center, *124 Le Loi Street, Pleiku, Tel/Fax (84 59) 824891.*

PRACTICAL INFORMATION

· **Bank of Gia Lai Province**, *Tran Hung Dao Street, Pleiku.*
· **Post Office**, *69 Hung Vuong, Pleiku. Tel. (84 59) 824006 or 824129.*
· **Gia Lai Tourist**, *77 Tran Phu Street, Pleiku. Tel. (84 59) 8824271 or 824645. Fax (84 59) 824891.*
· **Gialai Travel Service Center**, *124 Le Loi Street, Pleiku. Tel./Fax (84 59) 824891.* Located in a large office in the lobby of the Pleiku hotel. The fax number for area hotels is actually this office. The travel center specializes in tours to the Bahnar and Jarai tribes. Not only will this agency book a room, rent a vehicle or change money, but the staff

specializes in arranging treks on foot, by bicycle or elephant. Special tours for veterans can be arranged. Overnight treks cost from $55 to $65 per night, per person.
- **Vietnam Airlines Booking Office**, *Yaly Hotel, 89 Hung Vuong Street, Pleiku. Tel. (84 59) 823 834.*
- **Medical Clinic**, *Tran Hung Dao Street, Pleiku. Tel. (84 59) 82411.*

Kontum

In the language of the Bana people, **Kontum** means "village by the water." The **Po Co River** cuts through the dry, basalt land. Kontum is the capital of Kontum province, which is bordered by Cambodia and Laos. Although the province appears quite poor, the region has extensive plantations of sugar cane, rubber trees and tea shrubs. Ethnic minority people, including the Bana, Brau and So Dang, constitute over half the population.

The French came to the area in the seventeenth century, and from the nineteenth century onward, carried on the administration of the Central Highlands from Kontum.

Kontum is a the best town to use as a base for a tour of the Central Highlands. It is far lovelier that its southern neighbors, and the townspeople are welcoming of foreigners. The steady development and investment promises to make Kontum the tourist center of the area in the future.

ARRIVALS & DEPARTURES
By Air
The closest airport is in Pleiku, about 40 kilometers from Kontum. **Vietnam Airlines** runs flights from Pleiku to Ho Chi Minh City and Danang. Taxis between the Pleiku Airport to Kontum cost about $25. The nearest Vietnam Airlines office is in Pleiku, *Tel. (84 59) 823834.*

By Car
Highway 14 runs from Ho Chi Minh City, through Dalat and Kontum, to Danang Province. Since the highway is in disrepair, it is advisable to drop south and take Highway 19 to Qui Nhon or Highway 21 to Nha Trang. The Dakto hot springs are reached by this road.

ORIENTATION
Kontum has wide streets and palm trees. The streets run on a grid, so it is easy to find your way around. You can walk anywhere in the city you need to go.

WHERE TO STAY

BANK GUEST HOUSE, *90 Tran Phu Street, Kontum. Singles/doubles $10 to $15.*

The friendly manager of the Bank Guest House runs a comfortable hotel, which gives you the most for your money of any hotel in the Central Highlands. The casual atmosphere lets you relax. The rooms are clean and pleasant. Tours of the minority villages and war sites can be arranged upon arrival.

DAKBLA HOTEL, *Phan Dinh Phung Road, Kontum.*

Presently under construction, this new hotel will open its doors sometime in 1997.

NGOC LINH HOTEL, *12-A Phan Dinh Phung Street, Kontum. Tel. (84 60) 864560. Singles $7/doubles $13 to $16. Including a $1 charge for tourist insurance.*

This is the first hotel as you enter town. Rooms without hot water are about three dollars less than the "with hot water" variety. After a night on one of the dingy beds, chances are you will want a hot shower. The tourist insurance charge at this hotel is unique, and could not be explained by the staff.

QUANG TRUNG HOTEL, *168 Ba Trieu Street, Kontum. Tel. (84 60) 862249 or 862703, Fax (84 60) 862493. Singles $18; doubles $22.*

This is a large tourist hotel. Three meals at the hotel restaurant may be purchased for $8 per day. The restaurant will also cater picnics for $10 per person. The hotel's tourist office offers a variety of options for tours in the region.

WHERE TO EAT

Nguyen Hue Street is lined with cafes. All serve Vietnamese food for inexpensive prices. The best restaurant in town, which does not have a name, is located at *90 Nguyen Hue Street.*

DAY TRIPS & EXCURSIONS

Dak Glei Jail, one of the jails which housed Vietnamese prisoners who built highways during the French occupation, is open to visitors.

About 40 kilometers north of Kontum, you can visit the **Dakto** battlefield, which saw fierce fighting toward the end of the Vietnam War. The backbone of the American campaign here was unrelenting air raids.

Yaly Waterfall, a 60 meter fall on the Po River, is the site of a new hydro-electric plant. Tours take curious Vietnamese tourists to the once-spectacular fall. The falls are about 20 kilometers south of Kontum, just off the highway.

PRACTICAL INFORMATION

· **Kontum Province State Bank**, *88 Tran Phu, Kontum. Tel (84 60) 862556.* This bank has a currency exchange service.
· **Post Office**, *205 Le Hong Phong Street, Kontum. Tel. (84 60) 862279.*
· **Kontum Trade and Tourism Company**, *218 Tran Hung Dao, Kontum. Tel. (84 60) 862222 or 862434 or 862508, Fax (84 60) 862462.* Branch office located at 180 Nguyen Hue Street, Kontum.
· **Quang Trung Tourist**, *Quang Trung Hotel, 168 Ba Trieu Street, Kontum. Tel. (84 60) 862249 or 862703, Fax (84 60) 862493.* This tourist office arranges tours for both small and large groups. You must hire a guide, either have or hire a car, and pay an insurance fee. Here are some sample prices: six seat car $50 per day; guide $20 per day, tourism fee $5 per site visited; insurance $1 per person. So a tour for five people visiting four places would start at $95. The tourist office will work out a one day itinerary for $25 to $40, depending on the size of your group.

ARRANGE YOUR OWN GONG CONCERT

Should you want an orchestrated viewing of local culture, a Gong concert can be arranged upon request for groups. The two hours performance, held in a village long-house, includes folk songs and dances, the gong concert, and a drink from the communal wine jars. Prices range from $150 to $200, depending on the size of your group. Contact the **Quang Trung Tourist** *(see Practical Information above) and they will take care of the rest.*

---

14. CENTRAL COAST

Nha Trang

The best way to spend time in the fun and exciting city of **Nha Trang** is in the water. The clear blue-green **South China Sea** is inviting year-round. Rugged coral reefs offer good snorkeling and diving. Tourists boats crowd the harbor shuttling groups to island beaches.

Tourists come to Nha Trang just to be tourists: to eat, sleep and occasionally swim in the warm, salty sea. Hotels are inexpensive, fresh seafood is excellent and cheap, and almost every hotel has a tourist office which books boat trips and transportation or tours to areas beyond the city. Nha Trang is a good starting point for a trip through the Central Highlands.

For some 5,000 years humans have lived on this part of Vietnam's coast. The Cham extended through these lands. Their monuments, the exotic brick temples, remain. The French doctor Yersin docked at Nha Trang when he made his first trip of exploration into central Vietnam.

In 1924 a royal decree established the town of Nha Trang. Today the capital of Khanh Hoa Province has a population of over 200,000. Commercial fishing and salt extraction (from sea water) are major industries.

The flip-side of a tourist area—beggars, prostitution and commercialization—is also found here. Visiting the near-by Cham site, pagoda, or marina may become an exercise in tolerance. How so many children escape school and acquire postcards and trinkets to sell is anyone's guess. Usually a firm "no," will send them on their way; however in this town both professional peddlers and cyclo drivers grow more aggressive seemingly each day.

Average temperatures range from about 23°C to 33°C (73.4°F to 91.4°F). The rainy season, from June to October, is marked by wet mornings and evenings.

ARRIVALS & DEPARTURES

The Nha Trang airport is located a few kilometers outside the city. Taxi service is available; the ride between the city and the airport costs $7. Vietnam Airlines has direct flights between Nha Trang and Ho Chi Minh City or Danang. The standard passenger tax of 15,000 dong ($1.37) applies.

Nha Trang is 450 kilometers north of Ho Chi Minh City on Highway 1. The open ticket (cafe) tourist buses stop in Nha Trang. The local bus station is on Le Than Ton Street. On the continuation of that street, you will find the train station on Thai Nguyen Street.

ORIENTATION

Nha Trang is a city of about 250,000 which sits directly on the beach. Most hotels are located in the area behind the city's beach. Tran Phu Street runs along the seaside; boats dock at the southern end of this street.

GETTING AROUND TOWN

While in the city of Nha Trang, you do not need transportation, since most restaurants and the beach are all centrally located. The boat dock is some distance from the center of town, so if you take a boat tour of the bay, you may need to take a taxi to the dock.

If you plan to stay a few days to explore, Nha Trang is an excellent city for bicycle riding. The calm traffic and warm sea breezes make for leisurely rides. The good spots are the surrounding islands and the Cham temples.

WHERE TO STAY

BAO DAI VILLAS, *Tran Phu Street, Nha Trang. Tel. (84 58) 81049, Fax (84 58) 81471. Singles/doubles $25 to $70.*

This is one of the most attractive settings imaginable for a vacation stay. Once a vacation residence for the Emperor Bao Dai, the five spacious villas perched on a hill overlooking the harbor are now a hotel. The villas were built in 1920, and retain their period decoration. During the war, the elite of the South Vietnamese government used the villas. The hotel is also a museum, and open to the public.

The distance from the city (6 kilometers) allows you to completely enjoy the beauty of the setting without the noise and hassles of an urban environment. The hotel restaurant serves the freshest and most delicious seafood in the city. Boats are available for rental at the hotel, as are bicycles and cars. The hotel provides all services on a cash-only basis.

THE GRAND HOTEL, *44 Tran Phu Street, Nha Trang. Tel. (84 58) 822445 or 826944 or 826940, Fax (84 58) 825395. Singles $18 to $64/doubles $23 to $68.*

This solid yellow building has been a hotel since its opening in the early 1930s. From the outside you would guess it is a government building. The hotel does not offer enough to get away with the top-end prices. That is to say the $23 dollar double is a good deal and the $64 single is near robbery. While the rooms are renovated, the decor is far from first-class. Budget rooms are available for $10 per night (with a private bath and fan, but no air-conditioning).

HAI DAN HOTEL, *84 Tran Phu Street, Nha Trang. Tel. (84 58) 825023. Singles/doubles $15 to $25.*

The mini-hotel, located on the main street, has refreshing views of the water. The staff is very friendly and staying here has the advantages of staying in a newly built hotels with modern bathrooms, amenities such as air conditioning, IDD telephones, television with satellite, and a fresh atmosphere. To have a view of the sea, ask for a room with a balcony.

HAI YEN HOTEL, *40 Tran Phu Street, Nha Trang. Tel. (84 58) 822974 or 822828, Fax (84 58) 821902. Singles $30 to $40/doubles $35 to $40. Credit cards accepted.*

This hotel is connected to the nicer and less expensive Vien Dong Hotel. The salon downstairs gives a decent haircut for $4. The restaurant specializes in seafood.

NAVY GUEST HOUSE, *58 Tran Phu Street, Nha Trang. Tel. (84 58) 881705. Singles/doubles $10.*

If you have ever dreamt of spending a night in prison this is the place to stay. It remains popular with European backpackers— but why? The only allure could be the very low price. You can put five in a room for $13 per night. Of course, that is without hot water. The stuffed wildlife in the "lobby" gives you a prelude to the rooms (which are eerie).

VIEN DONG HOTEL, *1 Tran Hung Dao Street, Nha Trang. Tel. (84 58) 821606, Fax (84 58) 821912. Singles $25 to $30/doubles $30 to $70/triples $35 to $75. Credit cards accepted.*

This 84-room tourist hotel is the most popular place to stay, and for good reason. The clean modern rooms have complete amenities. The hotel has a large, clear pool and tennis courts. The restaurant serves the a variety of excellent Western and Vietnamese seafood dishes. The fried shrimp melt in your mouth. Nightly shows of regional music are free. The tourist office can arrange cars and tours.

VINA HOTEL, *66 Tran Phu Street, Nha Trang. Tel. (84 58) 823099 or 827344 or 827345, Fax (84 58) 825137. Singles $14/doubles $16.*

The Vina Hotel is a rambling house-style motel. It offers excellent budget facilities and is located just across from the beach. The staff is very friendly and attempts to provide convenience for their guests. The front desk is a mini-mart, selling snacks, batteries and goggles.

Most rooms have air-conditioning and televisions. Rooms with only a fan and no hot water run $8 to $12.

WHERE TO EAT
Moderate

LAC CANH, *Vietnamese, 11 Hang Ca Street, Nha Trang. Tel. (84 58) 821391.*

Lac Canh remains the favorite eatery for locals and tourists alike. Small clay pots with hot coals are brought to the table and you cook you own food. Vegetarians are out of luck here, because not only is barbecue the best food of the house, it is the only food of the house. Seafood is served, and is nearly as good as the beef. The atmosphere is festive, and the open-air seating is reminiscent of a July 4th picnic. The restaurant is usually crowded and there is often a wait. Reservations accepted.

VIEN DONG HOTEL RESTAURANT, *Western and Vietnamese, 1 Tran Hung Dao Street, Nha Trang. Tel. (84 58) 821606.*

The patio restaurant makes excellent and reasonably priced seafood dishes, such as fried calamari. The salads are big, fresh and safe to eat. The dinner show of regional music and renditions of folk dances is recommended. The show begins at 7 pm. The restaurant fills up when celebrations (such as weddings) are held here. Locals say this is the fanciest restaurant in town.

Inexpensive

BANH XEO RESTAURANT, *Vietnamese, 15 Ng Tri Minh Khai Street, Nha Trang.*

Savory banh xeo is served in this inconspicuous restaurant. Banh xeo are rice-batter pancakes with meat that are fried to a crisp. Actually, the lady of the house cooks on a small grill on the street; her daughter rolls the banh xeo into salad rolls. You sit at a table in the living room to enjoy your banh xeo. The family does not speak much English, but manages to have good conversations with their guests. Eating here is a great experience and moreover the banh xeo are out of this world.

PHO HA NOI, *Vietnamese, 21 Le Thanh Phuong Street, Nha Trang.*

When you have eaten the last breakfast pancake you can stomach, head over to this noodle house. As the name promises, you can get excellent pho (soup) here at any time of the day.

VIETNAM RESTAURANT, *Vietnamese, 23 Hoang Van Thu Street, Nha Trang. Tel. (84 58) 822933.*

This is a good local restaurant that serves seafood prepared in the traditional Vietnamese style. Nothing fancy, but it is delicious.

SEEING THE SIGHTS

The **city beach** is nothing spectacular for sunbathing. It is frequently crowded. The coastline runs for 6 kilometers along the palm tree-lined Tran Phu Street.

Hire boats at the docks on the southern end of Tran Phu Street. There are 14 islands off the coast of Nha Trang. Some are regular stops for tourist boats; others are nearly deserted. A favorite stop is the **Island of Seven Pagodas**. The island is home to a fishing village which you can visit. You can visit **Monkey Island**, appropriately named for the many monkeys that live there.

If you do opt for a tour boat, take Mama Linh's, *Tel. (84 58) 826693 or stop by the Hai Yen Cafe.* It is the most professionally run of the many tour companies. The guides pick you up at your hotel, provide a seafood buffet cooked on the boat for lunch, and stop at relatively secluded spots for swimming. The tour takes all day, and includes a stop on an island beach where you can sunbathe. The cost of the trip is $7; the price for a massage is $4, but may be negotiable. Masks for snorkeling and fresh fruit are provided without charge.

Long Son Pagoda was built in 1898, and the white Buddha was added in 1963. When you arrive, walk to the left of the pagoda. Here you will find a winding staircase leading to the large white Buddha statue that over looks the city. The Buddha's eye-view of the city is worth the climb of 150 steps to reach the top.

After seeing the Buddha, check out the pagoda. The ornate painting on the ceiling in the altar area is extraordinary. The three statues of incarnations of the Buddha — Siddhartha, Amida and Mitreya — date from the turn of the century.

The large number of tourists here means you should exercise caution. If someone strikes up a conversation with you, you can be certain they are acting the role of a guide and will expect compensation for it. The reason for seeing the Buddha first is that it allows you a quick exit when persistent "guides" approach you in the pagoda. Tourists are often harassed by people following them, them demanding money. *Long Son pagoda is on the north side Highway 1 as you leave the city.*

Po Nagar temple, dedicated to the queen-goddess Po Nagar, is undergoing reconstruction and preservation. The original temple was built in the eighth century, but was destroyed. The present temple dates from a later period, but there is disagreement among archeologist as to the construction date. The main temple is a sanctuary which is still used to pay homage to Po Nagar. The wardrobe behind along the back wall holds the gowns and headdresses that adorn the statue. These are changed every month. The faithful who have success and wealth donate the outfits as a way of giving thanks. *To reach Po Nagar, take Highway 1 north. Just after you cross Xom Bong Bridge, about 2 kilometers from the city center, you will see the temple on the western hill.*

The **Oceanographic Institute** *is located between Bao Dai's Villa Hotel/ Museum and the docks at the end of Tran Hung Dao Street.* Cement tanks hold examples of local water life. Inside the building is the skeleton of a humpback whale that was found on the coast. The other building in the museum has walls of specimens in jars that are sure to bring back memories of the smell of formaldehyde in the high school biology lab. Admission is 10,000 dong.

The **Hon Chong Rock** is a tourist attraction and part of local folklore. A group of giant rocks stand on the seaside. The legend says that the giant who formed the land fell on one of these and left an imprint of his hand. Sure enough, when you walk out on the rocks that overlook the water, with a little imagination you can see what could be a hand print. An otherwise pristine atmosphere of rocks and waves is encroached upon by the kiosks selling souvenirs and drinks.

Hon Chong Rock is about 4 kilometers north of the center of Nha Trang. Take Quang Trung Street north; this will turn into Thang Street. Remain on this street until you reach Nguyen Dinh Street. The entrance is at the top of this street, which ends in a large parking lot.

NIGHTLIFE & ENTERTAINMENT

The tourists keep the local cafes lively into the evening. For those who prefer sweets, the best pancakes (crepes) with ice cream are served at **Banana Split** *on Quan Trung Street.*

The **Lizard Bar**, *across from the Vien Dong Hotel*, attracts foreigners out for a late-night beer.

SPORTS & RECREATION

By any means necessary, get to the water. Swim, sunbathe, relax by the beautiful blue sea, and enjoy the coast!

Scuba Diving & Snorkling

Snorkeling and skin diving areas abound of the coast of Nha Trang. You can rent equipment from the tourist office of **Nha Trang Ship Chandler Company**, *74 Tran Phu Street, Nha Trang, Tel. (84 58) 821195.*

Luxury scuba diving trips aboard an oriental junk boat are arranged by **Voiles Vietnam**, *17 Pham Ngoc Thach Street, District 3, Ho Chi Minh City, Tel. (84 8) 8296750, Fax (84 8) 8231591.* The trip includes sailing from Ho Chi Minh City, up the coast to Nha Trang.

Sailboarding

Ironically, the Nha Trang Sailing Club does not have sailboats. But you can rent the next best thing, a sailboard, for $5 per hour. Jet skis are available for $40 per hour. The friendly manager of the **Nha Tran Sailing Club**, *72-74 Than Phu Street, Nha Trang. Tel. (84 58) 826528, Fax (84 58) 821906.* speaks fluent English and can arrange tours of the Central Highlands.

SHOPPING

Cho Dam Market sells luscious regional fruit, such as dragon fruit and mangoes. The vendors sell sea shells and tortoise shells, without regard for endangered species.

DAY TRIPS & EXCURSIONS

The protege of Louis Pasteur, Dr. Alexander Yersin, spent a good part of his life vaccinating rural Vietnamese. He died in Nha Trang in 1943. You can visit **Dr. Yersin's tomb** in a small village off Highway 1 south of Nha Trang. Signs show the way from the highway.

There are a lovely set of waterfalls about 28 kilometers from Nha Trang. The **Ba Ho** Falls pour over large rounded rocks. The three falls, each one larger than the next, are reached by crawling and hiking around over the rocks, following a small stream. More tourists are discovering the falls; still you can have a secluded sun bath. Some boys that live in the area enjoy walking with visitors and practicing English. A half-kilometer shaded path leads to the water; it takes another half kilometer to reach the farthest fall. A small cafe at the parking area sells cold drinks. *To reach Ba Bo Falls, take Highway 1 north for about 27 kilometers. A dirt road leads to the falls, which are on the east side of the road.*

After working up an appetite at the falls, you can enjoy fresh seafood at the nearby restaurants. On Highway 1 about 25 kilometers from Nha Trang are crab farms. A few restaurants here serve whole crab for only a few dollars each. The **Quan Gio Restaurant** serves sweet, tangy crab in tamarind that makes the effort of tearing apart the shell worthwhile.

PRACTICAL INFORMATION

• **Bank for Foreign Trade**, *17 Quang Trung Street, Nha Trang. Tel. (84 58) 821054.*
• **Post Office**, *2 Tran Phu Street, Nha Trang. Tel. (84 58) 822333. Hours 6:30 am to 8:30 pm.*
• **Khanh Hoa Province Tourism**, *1 Tran Hung Dao Street, Nha Trang. Tel. (84 58) 822753 or 822757 or 823709, Fax (84 58) 821912 or 821902.*

- **Mama Linh Boat trip Office**, *Hai Yen Cafe on the beach. Tel. (84 58) 826693*. Mama Linh runs the best boat tour of the islands off Nha Trang, and can arrange tours of the Central Highlands.
- **Nha Tran Sailing Club**, *72-74 Than Phu Street, Nha Trang. Tel. (84 58) 826528. Fax (84 58) 821906*. Arranges tours of the Central Highlands and rents jet skis and sailboards.
- **Nha Trang Tourism**, *57-59 Phan Boi Chau Street, Nha Trang. Tel. (84 58) 821231*.
- **Tourist Office at the Vien Dong Hotel**, *1 Tran Hung Dao Street, Nha Trang. Tel. (84 58) 821606, Fax (84 58) 821912*. The hotel offers comprehensive services at reasonable prices.
- **Voiles Vietnam**, *17 Pham Ngoc Thach Street, District 3, Ho Chi Minh City. Tel. (84 8) 8296750, Fax (84 8) 8231591*. Runs scuba-sailing trips from Ho Chi Minh City, up the coast to Nha Trang.
- **Vietnam Airlines Office**, *12 Hoang Hoa Street, Nha Trang. Tel. (84 58) 823797*.
- **Benh Viet Tinh Clinic**, *Yersin Street, Tel. (84 58) 822175*, emergency medical care is available from the clinic.

Qui Nhon

Qui Nhon sits on a peninsula at the base of Ba Hoa Mountain. It has two ports and is primarily an industrial town. Qui Nhon is very popular with Vietnamese vacationers although the beaches here suffer from pollution. The city itself is very pleasant, especially in the evening when traffic slows to a trickle. One of the best activities in Qui Nhon is strolling along the quiet city streets and enjoying a simple meal or drink with the locals.

The area has a rich history. It was home to the Cham empire, and close to Qui Nhon there are many Cham temples to visit. The emperor Quang Trung, one of the leaders of the Tay Son Rebellion hails from this area.

Qui Nhon is also home to the nation's opera company, the **Dao Tan**, who perform traditional oriental opera called tuong. The Dao Tan presents only four operas per year—perhaps because the performances can last for weeks, with an installation of the story every night. Smaller amateur companies perform in the area as well.

ARRIVALS & DEPARTURES

Highway 19 connects Pleiku to Qui Nhon. The Qui Hhon Airport is quite a distance from the city. A cab ride from the airport to town costs about $30.

You must pay the domestic airport tax of 15,000 dong ($1.37).

ORIENTATION

The city's two ports are at the eastern end of the peninsula. Bach Dang Street runs the length of the city, along the water.

GETTING AROUND TOWN

Qui Nhon is a small town; you can walk anywhere in the city that you would want to go. To reach the interesting historical areas, you need a bicycle, motor bike or car.

WHERE TO STAY

BANK HOTEL, *257 Le Hong Phong Street, Qui Nhon. Tel. (84 56) 822779 or 823591, Fax (84 56) 821013. Singles/doubles $15 to $30.*

The official hotel of the Vietcom Bank offers budget and tourist-class accommodation. The $15 rooms have hot water and fans; the $30 rooms have televisions and air-conditioning. The hotel is slightly run-down yet still manages to be reasonably comfortable. It is located in the center of town, convenient to the highway but far from the beach. It is a good, budget choice.

HAI HA HOTEL, *14 Tran Binh Trong Street, Qui Nhon. Tel. (84 56) 824300, Fax (84 56) 824300. Singles/doubles $20 to $30.*

The Hai Ha has a good location, just off the beach on a quiet street. The 10 rooms in the mini-hotel have modern bathrooms, air-conditioning, televisions and phones. Small touches like the crisp, white bedspreads and a courtyard with a garden make this a special place. The sweet family who runs the hotel enjoys getting to know their guests. The restaurant specializes in fresh seafood and will cook special meals on request. Upstairs there is a dining room that can be used for private parties. Call ahead for reservations, the hotel often fills up.

QUI NHON HOTEL, *130 Nguyen Hue Street, Qui Nhon. Tel. (84 56) 822401 or 8224028, Fax (84 56) 821162. Singles $25 to 28; Doubles $29 to $32, including breakfast. Credit cards accepted.*

This is a large, typical tourist hotel with outdated furniture. The Vietcom Bank runs an currency exchange at the front desk; and in case you are searching for one, there is copy machine in the lobby. With a steady stream of tour groups coming through, the staff seems not to be compelled to cater to individual guests. You can dine inside or outside at the hotel restaurant. Suites available ($40 per night).

SEAGULL HOTEL, *489 Nguyen Hue Street, Qui Nhon. Tel. (84 56) 846473 or 846377, Fax (84 56) 846926. Singles $20 to $35/doubles $25 to $40. Breakfast included. Credit cards accepted.*

The five-year-old Seagull Hotel sits on a private piece of beach. Half of the 50 rooms have an ocean view. The hotel has a resort atmosphere because it is designed to let visitors enjoy the beach. From most parts of the hotel you can hear the relaxing sound of the surf. The hotel has tennis courts and an excellent restaurant. The front desk can arrange tours and car rental for seeing the Cham temples in the area.

WHERE TO EAT

Most tourists eat in the hotel restaurants which usually serve good seafood. Most of the restaurants in Qui Nhon are small cafes that serve standard Vietnamese fare.

SANH PHUONG CAFE, *Vietnamese/inexpensive, 251 Le Phuong Street, Qui Nhon.*

Sanh Phuong Cafe is among the better places to eat. This is a clean, nice cafe where you can enjoy good food. The fried noodles are particularly good, and the bamboo soup is full of fresh bamboo shoots in an aromatic broth.

SEEING THE SIGHTS

The **Quang Trung Museum** holds artifacts pertaining to Emperor Quang Trung (Nguyen Hue), the eighteenth century leader who hailed from a nearby village. The museum chronicles his reign and the Tay Son Rebellion (see sidebar below) that led to his taking the throne.

THE TAY SON REBELLION

*The **Tay Son Rebellion** lasted from 1771 to 1789. The uprising against the government that ruled the lands of southern Vietnam is remembered as a peasants' revolt. The three brothers, Nguyen Hue, Nguyen Hac and Nguyen Lu, started the revolt in Tay Son and eventually took the south to Ho Chi Minh City.*

Nguyen Hue was a brilliant military strategist who led the rebel army. Soon after the Nguyen brothers seized power in the south, Chinese forces descended upon the north. Nguyen Hue led his troops against the Chinese and soundly defeated them. He then installed himself as emperor and changed his name to Quang Trung.

One group of Cham towers is in the middle of a neighborhood close to downtown Qui Nhon. The **Two Towers**, or Thap Doi date from the 1200s, and have been partially reconstructed. The Two Towers have heavy lines and thick archways, distinctively different from other towers. The architecture looks more solid than other towers, in part because the layers and decoration are absent from the roof. Neighborhood children will find you as interesting as you find the towers.

ENTERTAINMENT & NIGHTLIFE

The **Dao Tan Opera Company**, *854 Nguyen Thai Hoc Street, Qui Nhon*, presents the traditional form of song and dance called troung.

Along Le Hong Phoung Street you will find many open-air bars with pool tables.

DAY TRIPS & EXCURSIONS

The name of the **Bahn It** Cham temple means "wedding cake." The four towers are also known as the Silver Towers. This group of four structures is an extremely well-preserved site in a lovely location overlooking a pagoda and rivers. To reach Bahn It, take Highway 1 north from Qui Nhon about 25 kilometers (15 miles), and turn at the sign to Tuy Phouc. From the road that leads to the site is just south of the towers. You can park at Nguyen Thieu Pagoda which is down the dirt road. The tranquil setting is the home of a monastery.

About 30 kilometers (18 miles) from Qui Nhon, in the coastal hills, lies the immense **Cu Mong Lake**. It is surrounded by numerous fishing villages. Since there are no places to spend the night in this area, a day-trip will put you in touch with the local life.

The birthplace of the eighteenth century Tay Son rebellion was in **Tay Son** town. The three Nguyen brothers who led the peasant uprising later united the country. You can reach Tay Son by traveling 45 kilometers (27 miles) north on Highway 19.

MY LAI

*The **My Lai massacre** was one of the most scandalous and dramatic events in the Vietnam War. In 1968, partly in response to the Tet Offensive, American troops destroyed the village of My Lai, killing all of the inhabitants. This event was not reported by the American press until about eight months later, in November 1968. The brutality of the My Lai Massacre shocked the American public. Outrage and anger over this atrocity fueled the anti-war movement in the Untied States and remains ingrained in the collective American memory as a horrifying tragedy. The site of the My Lai massacre is marked by a monument and a museum.*

My Lai can be reached from Highway 1, about 13 kilometers (8 miles) from Quang Ngai town, north of Qui Nhon.

About 30 kilometers (18 miles) from Qui Nhon you will find one of the oldest pagodas in the country. The **Thap Thap Pagoda** was constructed in 1665. It is an interesting mix of Buddhist and Cham influence. This was once the seat of the Cham Empire.

North of Qui Nhon along Highway 1 is the hamlet of **Sa Huynh**. This is little more than a strip of beach and a hotel. This is a good place to stop to take in the beautiful coastline and rest if you need to. Quite a few tourists find their way here. However, both the hotel and the restaurant have seen better days.

If you want to stay or eat here anyway, the address is: **SA HUYNH HOTEL**, *Highway 1, Sa Huynh, Tel. (84 55) 860311 or (84 55) 60401.*

PRACTICAL INFORMATION
- **Foreign Trade Bank**, *148 Le Loi Street, Quy Nhon. Tel. (84 56) 822266 or 822408, Fax (84 56) 823181.*
- **Hospital**, *309 Nguyen Hue Street, Qui Nhon.*
- **Binh Dinh Province Post Office**, *197 Phan Boi Chau Street, Qui Nhon. Tel. (84 56) 821441, Fax (84 56) 821555.*
- **Binh Dinh Tourist Office**, *10 Nguyen Hue Street, Qui Nhon. Tel. (84 56) 822524 or 822206.*
- **Vietnam Airlines Office**, *2 Ly Thoung Kiet Street, Qui Nhon. Tel. (84 56) 823125.*

Hoi An

For centuries, the small city of **Hoi An** (population 30,000) thrived as an international port. British, Dutch, French, Italian, and Portuguese merchants brought silk, cinnamon and other treasures of the orient from Hoi An to the rest of the world. When not restricted by isolationist policies, both China and Japan sent ships through the harbor.

Hoi An was then known as *Faifo*, a name of uncertain origin. The area may have been a Cham trading center as early as the second century AD. The town as we know it today was founded in the late sixteenth century. In the seventeenth and eighteenth centuries Hoi An experienced a golden era as one of the most active ports on the Asian continent.

Hoi An not only brought Vietnamese goods to the rest of the world, but western influence came through the harbor. European missionaries brought Catholicism to Vietnam in the seventeenth century. Portuguese missionary Alexander de Rhodes played a key role in developing the modern Vietnamese script, *quoc ngu*.

Attracted by trade, Chinese and Japanese settled in Hoi An. The city was divided in cultural quarters, the remnants of which are still evident in the historic buildings. The notable absence of a strong French component is due to their choosing Danang for a trade center. Different nationalities coexisted and preserved their identities through local councils and religious houses. A dialect unique to Hoi An has developed from these influences.

Most of the architecture dates from the nineteenth century, although the elements of construction are true to the older forms which were destroyed during the Tay Son rebellion. The buildings which line the old city streets are a living museum of Vietnamese, Chinese and Japanese architecture. The city holds 529 historic houses, 70 halls and religious complexes, and many ancient tombs and shrines.

The Chinese Assembly Halls, which are named for the regions that their congregations came from, provided a center for each immigrant community. Religious services and community meetings were held regularly.

Wealthy and powerful families built mansions, many which still stand. The family shrines in these house showcase the heads of household. Two types of family houses are predominant, the double house connected by a courtyard, and traditional houses, which have either three or five sections.

Certain wells are protected because their age makes them historically significant. Wells are very important since well water must be used in the preparation of *Cau Lau*, a dish of thick noodles prepared only in Hoi An.

For centuries Hoi An has been a center of craftsmanship, especially metal work and ceramics The temple bells made here are taller and straighter than traditional bells. Gongs are made just outside the city. Some of the finest silk cloth is woven locally.

Preservation is a primary concern in Hoi An, although economic conditions forced it to be overlooked for years. Less than a decade ago Hoi An was a depressed city whose residents could barely make enough money for subsistence. With the recent influx of tourists, the city is experiencing a renaissance. The streets are lined with shops, new hotels dot the map and the many cafes are famous for excellent food.

Another plus is the the **Hoi An Tourist Service and Monument Management Authority**, established in 1986. They are in the process of renovating the city's museums.

ARRIVALS & DEPARTURES

Since Hoi An is such a small city, it does not have its own airport. The closest airport is in Danang, and some hotels run vans to the Danang Airport. There is no **train station** in Hoi An.

Open ticket buses frequently travel from Nha Trang to Hoi An (11 hours) and Hoi An to Hue (six hours). Local buses run from the bus station located at *74 Huynh Thuc Khang Street*. The Hoi An Hotel has a bulletin board with sign-up sheets for travelers wanting to share a ride in a **van** to other cities

ORIENTATION

The historical district is concentrated along the waterfront and is closed to cars. Chances are you won't even need to take a cyclo to get around. Many historic houses which are not open to the public are found across the bridges, in the parts of town that few tourist go. Hoi An sits on the Tau Bon River. Cua Dai Beach is about 5 kilometers from town.

GETTING AROUND TOWN

Cyclo drivers hang out just outside the Hoi An Hotel. Bicycles and motorbikes may be rented from most hotels. At the docks by the market you can hire boats to take you along the river. A word of caution: the operators of the large tourist boats have been known to harass small, private boats.

WHERE TO STAY

CUA DAI HOTEL, *18A Cua Dai Street, Hoi An. Tel. (84 51) 861722. Singles/doubles $20 to $30.*

This new villa-style mini-hotel is on the road to the beach, about one-half kilometer from the old city. All the rooms have television, mini-bar and air-conditioning. The restaurant serves meals all day. You can dine under the umbrellas of outdoor tables. Cars and motor bikes can be rented at the front desk.

HOI AN HOTEL, *6 Tran Hung Dao Street, Hoi An. Tel. (84 51) 861574, Fax (84 51) 861636. Singles/doubles $12 to $50. Credit cards accepted.*

Before construction of hotels went into full bloom, this was the tourist hotel of choice. It is a rambling motel-style place with a restaurant that makes decent crepes. Tour groups often wind up here. The better rooms are comfortable. The economy rooms are on the outer wings by the parking lots. The doors lock by padlock only, and unless the weather is unusually mild the open air windows allow the climate to be overbearing.

HUY HOANG HOTEL, *73 Phan Boi Chau Street, Hoi An. Tel. (84 51) 861453. Singles/doubles $20 to $30.*

On the water, this hotel gives you a lot of comfort for a reasonable rate. The rooms are reasonably large and have new bathrooms. The terrace which overlooks the Tau Bon River is a great place to relax in the late afternoon. The staff is friendly.

PHO HOI (FAIFOO) HOTEL, *7/2 Tran Phu Street, Hoi An. Tel. (84 51) 861633 or 861338, Fax (84 51) 861382. Singles/doubles $10 to $12.*

This mini-hotel is on a quiet street which seems to be far from the touristed streets. Staying at the Faifoo allows you to feel that you are really residing in a Hoi An neighborhood for a while. The rooms are new, comfortable and all have modern bath facilities and air-conditioning. The cafe downstairs is often lively at night. Rooms for three people available for $18.

SEA STAR HOTEL, *15 Cua Dai Street, Hoi An. Tel. (84 51) 861589. Singles/doubles $25 to $40 with air conditioning; $15 to $20 without air-conditioning.*

The 11 room Sea Star mini-hotel is located on the only road to the beach, just 1/2 kilometer from the old city. From the ground up, this hotel is new. The cheery, yellow rooms are comfortable and breezy. Each room one has a window. The friendly family that runs the hotel is eager to cater to the needs of their guests. You can rent bicycles, motor bikes and make reservations for travel by plane and van. The hotel has a parking area.

THANH BINH HOTEL, *1 Le Loi Street, Hoi An. Tel. (84 51) 861740. Singles/doubles $10 to $25. Credit cards accepted.*

Located at the top of the city's shopping street, the Thanh Binh is an ideal place to stay. It has a cozy sitting area with Chinese tables and chairs in the lobby. The rooms are modern and very accommodating and the staff has a professional attitude. A taxi between the Than Binh and the Danang airport can be arranged for $10.

THUY DUONG I, *11 Le Loi, Hoi An. Tel. (84 51) 861574.*

Once a favorite of European travelers, the Thuy Duong is currently under renovation and will open in 1997.

THUY DUONG II, *68 Huynh Thuc Khang Street, Hoi An. Tel. (84 51) 861394. Singles/doubles $12 to $30. Breakfast included. Credit cards accepted.*

The family that runs Thuy Duong I also operates this hotel which is outside the old city. The white column terraces complement the fresh atmosphere. The rooms are new and the bathrooms have large bath tubs.

VINH HUNG HOTEL, *143 Tran Phu Street, Hoi An. Tel. (84 51) 861821, Fax (84 51) 861893. Singles/doubles $10 to $30. Credit cards accepted.*

This hotel lies in the heart of the old Japanese area, and is highly recommended. The beautiful foyer, decorated in traditional Chinese style, has a sitting area with tables and chairs looking onto the old city. This hotel allows you to savor the history around you. It is a great place to pass quiet hours reading or writing and taking in the atmosphere. The rooms are modern and comfortable.

WHERE TO EAT

Dining in Hoi An is a refreshingly informal experience. The city is known for its excellent and inexpensive food. Many informal cafes serve the European and American tastes of tourists. They provide the nightlife of conversation and drink. You will have no trouble finding vegetarian food here. The specialty dish of Hoi An is *cao lau*, a bowl of fat rice noodles in broth with either meat of tofu. Authentic *cao lau* is found only in Hoi An because correct preparation requires local well water.

Inexpensive

CAFE CAN, *Regional, 74 Bach Dang Street, Hoi An. Tel. (84 51) 861525.*
Located on the waterfront, Cafe Can serves good fish as well as seafood and vegetarian dishes at very reasonable prices. In the evening, you may be lucky enough to hear acoustic guitar while incense burns around the tables. Arrive early for diner, the place closes around 7 pm, or whenever the customers trickle out.

MERMAID RESTAURANT (Nhu Y), *Regional, 2 Tran Phu Street, Hoi An. Tel. (84 51) 861527.*
This cafe has the reputation of serving the best seafood in the city. The food does not quite live up to the stories, but the pizza here is better than average. Avoid the coffee at all costs.

MS. LY'S CAFETERIA, *Regional, 22 Ng Hue Street, Hoi An. Tel. (84 51) 861603.*
The beautiful Ms. Ly oversees the preparation of some of the best food in Hoi An for the cafe that bears her name. White rose, her specialty dish, is shrimp-filled wontons that melt on the palate.

SEEING THE SIGHTS

You can travel down the river by boat to visit villages that produce, and of course sell, crafts. The typical line up is ceramics village, weaving village and a tour around the old shipyard. The trips cost less than $5 per person.

The city of Hoi An is regulating tourism while it strives to renovate the historic sites in the **Old Town**. The ancient houses and assembly halls that are open to the public are controlled by the tourist authority, and you must purchase a ticket to visit these. The $5 (55,000 dong) ticket allows you to enter the **Museum of History and Culture**, one of three assembly halls, one of four family houses, and the Japanese Covered bridge. Purchase the ticket at the information office, *12 Phan Chu Trinh Street, at the intersection of Nguyen Hue Street.*

The **Hoi An Museum** is under renovation. It is a small place, with interesting period oil paintings that depict the city as a thriving port. It takes less than an half-hour to tour the few cases of artifacts even if you scrutinize everything. The Japanese house at 80 Tran Phu Street is soon to be the **Museum of Ceramics** once renovation is complete.

There are a number of old, **historic houses** in Hoi An. The **Truong Family House**, built in 1840, was expanded to its present size at the turn of the twentieth century. This Chinese was one of the most influential in the country.

The house at **1 Nguyen Thai Hoc Street** is actually a line of three Chinese houses, the middle one in the style of northern China, and the outer two in the style of southern China.

The house at **77 Tran Phu Street** is a house with four extraordinary wood carvings. Two represent the four social classes: scholar, laborer, fisherman, and shepherd; the other two are mythological creatures. The carvings are enhanced by the natural illumination of a skylight.

The **Cam Pho Communal House**, built in 1818 was expanded in 1875, 1903 and 1913. The temple in the house is dedicated to Confucius.

DOOR-EYES

As you step into the threshold of an ancient house take a moment to look up. A pair of eyes cast a gaze upon all who enter. These are ornamental elements known as "door-eyes." They serve to guard the dwelling against evil spirits. Some of the door-eyes are painted, others are carved. On some structures, the nails in the walls have eyes their the heads.

The Chinese **assembly halls** were the center of life for the Chinese merchant community in Hoi An. Each community employed architectural design that reflects their native province. **Chaozaou Assembly Hall**, built in 1887, stands on the site of an earlier building. **Chinese Assembly Hall** (1792) stands where the Kim Son Temple (1697) once did. **Duong Thuong Assembly Hall** contains a stele from 1741 which details guidelines for Vietnamese/Chinese business cooperation. **Hainan Assembly Hall** (1892) is a tribute to a group of Chinese who were mistaken for bandits and massacred.

The Japanese **Fujien Assembly Hall**, built in the seventeenth century and renovated in 1990, pays tribute to the shipping industry. In front of the hall stand two masts. The model ship is the type which sailed into the harbor at the turn of the nineteenth century. This hall was used by a Taoist congregation. Note the elaborate wooden ornamentation: two pairs of tigers, one worshipping the sun and the other the moon, surround the yin-yang symbol.

The **Japanese Covered Bridge** lies at the western end of Tran Phu Street, which was once known as "Japanese Street." As you approach the bridge, the guide is often not at the bridge, but can be found across the street. He will come over when you walk up to the locked door on what appears to be a deserted bridge. The bridge was rebuilt in 1763, 1817 and renovated in 1874 and 1917. The door-eye is a yin-yang symbol surrounded by lotus flowers (see sidebar above).

HOI AN'S TEMPLES

Hoi An has at least 54 historic religious structures, many of which are temples.

Guangong Temple, built in 1653, is one of the oldest structures in the city.

Hai Tang Temple is a Chinese Buddhist temple built in the seventeenth century

Quan An (Ming Huong) Temple is dedicated to Avalokitesvara Bodhisattva.

Tran Family Temple was built by the Tran family who fled the north during the civil war of the Nguyen Dynasty.

Vien Giac Temple, dating from the nineteenth century is a replica of an earlier temple.

SHOPPING

Another reason to stay a few days in Hoi An is the clothing. Small tailor shops fill the streets. Simple tailor made shirts and dresses take only 12 hours to make. As long as you stick to a basic design (suits are not a good idea) you can get a beautiful article of clothing made to fit your body. The prices could not be lower: silk dress $10, men's silk shirt $5 to $7, set of pajamas $12. Cotton goes for about one-half the price.

Two shops found to have the best workmanship are:
• **Elegant Cloth Shop**, *148 Tran Phu Street, Hoi An. Tel. (84 51) 861133.*
• **Ngan Ha Cloth Shop**, *37 Tran Phu Street, Hoi An. Tel. (84 51) 861764.*

If you do not have time to spare, **Thu Thuy Cloth Shop**, *60 Le Loi Street, Hoi An, Tel. (84 51) 861699*, has a large selection of clothes on the rack.

The finest silk in Vietnam is made in Hoi An. You can buy fabric by the yard or by the bolt. The prices are considerably lower (and the selection better) than in Hanoi or Ho Chi Minh City.

Hoi An is famous for the beautiful blue ceramics made nearby. Many of the pieces in Hue shops, which are called "Hue blue" ceramics, are actually from here. Hoi An's shop owners are also famous—for passing off new ceramics as antique. The ceramics are beautiful in their own right, and the "antiques" do look old. But the odds of coming across genuine article are worse than winning the lottery. And this is the case for nearly all the "antiques" you will find behind shop cases.

The irony of the scam is that it is forbidden to remove any antique from the country. For a while the blue ceramics were being confiscated at the airport. This seems to have eased up a bit; perhaps fewer tourists are being searched upon leaving.

Many people fall in love with the traditional water color paintings on silk. The proprietor of **Hiep Art Gallery**, *19 Tran Phu, Hoi An*, is an artist who sells his work. You will not find better examples of this type of painting and his prices are reasonable.

DAY TRIPS & EXCURSIONS

Cua Dai Beach, about 5 kilometers outside of town at the end of Cua Dai Road, is worth the trip for the pleasant drive, not for the sand and surf which rates less than average. The seaside often becomes polluted from beach-goers during the summer. There is a 10,000 dong admission charge per person, plus 2,000 dong per bicycle, and 5,000 dong per motorbike.

Dien Ban Citadel was surrounded by moats 15 to 20 meters wide. It was built during an wave of fortification under Emperor Minh Mang (1821-1841). The site of the citadel is in Dien Phuong Village, about six kilometers from Hoi An. **Thanh Chiem Citadel** lies in ruins in Thanh Chiem town. Although the buildings are long gone, fragments of the ruined ramparts remain

Chuc Thanh Temple (Cam Ha Village) dates from 1454, and is the oldest building in Hoi An. It lies at the end of Nguyen Truong To Street.

My Son

My Son, the largest Cham site, lies just 25 kilometers from Hoi An. Many of the temples were destroyed during the war. UNESCO has pledged $50,000 for the preservation of My Son and Hoi An. My Son is a worthwhile trip, since the remaining towers are some of the largest. Tourist vans charge $10 for a trip to the site. Once there, you must pay another $5 which includes a jeep ride down a dirt road to the entrance. Even if you say "thanks, I'll walk," you will still have to fork over $5.

My Son is the largest and the only monumental site of the Cham civilization. The temples were built from the seventh to the thirteenth century. Even before that time, My Son was used as the burial site of kings. The immense complex once had 70 buildings, including the oldest remaining Cham temple.

The Ecole Francaise d'Extreme Orient dedicated seven years to the restoration of My Son, which concluded in the 1940s. Unfortunately much of My Son was destroyed by bombings in the wars that followed. Recent renovation by Polish archaeologists ended in 1990.

The main area of My Son is composed of eight temple groups, denoted by the letters A through H. The A group dates from the ninth century and has 13 towers. The Buddhist influence is notably strong in

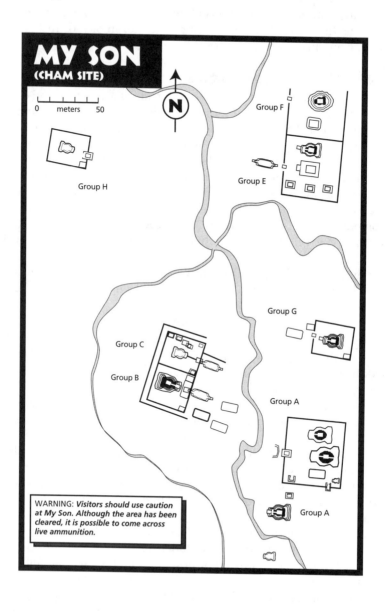

MY SON
(CHAM SITE)

0 meters 50

Group F

Group E

Group H

Group G

Group C

Group B

Group A

Group A

WARNING: *Visitors should use caution at My Son. Although the area has been cleared, it is possible to come across live ammunition.*

these buildings.

To the northeast of A, groups B, C and D stand together. Group C is south of B with group D standing in front of them both. It is believed that D actually dates from the tenth century and is part of the B complex.

The towers in group B were built in the tenth and eleventh centuries, and the stone carving on these is exemplary. The Hindu influence is particularly strong, with depictions of Vishnu appearing on the temple.

Group C is the earliest of the three. It dates from the ninth century, and pays homage to the Hindu god Shiva.

Just north of group A, you will find the small temple of group G. This consists of five simple towers with little decoration. The group dates from the twelfth century.

Beyond group G, to the north, sits the walled groups E and F. Group E, on the south, is the larger of the two. The seven buildings of group E are dedicated to Vishnu and date from the eleventh century. Sculptures recovered from this group are preserved at the Cham museum in Danang.

Group H is the northwestern group. This group is thought to be from the twelfth century. It was nearly completely destroyed in the war.

My Son spans over two kilometers (1.25 miles), and it takes a full day to see the main temples. Bring plenty of water on this trip, the area is usually very hot.

You can reach My Son by Highway 1 to road 537, which leads through Tra Kieu town. A gate has been constructed at the entrance to My Son. At one time you could walk to the temples; now you must pay an admission fee ($5) which includes a ride to the temples. Mini-vans take tourists to My Son from Hoi An and Danang.

PRACTICAL INFORMATION

- **Post Office**, *11 Tran Hung Dao Street, Hoi An*, sells post cards, writing paper, and pens plus the usual stamps. A pay-per-call international telephone is available.

Tourist Agencies
- **Hoi An Tourism**, *6 Tran Hung Dao Street, Hoi An, Tel. (84 51) 861373 or 861362 or 861248, Fax (84 51) 861636.* This is the official tourism office for the area, located in the Hoi An Hotel reception area. Tours of My Son, Marble Mountain, and the Cham Museum in Danang can be arranged.
- **Ninteen's Tourist Office**, *19 Tran Hung Dao, Hoi An. Tel. (84 51) 861937.* The young, friendly staff delivers the warm welcome promised on the business cards. Expect to spend awhile over conversation and coffee. Tours to My Son, Marble Mountain, China Beach, and

Danang can be arranged, as well as train and plane tickets. Cars and motor bikes are also for rent.

• **Sinh Cafe Representative Office**, *Vinh Hung Hotel, Tran Phu Street, Hoi An. Tel (84 51) 861621, Fax (81 51) 861893.*

Danang

Throughout Vietnam's history, **Danang** has been a center of commerce, in part due to its strategic location in the middle of the coast of the South China Sea. Danang is the capital of Quang Nam Province, which lies in the center of the country. Cinnamon, pepper and silk are produced here. Cham, Hoa, Mnong and other minority groups compose about four percent of the province's population. Today, Danang is a well-developed industrial center with a major port. The city has a fast-paced urban atmosphere and is a good place to use as a base for day trips around the region.

The Cham occupied developed cities in the Danang region by the second century AD, including Tra Kieu, (40 kilometers south), Dong Duong (60 kilometers south), and My Son (70 kilometers southwest). However, the Cham did not develop the area that is present-day Danang.

For centuries Hoi An was the focal point of Asian and European commerce in the region. Danang did not grow to economic importance until the nineteenth century, when the French colonial administration established the city as its main port. In 1945, during the uprising against the French, Japanese forces occupied Danang. The Geneva Agreement divided the country and placed the area under the jurisdiction of the South Vietnamese government, which paved the way for American forces to establish Danang as a focal point of military operations.

Americans know Danang from the Vietnam War as the home of the **95th Evacuation Hospital** and the center of air and naval operations. At near-by **China Beach**, the subject of the TV series with the same name, American officers took rest and relaxation. During the Vietnam War, over 600,000 refugees fled to Danang, seeking political asylum and relocation.

With the Marble Mountains to the south and the Hai Van Pass to the north, Danang is sandwiched in spectacular countryside. The 20 kilometers of coastline between Danang and Hue is some of the best beach in the country. At Nam O Beach, just before Hai Van Pass, frothy waves crash onto clean, coarse sand where few tourist visit.

Today Danang seeks to leave its turbulent past behind. With its scenic mountain passes and long, rugged beaches, Quang Nam Province aspire to joint the world's resort locations. New luxury and resort hotels are being built in and around Danang. This should make up for the current notable lack of luxury hotels. Tourism insiders anticipate Danang will soon be a hub for international travelers, especially those in tour groups and on cruises.

ARRIVALS & DEPARTURES

By Air

The **Danang Airport** serves domestic and international flights. A taxi to the city center costs $5, and a cyclo $1. The **Vietnam Airlines Office**, *35 Tran Phu Street, Danang, Tel. (84 51) 821130*, is a full-service booking office. The airport charges a 15,000 dong ($1.37) tax to each passenger.

By Bus

The open ticket buses do not go to Danang.

By Train

The train station, which lies on the west side of the city at the end of Haiphong Street, is a short taxi or cyclo ride from the hotel district.

ORIENTATION

Danang sits on the Han River. You will find cafes, restaurants and hotels along

Bach Dang Street, which runs north-south along the river. Tran Phu and Le Loi Streets run parallel to the river and are where you will find restaurants and bars. My Khe beach has good waves and is popular with the locals during the summer.

GETTING AROUND TOWN

Danang is an urban town and the easiest way to get around is by taxi and cyclos are also available. If you stay outside the city center at the beach, renting a motorbike would be the most economical.

WHERE TO STAY

BACH DANG HOTEL, *50 Bach Dang Street, Danang. Tel. (84 51) 823649 or 823034 or 825318, Fax (84 51) 821659. Singles $45 to $100; doubles $53 to $120. Credit cards accepted.*

The Bach Dang is a 91 room tourist hotel which is described in its own brochure as "adequate." Rooms have standard amenities; breakfast is an extra $3 per person. While all your needs are sure to be met by the facilities, if you do not want to feel like just another tourist in the crowd, try a smaller, newer hotel. Moreover, the prices for this hotel are rather high. The restaurant overlooks the Han River and specializes in seafood.

BINH HUONG HOTEL, *32 Tran Phu Street, Danang. Tel. (84 51) 821930, Fax (84 51) 827666. Singles/doubles $25 to $35.*

Rooms are priced according to the size and will meet the needs of most travelers. This is a comfortable mini-hotel with a restaurant comparable to others in the area; the room rates are a bit higher, though.

DANANG HOTEL, *3-5 Dong Da Street, Danang. Tel. (84 51) 823258 or 821986 or 823122, Fax (84 51) 823431. Singles/doubles $30 to $50. Credit cards accepted.*

The Danang Hotel recently opened the doors of the newly renovated wing. This is probably the most comfortable large hotel in the city. It is popular with foreign veterans groups, and can arrange guided tours geared for American veterans. Part of the old building was the administrative offices the US Army, and remained unrenovated for nearly 30 years. The hotel restaurant serves huge dishes of excellent Vietnamese food which has a distinct European influence. The renovated building is one of the most comfortable places to stay in Danang. Prices are lower in the old wing.

HAI AU HOTEL, *177 Tran Phu Street, Danang. Tel. (84 51) 822722 or 823942, Fax (84 51) 824165. Singles from $35 to $55; doubles $45 to $65. Credit cards accepted.*

The luster has worn off this establishment which opened a few years ago, and was then the largest hotel in the city. As a standard tourist hotel there is little personality or charm in this establishment, but it has all the standard amenities: air conditioning, telephone, television and modern bath. Gift shop, massage rooms, restaurant on the water.

HOA BINH HOTEL, *3 Tran Quy Cap Street, Danang. Tel. (84 51) 823984 or 820294, Fax (84 51) 823161. Singles/doubles $25 to $50.*

The Hoa Binh Hotel has 30 rooms, each with shiny satin bedspreads. A brochure claims the hotel has hosted foreign heads-of-state such as an "Indian vice-president and a Thai Princess." Perhaps they visited during a time when a giant photo mural of a swimming pool was considered elegant decor. The hotel does have modern amenities and a good restaurant. The garden cafe is a quiet and lovely retreat from the busy city streets.

HOA SEN HOTEL, *103-105 Hung Vuong Street, Danang. Tel. (84 51) 824505 or 829000, Fax (84 51) 829001. Singles/doubles $15 to $70. Credit cards accepted.*

This small, new, family-run mini-hotel is a good value. Large, comfortable rooms offer amenities of larger hotels, like built-in hair dryers and full-size ruby red bathtubs. The hoteliers will go out of their way to make sure your stay is pleasant. Take the elevator to the terrace on the 8th floor for a good view of the city. The hotel has a restaurant and garage.

HOANG LAN HOTEL, *275 Nguyen Van Troi Street, Danang. Tel. (84 51) 836377. Singles/doubles $15 to $20.*

The 10 room mini-hotel is close to My Khe Beach, and 8 kilometers from Danang city center. The building shows its age, but all rooms have modern baths and air conditioning.

HOTEL 32 (KATCH SAN), *32 Phan Dinh Phung Street, Danang. Tel. (84 51) 823928. Singles/doubles $15/triples $17 with air conditioning; singles $8/doubles $14 without air conditioning.*

This simple hotel offers reasonable rooms for budget travelers. It seems to be safe and well kept. All rooms have hot water.

HUNG VUONG HOTEL, *95 Hung Vuong Street, Danang. Tel. (84 51) 823967, Fax (84 51) 824023. Singles $7/doubles $12 to $15.*

A favorite of backpackers, the Hung Vuong appears abandoned from the outside. The hotel is dingy, but manages to retain a bit of the charm of a formerly nice, old building.

LAN PHUONG HOTEL, *825 Phan Chau Trinh Street, Danang. Tel. (84 51) 835001 or 832556, Fax (84 51) 823733. Singles/doubles $22 to $35, breakfast included.*

This twenty room hotel is on a quiet street, which lets you feel that you are staying in a neighborhood. The friendly staff makes up for the need of fresh paint on the walls.

MINH TAM II HOTEL, *63 Hoang Dieu Street, Danang. Tel. (84 51) 826687, Fax (84 51) 824339. Singles/doubles $15 to $20.*

The mini-hotel has air conditioning and a telephone in each of its 20 rooms. The interior is very nice and the hotel is centrally located.

MODERN HOTEL, *182 Bach Dang Street, Danang. Tel. (84 51) 820113 or 820550, Fax (84 51) 821842. Singles $30 to $64/doubles $35 to $69, breakfast included. Credit cards accepted.*

The Modern Hotel has a fitting name, since it very new. The freshness has not yet warn off the white exterior or the 40 rooms. The hotel is across the street from the waterfront, and walking distance from restaurants. The white pillared "Main Hall" is a sparse lobby/lounge with large windows that provides solitude for afternoon tea or writing letters. A garden cafe outside serves snacks, and the restaurant has a large dining room. The restaurant serves good Vietnamese and Western dishes. Complete tourist services are offered including safe deposit boxes, sauna and tour arrangements.

MY KHE HOTEL, *My Khe Beach, Danang. Singles/doubles $25 to $40. Credit cards accepted.*

This large hotel is a complex of five buildings right on My Khe Beach, about 10 kilometers from the city center. Its a good place to stay if you want to enjoy the surf, and don't have much interest in hanging out in the city. Many rooms have balconies overlooking the beach, and the sound of the surf is the main distraction here. During summer the beach is full of locals and parked motorbikes. This is a far nicer establishment than the old Soviet "resort" on China Beach.

PHUNOG DONG HOTEL, *93 Phan Chu Trinh Street, Danang. Tel. (84 51) 821266 or 822184 or 822185, Fax (84 51) 822854. Singles $35 to $55/ doubles $ 40 to $65. Breakfast included.*

A good 36 room tourist-class hotel, is clean and well managed. The decor is out of step with the times, which gives the hotel an off-beat feel. The restaurant on the fifth floor makes excellent spring rolls. Room prices vary according to season. Low season brings runs from May 1 to July 31 and brings prices down about 20 percent.

PHUNOG NAM HOTEL, *205 Tran Phu Street, Danang. Tel. (84 51) 835008 or 834746, Fax (84 51) 824609. Singles/doubles $15 to $35.*

Good, clean, standard rooms. The hotel is close to restaurants and the waterfront.

SON TRA HOTEL, *815 Ngo Quyen Street, Danang. Tel. (84 51) 831217, Fax (84 51) 831312. Singles $5 to $25/doubles $7 to $30.*

Breakfast and air conditioning included. The Son Tra is right between the beach and downtown, which is a convenient location but means that you will need to have transportation. A musty smells lingers in the rooms, which matches the decor which is straight out of the 1970's. Lovers of kitsch will not mind the flash from the past, which is the only disadvantage to staying in this clean budget hotel. The bathrooms are newly renovated. Restaurant, karaoke and 24-hour room service and laundry are some of the perks that make the budget rooms a good deal. You can rent bicycles and motor bikes at the front desk.

SONG HAN HOTEL, *36 Bach Dang Street, Danang. Tel. (84 51) 822540 or 821487, Fax (84 51) 821109. Singles/doubles $25 to $50. Credit cards accepted.*

The hotel has 61 renovated rooms and is located on one of the main streets and right next to tennis courts. The rooms are quite plain with accents of nice wooden chairs in the larger accommodations. The dining rooms seats 200 and serves Vietnamese food.

TAN MINH HOTEL, *142 Bach Dang Street, Danang. Tel. (84 51) 823427 or 827456, Fax (84 51) 830172. Singles $20 to $40/doubles $30 to $40.*

The ten room Tan Minh mini-hotel offers pleasant rooms with modern facilities. The price of your room depends on the view: a garden view adds a few dollars to the price and river views have the highest price. If you call ahead for a reservation you may be able to get a better price.

THANH THANH HOTEL, *50 Phan Chu Trinh Street, Danang. Tel. (84 51) 830684 or 821230 or 823684. Singles/doubles $12 to $39; $9 without hot water.*

This 53 room budget accommodation will not add any zest to your stay in Danang. You can find better budget rooms, but the hotel is up to date enough so you will be comfortable.

WHERE TO EAT

You will find quite a few restaurants in Danang. On average, the food is good in this city, but not spectacular. Many hotels have restaurants with surprisingly extensive menus. The food stands at the market serve cheap, good food that is reportedly safe to eat.

Expensive

HANA KIM RESTAURANT, *Vietnamese, 7 Bach Dang Street, Danang. Tel. (84 51) 830024, Fax (84 51) 834219. Lunch 11 am to 2 pm; Dinner 5 pm to 10 pm. Bar open from 11 am to 11 pm. Credit cards accepted.*

This large patio restaurant on the waterfront serves Vietnamese and Western food. The snazzy atmosphere surpasses the food; the outdoor seating is a perfect setting for an early evening cocktail. The food is good, but the atmosphere is better. Plan to take a long meal here; this is probably the best waterfront view of Danang available.

KIM DO RESTAURANT, *Chinese, 176 Tran Phu Street, Danang. Tel. (84 51) 821846. Credit cards accepted.*

The Kim Do offers excellent and authentic Chinese food in an elegant setting. The restaurant is one of the trendy places that concentrates on image. The specialty of the house is cooking your order right at the table. The crab is especially succulent. Prices are high, but the food is not disappointing. So this is a good place to have a nice, relaxing meal.

Moderate

TU DO RESTAURANT, *Vietnamese, 172 Tran Phu Street, Danang. Tel. (84 51) 821869.*

This unassuming restaurant has a reputation for serving the best Vietnamese food in town. You will have a difficult time choosing from the many dishes that are served here. Rest assured you will not go wrong with the shrimp, it is the best around. If you are inspired to come back here for every meal do not worry that you are missing anything; you found the tastiest morsels right here.

SEEING THE SIGHTS

Cao Dai Temple, *Hai Phoung Street, Danang*, is the second largest place of worship for the Cao Dai faith; the main temple is in Tay Ninh, about 70 kilometers from Saigon. The Cao Dai faith is active in this area, with over 50,000 faithful. You can observe one of four daily prayer services (6 am, noon, 6 pm , midnight). The advantage of visiting this temple is that you will be free of the tour groups that frequent the noon services of the Tay Ninh Temple.

The Cham Museum, *Bach Dan Street at the intersection of Trung Nu Vuong Street, Danang, hours 8 am to 11 am; 1 pm to 5 pm, admission 20,000 dong*, established by the Ecole Française d'Extrême-Orient in 1915, houses the most extensive collection of sandstone Cham monuments from the seventh to the fifteenth century. The open-air museum does not have descriptions (in any language) on the nearly 300 carvings and statues. You may purchase a guide book at the entrance, however, this offers only dates and names, no history or background. Despite the lack of information, the collection is still very worthwhile to anyone with an interest in ancient civilizations.

For those who are interested in the culture of the ancient Cham, this collection is a mandatory stop. Although there are few artifacts considering this is the national archive of Cham sculpture, you cannot see such a comprehensive collection anywhere else. No statuary and few reliefs remain at the temples.

The **Statue of the Martyr of Vietnam**, a tribute to the sacrifice for war, stands proudly on Dien Bien Phu Street, 3 kilometers north of the city.

NIGHTLIFE & ENTERTAINMENT

For a taste of cha cha, spend an evening at the **Danang Hotel's nightclub**. It's popular with locals who enjoy dancing to renditions of songs ranging from disco to waltzes. Many young couples come here on Friday and Saturday nights, giving the place a far more wholesome atmosphere than the "pay-per-dance" bars.

Cafes and bars that stay open late are found around the intersection of Hung Vuong and Phan Chu Thinh Streets. A few outdoor cafes on Bach Dang Street have chairs lined up to watch the cars go by in the evenings.

SHOPPING

Along **Phan Chu Trinh Street**, you will find many tailor shops and stores that sell silk. Souvenir shops and cafes abound on the streets close to the central market.

DAY TRIPS & EXCURSIONS

Today, most of the **Demilitarized Zone (DMZ)** is farmland. Due to the poor roads, which wash out in heavy rains, and the numerous checkpoints which control tourist groups, the most efficient way to visit the DMZ and the **Ho Chi Minh Trail** is to take a tour. Most hotels and tourist offices arrange tours. The DMZ can also be visited from Hue.

THE DEMILITARIZED ZONE

In 1954, The Geneva Agreement split the nation of Vietnam into two entities: North and South Vietnam. The 17th parallel served as the diving line, and the area around this was classified as a demilitarized zone, or DMZ. The DMZ was intended to be a temporary buffer zone; however, it lasted until the reunification of the country in 1975.

The DMZ was the focus of a large military build-up by the South Vietnamese and American forces. Live ammunition has caused needless losses over the years. Most remnants of the war have been scavenged by peasants who sell the macabre keepsakes. This led to a tourist trade in reproductions which are sold as genuine war remains. The defoliants which were sprayed throughout the area over time washed out of the soil and flora.

Today the land, for the most part, is cultivated. As you drive through the area you will see large sink-holes, lasting reminders of the harsh bombings that took place. The Hien Long Bridge is the site of a monument to reunification. The remains of small bunkers are visible from the roads. The Rockpile, a hill used as an American base, can be see from an observation point.

For a number of reasons, the easiest way to visit the DMZ is on an organized tour from Danang or Hue. The roads in the DMZ area are in poor condition and wash-out in the rain. Gates have been set up throughout the area to check travel permits and charge fees to tourists. Finally, it is difficult to find maps of the area. Unless you know how to get around in the DMZ, you may not be able to see the war sites.

China Beach is the name given to a 150 kilometer stretch of rugged beach close to Danang. During the war, American officers were given vacation time at the beach which was close to the area with the largest American military facilities in the country. In 1985, the Russians built a large tourist resort (Nuoc Hotel) about 17 kilometers from Danang. The actual site of China Beach is supposedly further toward Danang. You will see the remains of the American military facilities as you drive into Danang. An American group has plans to build a new resort on China Beach. Rumor has it that they are not on precisely the right spot, either.

If you want to stay in the China Beach area, go to the **NUOC HOTEL**, *10 Ly Thuong Kiet Street, Danang. Tel. (84 51) 836214. Singles $34 to $50/ doubles $40 to $56. Credit cards accepted.* At Nuoc Hotel, no less than three rambling concrete buildings make up the "resort," which is now ten years old. Many tourists come here to catch a glimpse of China Beach and take a look at the legacy of Russian vacations.

If you want to stay on the beach, go to My Khe Hotel on the same stretch of beach in Danang city limits.

Marble Mountain is home to a series of shrines built into the caves of Ngu Hanh Son mountain. Trails lead to Tam Thai, Tu Tam and Linh Ung Pagodas. A visit to Marble Mountain takes about three hours. The best time to visit Marble Mountain is in the early morning, before the onset of the day's heat and tour groups. A visit to nearby Non Nuoc Beach gives a weary trekker a cool break. The eight kilometer trip from Danang to Marble Mountain can be made easily by bicycle since the road is in good condition.

Tam Thai Pagoda is the largest of the pagodas on Marble Mountain and was built by Emperor Gia Long in 1825. **Linh Ung Pagoda** holds a set of striking statues; King Minh Mang built this pagoda. From the Vong Hai Dai Pavilion you can see the tranquil Non Nuoc Beach. Marble sculptors work at the base of the mountain, making souvenir carvings for eager tourists.

Quang Minh Nith Pagoda, which is both a pagoda and monastery, is a tranquil place to visit. It's only 7 kilometers from the city. The monks here make incense and cultivate flowers. You can enter the large, white Buddha and climb stairs all the way to the very top.

Both the Reunification rail line and Highway 1 cut through **Hai Van Pass**. The French called Hai Van "the Pass of the Clouds." A lookout point, complete with kiosks and refreshment stands, mark the point where tourists stop to take in the view. However, the countryside surrounding the pass is even more spectacular. Waterfalls accent the mountainsides, tumbling down toward the coastline. Remains of a Nguyen Dynasty wall are found along the pass.

Lang Co, just north of Hai Van Pass, has little more than a single hotel on a nearly deserted beach. And that's the beauty of the place. The train makes a stop in Lang Co town. The hotel is a 20 minute walk from the train stop; look for a sign along the roadside. The **LANG CO HOTEL**, *Tel. (84 54) 874456*, has basic, rather run down rooms with no amenities and only cold showers at $15 per night. You have the beach to yourself, and that is the reason to come here. If you are traveling by car, this is a good mid-point break between Danang and Hue. The open ticket buses usually stops here for lunch. The restaurant serves excellent sea food, the spring rolls are especially tasty.

My Son lies seventy kilometers south of Danang. This is the largest Cham archaeological site in the country. My Son served as the capital city of the Cham empire for 7 centuries, until the 13th century. French excavations explored and documented 68 structures, over half of which were destroyed during the wars of this century. Once you arrive at the site, you must travel 5 kilometers by jeep to reach the ruins. Tourists are not permitted to walk. The site is closer to and more easily visited from Hoi An. There is more information on My Son in the Day Trips and Excursions section of the *Hoi An* section of this chapter, above.

The beautiful old city of **Hoi An** is only 30 kilometers from Danang, and can be visited as a day trip. If time permits a stay of at least three days is recommend. For more information, see the section on Hoi An.

PRACTICAL INFORMATION

- **Dana Tours**, *3 Dong Da Street, Danang. Tel. (84 51) 823833 or 822516, Fax (84 51) 822854.*
- **Post Office**, *46 Bach Dang Street, Danang. Tel. (84 51) 821522 or 821877. Hours: 7:30 am to 11:30 am; 1:00 pm to 3:00 pm.*
- **Danang City Tourist Company**, *76 Hung Vuong Street, Danang. Tel. (84 51) 821969, Fax (84 51) 821213.*
- **Danang Hotel Company Tourist Office**, *3-5 Dong Da Street, Danang. Tel. (84 51) 823298 or 823122 or 824555 or 823258, Fax (84 51) 823431.* This agency offers individual guides and group tours of the region or the entire country. Package tours run from four to fourteen days and include transfers and lodging.
- **Danang Tourism**, *92 Phan Chu Trinh, Danang. Tel. (84 51) 821423 or 822112, Fax (84 51) 821560.*
- **Quang Nam/Danang Tourism Service Company**, *95 Hung Vuong Street, Danang. Tel. (84 51) 823993, Fax (84 51) 824023.*
- **Vietcom Bank**, *104 Le Loi Street, Danang. Tel. (84 51) 821975.*

Hue

The beautiful city of **Hue**, shadowed by wet weather, lies on both banks of the **Song Huong** or Perfume River and is connected by a series of bridges. The citadel sits on the left bank, and the main tourist area of hotels and restaurants, sits on the right. The mix of relics and a new thriving city is tinted by Hue's spiritual elements. Hue is known for its deep-rooted traditions and unique history as the seat of the last kings of the Nguyen Dynasty.

Hue served as the seat of southern feudal lords from the 16th century until the 19th century, when it became the imperial capital of the reunified Vietnam. Emperor Gia Long broke ground on modern Hue in 1802, razing the villages in the area and thus founding the Nguyen Dynasty. During French colonialism, the Nguyen kings remained puppet rulers. The Nguyen Dynasty is known for architectural tributes to itself— the imperial tombs that lie outside the city.

HO CHI MINH IN HUE

Hue bred more than Nguyen Kings. The country's greatest modern leader, Ho Chi Minh, born Nguyen Sing Cung, was raised here. His family moved to Duong No Village, about 10 kilometers from Hue, when his father took an appointment as a teacher in the town's French-Vietnamese Primary School. His mother remained in Hue.

It was under his father's tutelage that Ho Chi Minh began his formal education. A replica of the house where father and son lived holds a collection of Ho Chi Minh's childhood memorabilia. (The original house burned down.)

Ho Chi Minh later attended Quoc Hoc high school in Hue. The school was a colonial institution where children were schooled in French. You can see the school on Le Loi Street, but since it is still in use no visitors are permitted.

Today Hue is a thoroughly modern city. You will have to venture out of the city center to surround yourself with history and beauty. Traces of the past, such as the dragon boats which carry tourists along the Perfume River, decorate the city.

It is more common for men to wear traditional *ao dai* outfits in Hue than anywhere else in Vietnam. The male tunics are similar to those worn by women throughout the country. The color of the ao dai has meaning. For example, black signifies age, boys wear blue or green, and women wear red *ao dais* for weddings.

Hue's cuisine offers some of the best food in Vietnam. The simple dish *bun bo*, which is made of thick rice noodles with fragrant beef and spicy sauce, is delicious and cheap. Ruon Minh Mang is the regional wine prepared in the tradition begun with Emperor Ming Mang. Restaurants and hotels hold Imperial Dinners, which are banquets during which a king is crowned amid traditional dancing and music.

The region has a tropical climate, with highs of 40°C (104°F) from March to September. Europeans love Hue, and high season for tourism runs from February to April. For the lowest prices, visit during late April or May lull. Since the countryside north of Hue is not known for either beauty or diversity, many travelers do not journey further north, and many opt to take the night train to Hanoi.

ARRIVALS & DEPARTURES
By Air

Vietnam Airlines, *Tel. (84) 54 823249*, runs direct flights between Hue and Dalat (Wednesday, Friday and Sunday), Hanoi (daily) and Ho

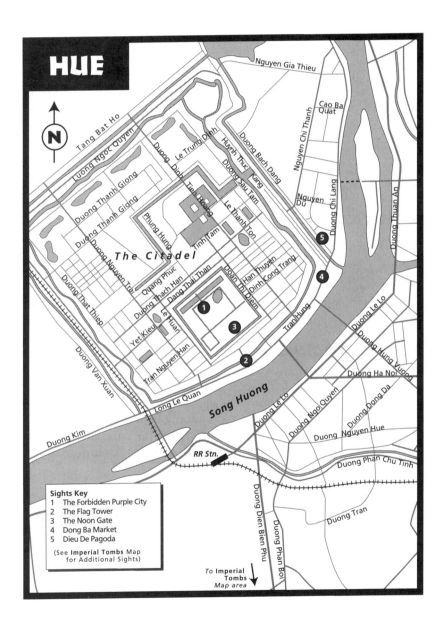

HUE

N

Nguyen Gia Thieu

Tang Bat Ho

Luong Ngoc Quyen

Cao Ba
Quat

Nguyen Chi Thanh

Le Trung Dinh

Duong Dinh Tien Hoang

Duong Bach Dang

Huynh Thuc Kang

Duong Sau Tam

Nguyen
Du

Duong Chi Lang

Duong Thuan An

Duong Thanh Giong

Duong Thanh Giong

Phung Hung

Le Thanh Ton

Tinh Tam

Duong Nguyen Tra

The Citadel

Quang Phuc

Duong Thach Han

Han Thuyen

Dinh Cong Trang

Dang Thai Than

Doan Thi Diem

⑤

④

Duong That Thieu

Le Huan

Yet Kieu

①

③

Tran Hung

Duong Le Lo

Duong Hung Vuong

Tran Nguyen Han

②

Duong Ha Noi

Duong Van Xuan

Long Le Quan

Song Huong

Duong Le to

Duong Ngo Quyen

Duong Dong Da

Duong Kim

RR Stn.

Duong Nguyen Hue

Duong Phan Chu Tinh

Duong Tran

Duong Dien Bien Phu

Duong Phan Boi

Sights Key
1 The Forbidden Purple City
2 The Flag Tower
3 The Noon Gate
4 Dong Ba Market
5 Dieu De Pagoda

(See **Imperial Tombs** Map
  for Additional Sights)

To **Imperial
Tombs**
Map area

Chi Minh City (daily). Phu Bai Airport is 15 kilometers from the city. Taxis charge $10 for the ride; Vietnam Airlines runs a shuttle between the airport and the airline office at *12 Hanoi Street, Hue*. An airport tax of 15,000 dong ($1.37) is levied on all passengers.

By Bus

To catch a bus heading south, go to the An Cuu Bus Station at the corner of Ba Trieu and Hung Voung Streets; buses going north leave from An Hoa Bus Station at the corner of Le Duan and Tang Bat Ho Streets.

By Train

The train station is in the city center, at the western end of Le Loi Street. The ticket office is open daily from 8 am to 5 pm. You need to reserve overnight sleepers to Hanoi a few days in advance, as they fill up.

ORIENTATION

The Perfume River, which may be named for the fragrant bushes that grow along its banks, flows through Hue. It is both a commercial pathway, and a beautiful recreation area for tourists. From the riverbank, the Troung Son Mountains rise along the horizon.

The best view of Hue is from Ngu Binh Hill, which rises over 100 meters above the city.

GETTING AROUND TOWN

By Car & Driver

Cars can be rented from most hotels and tourist offices. The Hue police force has the reputation of being heavy-handed when it comes to tourists. They are likely to stop a car simply because a foreigner is a passenger. So be certain your driver/guide has the appropriate papers and permits for Hue, especially if you are driving to Hue from out of town.

By Dragon Boat

Dragon boats are a popular mode of transportation to take down the Perfume River. They are large wooden boats, similar to gondolas that hold 10 to 12 people, adorned with a gold and red dragon head. You can combine this with a tour which includes the Imperial Tombs. Be prepared to walk on these tours because you will have to get from the river to the tomb on foot. Saving the river trip for the evening is another option.

Tour boats on the Perfume River can be hired from most hotel tourist offices. The **Hoa Hong Hotel**, *Pham Ngu Lao Street, Hue, Tel. (84 54) 824377 or 826943, Fax (84 54) 826949 or 8269501*, rents dragon boats with a seating capacity of 9 people for $8 per hour.

By Motor bike

Hue is the perfect place to rent motor bikes. The many interesting sites that lie outside the city center are best explored without the time constraints of a tour group's agenda. Also, you can venture to places most tourists do not go if you have your own transportation.

Two British friends of mine reported that they saw the entire city and then some in only two days. Most hotels and all tourist offices can arrange a car and driver or rent you motor bikes.

By Taxi

Hue Taxi operates 30 cars in the city, so you should be able to flag one down along major streets.

WHERE TO STAY

A DONG HOTEL, *7 Doi Cung Street* and **A DONG II HOTEL**, *1 Bis Chu Van An Street, Hue. Tel. (84 54) 822765 or 822766, Fax (84 54) 828074. Singles $25 to $40/doubles $30 to 50. Credit cards accepted.*

These two mini-hotels are virtually indistinguishable from one another. Both have neat, clean rooms with quaint furnishings and modern amenities like mini-bars, telephones and televisions. The restaurants serve meals all day; there is an extra charge of $2 for breakfast. Both the A Dong I and II are a few blocks from the Perfume River. The staff can arrange cars, tours, boat rides and book train and plane tickets.

CENTURY HOTEL RIVERSIDE, *49 Le Loi, Hue. Tel. (84 54) 823390, Fax (84 54) 823399. Singles $60 to $80/doubles $65 to $85/suites $150. Credit cards accepted.*

This hotel is the choice of business travelers, since it is run by the French Century Group and is one of the few places in Hue to have a business center. The hotel offers a full business center, with a professional and attentive staff. The hotel was built eight years ago in utilitarian "luxury" style. The staff attempts to provide guests with the finest service, despite the limitations of the 147 cramped rooms and simple decor. There is plenty to do for recreation at the hotel since it has a pool and tennis courts overlooking the river, as well as gym and sauna facilities. The indoor waterfront cafe, formerly a disco, is a great place to relax and take in the view.

DONG DA HOTEL, *15 Ly Thuong Kiet Street, Hue. Tel. (84 54) 823071, Fax (84 54) 823204. Credit cards accepted. Singles/doubles $50.*

The Dong Da strives to fill the void of glitzy hotels. In the evenings, the exterior is awash in strings of light. With 37 rooms and no less than five karaoke rooms which offer multi-lingual repertoires, it does come as close as you can get to Las Vegas in Hue.

DONG PHUONG HOTEL, *26 Nguyen Tru Phuong Street, Hue. Tel. (84 54) 825333 or 825480. Singles/doubles $8 to $20. Breakfast included.*

The 15-room mini-hotel is very popular with European travelers. The rooms are clean and equipped with TVs. Although slightly run-down, the Dong Phuong is a good bargain. Especially during the off-season, you may be able to get a triple for the price of a double.

DUY TAN HOTEL, *12 Hung Vuong Street, Hue. Tel. (84 54) 82500. Singles/doubles $20 to $35. Credit cards accepted.*

In this fresh, new hotel you can have a room with a balcony. The 58 rooms are notably large, although plain. Bathrooms have full-size tubs. Not all rooms have a television or phone. Breakfast is included in the higher rates.

GOVERNMENT GUEST HOUSE, *5 Le Loi Street, Hue. For reservations you must call the Hue City Tourism Office, Tel. (84 54) 823577, Fax (84 54) 825814. Singles $25/doubles $40 to $60.*

The estate-like hotel was built in 1865 for visiting French government officials. The 16 large rooms with high ceilings and beautiful wood moldings transport you to genteel, bygone days. Remember, this place offers charm, not grandeur. The hotel is surrounded by a substantial lawn and gardens and sits right on the Perfume River.

There is no restaurant, but this is a minor inconvenience, easily outweighed by the unique surroundings. For a perfect sunset, sip tea on the large balcony off the main hall. Rooms have refrigerators and televisions. People traveling solo during the off season may be able to get a slight reduction in the price.

HOA HONG HOTEL, *1 Pham Ngu Lao Street, Hue. Tel. (84 54) 824377 or 826943, Fax (84 54) 826949 or 826950. Singles $30 to $80/doubles $35 to $90.*

The airy lobby gives you a good idea of what to expect from a stay at the Hoa Hong. The decoration is elegant in its understatement. The rooms are large, airy and priced according to view. The least expensive, or "standard city view," is a bargain at the rate for double occupancy. The 60-room, seven-story building (with elevators) easily earns its self-appointed three stars. You may purchase three meals a day at a set rate which ranges from $12 to $20. The tourist office arranges tours, cars and boats for hire.

HUONG GIANG HOTEL, *51 Le Loi Street, Hue. Tel. (84 54) 822122 or 823958, Fax (84 54) 823424 or 23102. Singles $50 to $75/doubles $55 to $80/suites $150 to $230. Credit cards accepted.*

The hotel's name is "Perfume River" in English. This 160-room establishment has the city's best view of the river, and when built was the city's luxury accommodation. The third floor restaurant has good seafood dishes and a lovely atmosphere. The staff is very service-oriented.

The hotel can arrange guided tours, provide cars or bicycles for rent, and can put on a Royal Dinner for two or more.

HUONG VUNG HOTEL, *2-8 Hung Vuong Street, Hue. Tel. (84 54) 823866, Fax (84 54)825910. Singles $20 to $30/doubles $25 to $35. Breakfast included. Credit cards accepted.*

The best part of staying at this hotel is that the Sinh Cafe Tour office is right next door. The Houng Vung resembles a Vietnamese version of a Motel 6. The atmosphere is not bland, since the people hanging out in the lobby give it a bar-room ambiance.

KINH DO HOTEL, *1 Nguyen Thai Hoc Street, Hue. Tel. (84 54) 823566, Fax (84 54) 823858 or 821190. Singles/doubles $30 to $55. Service charge and tax included. Credit cards accepted.*

The Kinh Do sits in the main hotel district, and takes pride in its tourist services. Many groups choose the 50 room Kinh Do. Some of the rooms are particularly spacious, with a sitting area with carved tables and chairs, although most have less desirable modern furnishings. The hotel has full amenities - air, telephone, television with satellite, and all bathrooms are renovated. The restaurant seats 300, serves Asian and European dishes and will organize music or an Imperial Dinner for large parties. For those who need to unwind after a long day of hiking around tombs, try the sauna and massage facilities.

NGO QUYEN HOTEL, *9 Ngo Quyen Street, Hue. Tel. (84 54) 823278 or 822476, Fax (84 54) 28372. Singles/doubles $19 to $40. Credit cards accepted.*

This 56-room tourist hotel with its slightly shabby rooms is no great deal. It is located off the main street under lots of shady trees. The rooms are modest and not quite comfortable.

PHOENIX HOTEL (Phuong Hoang), *48/3 Le Loi Street, Hue. Tel. (84 54) 26736 or 826902, Fax (84 54) 828999. Singles $15 to $30/doubles $30 to $40. Credit cards accepted.*

One of the newest hotels in the city, the Phoenix is also one of the best values. The 30 immaculate rooms and friendly staff who speak English make for a comfortable stay. The hotel is actually located on a small alley off Le Loi Street, which is the main thoroughfare. A sign just across from the Century Riverside Hotel marks the place to turn. The hotel has a small parking lot.

ROYAL (HOANG GIA) HOTEL, *185 B Thuan An Street, Hue. Tel. (84 54) 25246 or 25820, Fax (84 54) 26691. Singles $30 to $40/doubles $35 to $45.*

This hotel is located about five kilometers from the city center, on the bank of the Perfume River. The new eight room villa-style mini-hotel has comfortable rooms, a cafe and garden. The homey atmosphere is a good switch from the tourist hustle and bustle of Hue city.

GUEST HOUSES IN HUE

Many of the French colonial villas on Ly Toung Kiet Street are run as small guest houses. Although the facilities are not as new and spiffy as those in hotels, certain details, such as original wood floors can be much appreciated. The guest houses do not offer restaurants or tourist offices. Each is independently operated, and they are identified by street number. Leave the credit card in your wallet and forget sending a fax for reservations. These places are run in Old-World style, meaning show up and hope for the best. The following two guest houses are your best bets:

Number 5, 5 Ly Toung Kiet Street, Hue. Singles/doubles $20. Tel. (84 54) 823945.

This lovely 70-year-old house has a mere 4 rooms, each with air conditioning and a telephone. The baths are remodeled and the furniture is worthy of the beautiful house. The old staircase with its heavy antique banister is the centerpiece of the house. Certainly this is the nicest of the guest houses and one of the best values for accommodation.

Number 16, 16 Ly Toung Kiet Street, Hue. Tel. (84 54) 823964. Singles/doubles $10 to $20.

The 15-room, single-story hotel offers less personality than Guest House 5, but it's a good deal for budget travelers. The most expensive room has 3 beds, air conditioning and telephone. The least expensive has a ceiling fan and no phone. All baths are modern.

THANG LOI HOTEL, *7 Dinh Tien Hoang Street, Hue. Tel. (84 54) 824803. Singles/doubles $12 to $18.*

The 36-room Than Loi Hotel services many tour groups with plenty of space and ample parking. The bathrooms are new and some rooms have a TV. Garden tables at outdoor patios let you sit back and enjoy the evening breeze. This is a sure bet for budget travelers, and a favorite of American and Australian backpackers. A room with three beds runs $18 and six beds, $30.

THUAN HOA HOTEL, *7B Nguyen Tri Phuong Street, Hue. Tel. (84 54) 822553 or 22576. Singles $25 to $45/doubles $30 to $75.*

Budget rooms from $8 to $14 are available. However, the hotel adds a service charge of 5 percent to all prices. This 80-room hotel has tennis courts and sauna rooms, and complete tourist facilities including a restaurant, coffee shops and a bar. The deluxe rooms are new and clean with rattan furniture.

TRANG TIEN HOTEL, *46A Le Loi Street, Hue. Tel. (84 54) 822128 or 82677, Fax (84 54) 826772. Singles $15 to $20, doubles $20 to $35.*

This tourist hotel offers nothing notable, except that it has large rooms that can accommodate groups of 3 to 5 people for $35 to $45 per night. The hotel restaurant serves breakfast, which can be added on to the price of the room.

VIDA HOTEL, *31 Thuan An Street, Hue. Tel. (84 54) 826145 or 826146, Fax (84 54) 826147. Singles $30 to $40/doubles $40 to $45/triples $40 to $50.*

Prices are reduced during the summer. The exterior of the Vida Hotel looks like a house, and the staff is so welcoming you will feel as though you are visiting a family. The tourist office can arrange tours or rent bicycles, motor bikes or cars. This hotel is just outside the city center.

WHERE TO EAT

Moderate

HUONG GIANG HOTEL RESTAURANT, *Vietnamese, 51 Le Loi Street, Hue.*

This third floor restaurant has excellent seafood dishes and impeccable service. Depending on what you order, you can find the prices on the high end of moderate. Imperial dinners can be arranged, but the elegance of the oriental decor is best enjoyed over a quiet meal.

ONG TAO RESTAURANT, *Vietnamese, at the Citadel, just outside the Hien Nhon Gate. Tel. (84 54) 23031.* Or try the other location at *134 Ngo Duc Ke Street, Hue. Tel. (84 54) 22037.*

The garden setting provides a peaceful setting for a meal. Mr. Tao, the owner, has been serving some of the best food in Hue for over 20 years. Depending on what you order, you can find the prices on the high end of moderate.

SONG HUONG FLOATING RESTAURANT, *Vietnamese, by Le Loi and Hung Vuong Streets. Tel. (84 54) 3738.*

The floating restaurant is a favorite spot for tourists. The waitpeople have a difficult time getting the orders right and the food is average at best.

Inexpensive

DZACH LAU RESTAURANT, *Vietnamese, 23 Ben Nghe Street, Hue. Tel. (84 54) 822831.*

The name is Chinese for "number one," and locals find that this family-run restaurant serves some of the best Vietnamese food around. Seafood is the house specialty. Shrimp rocket-style are out-of-this-world, as are the spring rolls stuffed with seasoned seafood.

VEGETARIAN RESTAURANT, *Regional, 42B Hung Vuong, Hue. Tel. (84 54) 23226.*

Eating at Hue's best vegetarian restaurant is a real treat for omnivores and herbivores alike. The proprietor prepares specialties of Hue with

100% vegetarian food. Some of the tofu dishes taste even more delicious than the chicken or duck they are supposed to replicate. You may order from the menu, or have course after course brought out until you are satisfied.

SEEING THE SIGHTS

The **Imperial Citadel** on the left bank of the Perfume River is a giant complex begun in 1805 during the reign of Emperor Gia Long and is presently undergoing major renovation. The original Citadel, which was smaller than the one standing today, took 30 years to complete. The entire area spans over 10 kilometers (6.2 miles) and is surrounded by an immense fortifying wall, which is 21 meters at its thickest point. During the most intense phases of construction, over 75,000 workers labored on this project.

Within the citadel walls, the Nguyen Emperors, their families and courts lived and conducted affairs of state. The many structures within the Citadel are designed according to Chinese principles and laid out by geomancy, the harmonious placement of buildings in nature. The once grand royal city suffered during the Vietnam War, as great sections were completely destroyed. With funding from international humanitarian associations and various grants, the city is being quickly renovated for tourism. You can walk under the scaffolding and watch fresh designs being painted on the interior of the royal buildings. Much of the grounds still remain empty park land or are used for the practical pursuit of gardening.

During the later half of the nineteenth century, the emperor lived and carried out all official functions in the walled citadel. The **Emperor's City**, *Dai Noi*, is a square walled area within the Citadel where the emperor carried out administrative duties. The Throne Room, *Thai Hoa Dien*, and the Reception Hall, *Can Chanh Dien*, were the areas where guests of the court were received. The gates to this area were permitted to open only for ceremonies.

Within the Emperor's City is the **Forbidden Purple City** which is surrounded by ten gates. Originally there were numerous buildings, gateways and halls of worship, most of which no longer exist. This was the residential area for the royal family, and includes apartments for family members and the king's concubines.

The Citadel, which was constructed from 1805 to 1832, has ten gates in all. The **South Gate** structure served as the main entrance and has three entrance ways. The middle of the three, the Noon Gate, *Ngo Mon*, was the portal reserved for the emperor. The Phoenix Tower, which is the upper part of the South Gate complex, is supported by 100 red columns and was designed for members of the court to observe processions.

Just inside the South Gate, is the **Palace of Harmony**. This is where the Emperor held court. Amid glorious displays of wealth and power, the king sat over his mandarins, welcoming foreign dignitaries. A major renovation project aims to refinish the bright red-and-gold painted interior.

The **Flag Tower** is a three-story tower built in 1807. Once, guns stood on the platform. The flag pole stands 54 meters tall.

The large **Temple** is composed of two buildings. The front building has 11 rooms, and the back has nine. Within each room is an altar dedicated to an emperor. In front of the Temple stands **Hien Lam Pavilion**, built by Emperor Minh Mang.

The nine immense **bronze urns** in front of the temple were made in the mid-nineteenth century in Hue. Each urn pays tribute to one Nguyen emperor, and the royal names are written in Chinese characters. They are roughly 2.5 meters tall. Nine bronze cannons were made in 1803, on orders of Emperor Gia Long.

Dien Tho Palace is the residence of the Emperor's mother. The ten buildings served as both her home and place of worship.

Tang Tho Library, the Nguyen archives, was built in 1825 and is surrounded by water as a guard against fire. From 1826 to 1945, this was the royal library and archives and held over 12,000 documents, many of which have not been preserved.

The **Museum of Hue** is in the Citadel, and holds artifacts from the Nguyen Dynasties and some Cham artifacts. Even if you skip the museum, the bronze statuary in the courtyard is not to be missed.

The **Imperial** (or Royal) **Tombs** lie 7 to 16 kilometers south of the city center. The best way to get to the tombs is by motor bike, since this allows you to get off the beaten path and move at your own pace. The tombs are set in the pine-covered hills spotted with small lakes. Thien An Hill is the most recognizable landmark and is found southwest of Hue. Even with a map, difficulty arises in maneuvering around confusing, unmarked roads. If you're at all concerned about this, you can hire a guide, but you don't have has as much flexibility as you would on a motorbike. If you go to the tombs by boat, keep in mind you will have to walk a few kilometers from the river to the tombs.

The **Tomb of Gia Long** is a nearly 20 kilometers from Hue. Gia Long is a legendary war hero, the founder of the Nguyen Dynasty and is responsible for moving the imperial seat to Hue. He reigned only 18 years, from 1802 to 1820. Construction on the tomb began at the time of the queen's death, in 1814 , and lasted six years. This is the oldest and one of the most simple burial complexes. On the left is a group of stelae erected by Emperor Minh Mang, which chronicles the reign of Gia Long.

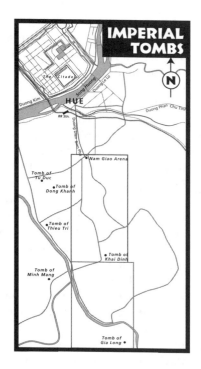

The burial complexes of the king and queen rest in the center. And on the right is a temple dedicated to the queen.

The **Tomb of Minh Mang** sits by Kim Phung Hill, about 14 kilometers from Hue. Minh Mang, son of Gia Long, was one of the most powerful Nguyen kings. Minh Mang died before the completion of this elaborate complex of temples and tributes. Although most of the over 50 structures are now in ruin, set aside about two hours to walk the grounds. Paths lead around two ponds and through the temples. Many visitors find this the most striking and interesting of the Imperial Tombs.

The Tomb of Tu Duc is unusual because Tu Duc originally used the peaceful grounds as a vacation retreat. The poet-king spent hours composing verse here and enjoyed the seclusion and natural beauty. The royal family spent recreational time here, and you can visit the apartments of the queen, the king and the king's concubines. The park-like surroundings, full of foliage and lakes, is a pleasant place for a leisurely afternoon stroll.

Thieu Tri's Tomb, in Chu Chanh Village, was built by his son, Emperor Tu Duc. Most Imperial tombs are the result of the ruler's vision, but Thieu Tri died suddenly and without plans for his own tomb. Thieu Tri's Tomb stands as a son's tribute to his father and is built in the same grand style as the Tomb of Tu Duc.

The **Tomb of Dong Khanh**, in Thuong Hai village, is a family memorial. Dong Khanh died suddenly in 1888 at the age of 25, after only three years on the throne. The monumental tomb was not finished until 1924.

Finally the **Tomb of Khai Dinh** is the latest, and the least notable of them all. Finished in 1931, this tomb is not a family temple, but a monument to the king alone, who was then a puppet king of the French colonial government. The giant white mausoleum sits perched atop a hill. Its ostentatious ornate decoration is an ironic attempt at grandeur.

ONE DAY IN HUE

If you must limit your stay to only one day, which is often the case for tourists who must move through quickly to get to Hanoi, here is a list of the essential sights.

*The **Citadel** covers an area practically equal to that of the entire new city of Hue. You can appreciate its size only by devoting time to walking the grounds. But if time does not permit that, go straight to the **Emperor's City**. This was the heart of official functions, and is the center of the reconstruction efforts. This area is relatively small, and contains some of the few remaining buildings that survived the war.*

*On the way out to visit the tombs stop at the **Tiger Arena**, one of the most unusual structures in all of Asia. Try to imagine the king watching the pageantry of the tiger contests.*

*The **Tomb of Tu Duc**, most often described as harmonious with its natural surrounding, gives the visitor peaceful solitude. The combination of power and art is reflected in the sprawling layout of the temples. You will feel the beauty of the oriental tradition of royalty here.*

*Finally, end the day at **Thien Mu Pagoda**. The 21-meter tower which overlooks the Perfume River is one of the most striking images of Vietnam. If you arrive just before sunset you may hear the ringing of the monastery's bronze bell.*

Nam Giao Arena is not an arena in the Roman sense, although worship and sacrificial offerings did take place here. The terraced arena is a representation of the hierarchy of man, earth and heaven, from bottom to top. For most of the nineteenth century, ceremonies took place here regularly. Elaborate processions, colorful decorations and animal sacrifice made up the long ritual. Nam Giao is one of the country's most unusual most interesting monuments.

The **Tiger Arena** (Ho Quyen) looks more like a fortification than an arena. The 4.5 meter thick walls encircle a 35 meter arena. It is found on the southern bank of the Perfume River, about 7 kilometers from Hue. The six meter-thick wall encloses the 54-meter area where elephants and tigers fought each other. This form of entertainment was a favorite of Vietnamese kings who ruled in Hue, and is unique to the area. The arena was built in 1830 during the reign of Gia Long, and remained in use until 1904.

The **Temple of Literature** (Van Mieu), erected during the Nguyen Dynasty, pays homage to Confucian scholars. In 1808 the emperor moved the Temple of Literature from Long Ho Village to its present site, and constructed a national university. The university remained open for 100 years. During this time more stelae, recording the names of graduates, were erected. Although the temple itself is the victim of time, the stelae remain intact. The two small structures hold stelae inscribed with imperial decrees. Minh Mang's stelae (on the left), dated 1936, dictates the role of eunuchs in court; Theiu Tri's stelae, dated 1844, restricts the roles of female leaders. The Temple of Literature is located on the southern bank of the Perfume River, about 5 kilometers from the center of Hue (near the Thien Mu Pagoda).

Dieu De Pagoda has three temples, the main temple for prayer, and two smaller temples for meditation. In 1842, Emperor Thieu Tri decreed Dieu De Pagoda as one of the treasures of the nation. Just 43 years later, in 1885, much of the temple complex was destroyed and the statuary was removed. The pagoda was reconstructed in 1960. Dieu De Pagoda is located on Bach Dang Street, just south of Chua Ong Street, just across from the eastern wall of the citadel.

Thien Mu Pagoda sits on the north bank of the Perfume River, about 5 kilometers from the city center. The name means "heavenly lady" which is a tribute to the woman who, according to legend, ordered the pagoda built then ascended to heaven some four centuries ago. The original structure from 1604 is now but a legend itself, since many reconstructions have taken place over the years. The most significant building on the grounds is the tall. octagonal pagoda which is as mysterious as it is beautiful. Built in 1844, the pagoda remains part of an active monastery. The monks who live here are warm and friendly. If you visit in the twilight of sunset, you may be asked in for tea. To get to Thien Mu Pagoda take Le Duan Street west, away from the city (near the Temple of Literature).

Nearby, in the tiny town of **Thuy Toan** (Huong Thuy District), you will find one Vietnam's few tile-roofed bridges. The bridge took six years to build. An altar on the Thanh Toan Bridge is dedicated to the wife of a local official who donated funds for the replacement of the original bridge.

Ho Chi Minh Museum, *9 Le Loi Street* (at the intersection of Tran Truc Nhan Street on the southern bank of the Perfume River) pays tribute to the boy who would become the father of nation. The first room chronicles the first 10 years of Ho Chi Minh's life when he lived close to Hue. The bulk of the collection follows Ho Chi Minh's time abroad, the founding of the communist party, his leadership during war and finally, his funeral.

NIGHTLIFE & ENTERTAINMENT

You can take a moonlight ride on one of Hue's famous **dragon boats**. These small crafts have elaborate dragon heads on the stern; some have musicians playing traditional songs on evening cruises. Some tourists take dragon boats to the royal tombs, however there is a considerable walk from the riverbank to the sites. The **Thien Mu Pagoda** is a good boat trip, since it sits near the river.

Many places rent dragon boats and drivers, charging either by the hour or by the destination. Shop around since prices vary, and look for posted rates. The **Huong Giang Hotel Company**, *51 Le Loi Street, Hue, Tel. (84 54) 22122 or 23958 or 22818, Fax (84 54) 23102 or 23424*, has a good reputation and charges the not-so-trifling sum of $20 per hour for a boat.

Discos & Bars

If you just have to get out and dance, Hue has a few discos, including:
THAUN HOA, *7B Nguyen Tri Phuong Street, Tel. (84 54) 823340*
SO, *8 Hung Voung Street, Tel. (84 54) 828054*
DONG DA, *15 Ly Thuong Kiet Street, Tel. (84 54) 826177*
THE WATERING HOLE, *13 Hung Vuong Street*, which is a popular bar run by an Australian expatriate.

SHOPPING

Dong Ba Market, *Tran Hung Dao Street, east of the Troung Tien Bridge*, is the city's largest market and provides a highly recommended afternoon distraction. You can sample the sweet treats, which are a specialty of the region. A variety of small cakes are sold for about 2,000 dong each. Try *banh it danh*, a sweet cake wrapped in a banana leaf, or *banh xu xe*, a small wedding cake. The straw hats made in Hue are considered the finest in the country. If you hold one up to light you will see the fronds are interwoven; this is the mark of a Hue hat. Naturally, the best place to buy one is in the market. You can also find the silk tiara-like headdresses and the well-known distinctive blue pottery in the Dong Ba Market.

A strip of **souvenir shops** has sprung up on Le Loi Street, across from the Century Riverside Hotel. The selection in each shop is good. Prices are high, but negotiable.

DAY TRIPS & EXCURSIONS

Bach Mo Resort was founded by the French in 1942 on Bach Ma Mountain, and is surrounded by the Five Lakes (Ngu Ho), about 60 kilometers from Hue. The old resort has 139 old villas. Nearby, White Horse Mountain reaches an elevation of 1,450 meters. The climate here is cooler than Hue's, thanks to the altitude. A number of waterfalls, including the small Bac Waterfall, are located around Bach Ma Resort.

The larger Do Quyen waterfall is a half-hour walk from the 16 kilometer marker of the Cau-Hai-Bach Ma Road. Bach Mo was declared a national park in 1991.

Lang Co, just north of Hai Van Pass, has little more than a single hotel on a nearly deserted beach. And that's the beauty of the place. The Lang Co Hotel, *Tel. (84 54) 874456*, has basic, rather run down rooms with no amenities and only cold showers for $15 per night. You have the beach to yourself, and that is the reason to come here. If you are traveling by car, Lang Co is a good place to stop for lunch. The restaurant serves excellent sea food.

Ngu Binh Hill is a flat-topped hill, thick with pine trees, that offers good camping. Many people enjoy walking up the 100 meter Ngu Binh Hill to take in the city skyline. When Gia Long built the imperial city, the hill was incorporated into Hue's general design and defense strategy by geomancy, an oriental method of using the lay of the land as a map for spiritual and practical design.

PRACTICAL INFORMATION

· **Industrial and Commerce Bank**, *2A Le Quy Don Street, Hue. Tel. (84 54) 823275.*

· **Vietcom Bank**, *6 Hoang Hoa Tham Street, Hue. Tel. (84 54) 824572.*

· **Hue Hospital**, for medical emergencies, *16 Le Loi Street, Hue. Tel. (84 54) 822325.*

· **Thua Thien Province Tourism Office**, *9 Ngo Quyen Street, Hue. Tel. (84 54) 822369 or 822355, Fax (84 54) 823502 or 823424.*

· **Hue City Tourism**, *18 Le Loi Street, Hue. Tel. (84 54) 823577, Fax (84 54) 825814.* The city tourism authority runs 25 hotels, the city guest houses and many restaurants. The office books tours and has information about trains.

· **Sinh Tourist Office**, *2-8 Hung Vuong Street, Hue. Tel. (84 54) 822121 or 826918, Fax (84 54) 25910.* Hue is the final stop for the open ticket bus. The Sinh office runs tours to the DMZ (leaving at 6 am) and boat trips along the Perfume River which stop at the Imperial Tombs (leaving at 8 am).

· **Post Office**, *8 Hoang Hoa Tham Street, Hue. Tel. (84 54) 822572. Hours from 6 am to 9 pm.*

15. HANOI & NORTHERN VIETNAM

Hanoi

Vietnam's capital city of **Hanoi** retains some French influence in the facades of houses and storefronts along its shady boulevards. Hanoi, population 2 million, sits on the **Red River Delta**. The name Hanoi is a derivation of an ancient word which means "on the bend of the river ." The city is better known as a city of lakes, since is has 18 urban bodies of water. Of the lakes in Hanoi, **Ho Tay** is the largest and is used for fishing and leisure. The character of central Hanoi is enhanced by Hoan Kiem, Bay Mau, and Thien Quang Lakes and their surrounding parks.

Hanoi sits on the site of the ancient city Than Long; the name means flying dragon. First chosen as a capital city in the fifth century AD, the Ly Dynasty made Thang Long the imperial seat in the year 1010 AD. In 1407, the Chinese marched, took, and held the city for twenty years, until Le Loi pushed the invaders out and proclaimed himself king.

The country then once again fell into the hands of the Chinese. In the late eighteenth century the people revolted and the Chinese were defeated in the Hanoi suburb of Dong Da. The Nguyen Dynasty moved the royal court to Hue.

When King Minh Mang brought the capital back in 1831, the city was renamed Hanoi. Suddenly a new military power appeared; the French successfully took control of the Indochinese peninsula. The French left a lasting impression with the beautiful buildings they put up during their administration from 1888 to 1954.

Hanoi served as the North Vietnamese capital after the Geneva Agreement divided the country. During the Vietnam war, American forces bombed Hanoi in 1966 and 1972, causing substantial damage. After the end of the war, Hanoi became the capital of the united Vietnam.

Hanoi has four urban districts. The central business district, Hoan Kiem, holds commercial and governmental offices. French colonial architecture flavors the area. Dong Da, primarily a residential area, is also home to the National University and Institute for Foreign Languages. Hai Ba Trung is an urban residential district. Ho Chi Minh's mausoleum and other notable attractions are found in Ba Dinh District. Five large suburban districts surround the city.

The city is in an exciting period of flux, but unlike Ho Chi Minh City, which races toward development at a breakneck pace, Hanoi is easing into the future. An example of the transition is the new office building which stands where the Hanoi Hilton, *Hoa Lo*, the largest POW jail in the North during the Vietnam War, once stood.

Hanoi experiences a true winter with frost and temperatures near freezing in December and January. Summer is hot and humid although without rainfall; from April to September the thermometer may reach 40°C.

ARRIVALS & DEPARTURES
BY AIR
Noibai Airport is small and manageable. The airport building is quite old, but still functional. Although the airport has a reputation for hassling tourists, this is becoming a thing of the past.

A bus takes you from the plane to the arrivals area, where you pick up your bags right inside the door. Taxi drivers will try to pull you straight from the arrival area to their taxi, but you also have the option of a less expensive shuttle van.

From the Airport to the City By Mini-van
The **Noibai Car Transport Service**, *Tel. (84 4) 8254250 or 266666*, runs vans from Noibai Airport to Hanoi, a 35 kilometer trip. You can purchase a ticket from the stand nest to the baggage carousel (and do not be deterred by the taxi drivers who will tell you there is no shuttle).

Although not a luxury mode of transport, it is a good deal: for drop-off at the centrally-located Noibai Car Transport office, *1A Quang Trung Street or 60 Nguyen Du Street*, the fee is $4; for $6 you can be left at the door of your hotel. Rates are the same for rides to the airport.

From the Airport to the City By Taxi
You will have no trouble finding a taxi since the drivers will greet you right in the arrival area. The cost of taxi ride to downtown Hanoi is about $30.

TAXI SERVICE IN HANOI
Hanoi Taxi, Tel. (84 4) 8535252
PT Taxi, Tel. (84 4) 8533171
Red Taxi, Tel. (84 4) 8353686

BY BUS

Hanoi has three bus stations. The main station serving points south is the **Southern Bus Station,** *Kilometer 6, Giai Phong Road, Hanoi, Tel. (84 4) 641476.*

From **Kim Ma Bus Station**, *116 Nguyen Thai Hoc Street, Hanoi, Tel. (84 4) 8256735,* buses travel to the north. And the suburban station is **Gia Lam Bus Station**, *Nguyen Van Cu Street, Gia Lam Town, Tel. (84 4) 8271529.*

BY HELICOPTER

Every Saturday, **Heli-Jet Vietnam**, *15 Ngo Quyen Street (in the Hotel Sofitel), Hanoi, Tel. (84 4) 8266919, extension 8015, Fax (84 4) 8250168,* offers helicopter flights between Hanoi and Halong. The 45 minute flight leaves Gia Lan Airport in Hanoi at 8 am, the return trip departs from Halong at 3:30 pm. Charter trips to most major destinations in Vietnam can be arranged.

BY TRAIN

The **Railway Station**, *120 Le Duan Road, Hanoi, Tel. (84 4) 8253949,* is in the middle of Hanoi, about 3 kilometers from the Old Quarter. You can get information about international and domestic trains and purchase tickets at the information room in the left wing of the main building.

To get information and tickets for Lao Cai (Sapa and Bac Ha) you must go to the train station annex, which is located behind the main building.

ORIENTATION

Hanoi is an ancient city composed of many districts. The downtown lakes provide points of reference for visitors. In the northern area of the city, close to West Lake you will find many cultural landmarks and pagodas. Hoan Kiem Lake is in the city center; to its north is the Old Quarter, and just to its south are the central business district and many of the foreign embassies.

Hoan Kiem Lake, a small body of water with a man-made island in the center, stands just south of the Old Quarter. In the northern part of the city, **West Lake**, *Ho Tay*, historically called Misty Lake, was once the site of royal residences. The lake is the largest and most beautiful in the city, surrounded by flower growing villages (Nghi Tam and Tay Ho Villages) and peach orchards. West Lake is separated from the much smaller **Truc Bach Lake** by a tree-lined boulevard.

The Ho Chi Minh Mausoleum and many of the monuments you will want to visit are north, near Lenin Park.

GETTING AROUND TOWN

By Bicycle

Bicycle rental runs about $5 per day. You can rent bicycles from the following hotels: Bac-Nam Hotel, Bodega Hotel, Hoan Kiem Hotel, and Sofia Hotel.

By Cyclo

Remember to set the price of a cyclo ride before you begin. If the driver tries to change the price or "renegotiate" get out, even if the ride has begun. Hanoi's cyclo drivers are notorious for being difficult and underhanded. Fair prices are $1 (11,000 dong) for a 3 kilometer ride or $5 (55,000 dong) for a half-day of sightseeing.

By Motorcycle

Traffic in Hanoi is slightly less chaotic than in Ho Chi Minh City. Motor bike rental runs about $10 per day. You can rent motor bikes from the following hotels: Bac-Nam Hotel, Bodega Hotel, Hoan Kiem Hotel, and Sofia Hotel.

By Taxi

Taxi drivers in Hanoi are known to be less friendly than in other cities. This may be because the incidence of petty crime associated with taxis is higher in the capital city. Generally, the incidents are no more serious than overcharging.

The safest way to get a taxi is to call a known company, which have published rates. When you travel across town, it may be less expensive to take a taxi than a cyclo, since taxi rates are reasonable.

WHERE TO STAY

Hotels in the Old Quarter

The old quarter is a roughly defined area of winding streets, just north of Hoan Kiem Lake. This lake, set in a small urban park, buffers the old and new cities. The old quarter, with its Chinese-style roofs and tightly packed houses, feels like a market. Shops overflow with racks of clothes, toys and household goods. Parked motor-bikes and bicycles claim sidewalks, forcing pedestrians to become part of the traffic flow. The streets here are named for the various crafts that are produced on each one.

Moderate

FORTUNA (PHO DU) HOTEL, *68 Hang Bo Street, Hanoi. Tel. (84 4) 8281324, 8282187, 8246392, Fax (84 4) 8281323. Singles/doubles $50 to $130. Credit cards accepted.*

Don't be put off by the twinkling Christmas lights in the entryway. This hotel is modern, comfortable and quiet. It is set back from the street, which gives the inside a peaceful, noise-free air. The spacious rooms have rattan furnishings and plenty of space. This is a step above the average small hotel in the area. The Royal Suite ($130) has a balcony which overlooks the old quarter. Suites have a bathtub and the deluxe room has a half-sized tub; the standard rooms have only showers. Government tax (7%) and service charge (3%) will be added to your bill. Prices are negotiable for long stays and groups.

GOLD III HOTEL, *77 Hang Luoc Street, Hanoi. Tel. (84 4) 8283525 or 8265339, Fax (84 4) 8283526. Singles/doubles $80 to $100/suites $120. Breakfast, service charge and tax included. Credit cards accepted.*

The Gold III Hotel strives for an air of elegance, and achieves this with Vietnamese carved furnishings, a receptive staff and colorful bathrooms. This 20- room hotel is located on a busy street. Although in a tourist area, the hotel seems to handle primarily business travelers. If you want a better hotel in the old quarter, this is a good choice. Round the clock room service, and arrangements for services from medical assistance to dry cleaning set this hotel apart.

TRANG AN HOTEL, *58 Hang Gai Street, Hanoi. Tel. (84 4) 8268928 or 8261135, Fax (84 4) 8258511. Singles/doubles $50 to $100. Credit cards accepted.*

The lobby attempts to be an art gallery, just as this eleven room mini-hotel hopes to be worth the high rate it charges. The rooms are new, but the only real difference between this hotel and others in the area charging half-the-price seems to be the location. The Trang An is on one of the main strips of souvenir shops.

Inexpensive

BAAN THAN HOTEL, *3B Cha Ca Street, Hanoi. Tel. (84 4) 82821120, Fax (84 4) 8283503. Singles/doubles $30 to $50.*

The small hotel has covered parking that allows you to drive right into the reception area. The rooms are new and the hotel is comfortable. When you get tired of eating the fried fish that cafes on Cha Ca Street are famous for, try the hotel's Thai restaurant upstairs which has good food.

CAMELLA HOTEL, *81 Thus Bac Street, Hanoi. Tel. (84 4) 828376 or 8283128, Fax (84 4) 8282404. Singles $15/doubles $35.*

The Camella Hotel is recommended for budget tourists. It has 15 rooms and a pleasant lobby. The newly renovated rooms have full bathrooms and windows. Satellite television and air-conditioning are standard amenities.

GIA KHAN HOTEL, *2b Hang Ga Street, Hanoi. Singles/doubles $20 to $30.*

If you're not put off by the dark, musty lobby, just wait. The unprofessional staff and uneasy feeling of this hotel make it one to avoid. The cost of rooms may change depending on what time of the day you inquire.

HOA LINH HOTEL, *35 Hang Bo Street, Hanoi. Tel. (84 4) 8243887 or 8250034, Fax (84 4) 8243886. Singles $30/doubles $50.*

This is a standard tourist hotel which is safe yet unremarkable. The price is reasonable for the rooms, but you can find places with more personality.

HUNG NGOC HOTEL, *34 Hang Manh Street, Hanoi. Tel. (84 4) 8285053, Fax (84 4) 8285054. Singles/doubles $35 to $45. Breakfast included. Credit cards accepted.*

A friendly business-suit clad staff runs this 8 room mini-hotel. The rooms are furnished nicely with Oriental decoration. The more expensive rooms have a balcony and sitting area. From the roof you have a good view of the Old Quarter. The Hung Ngoc operates a similar hotel in the new city.

KIM QUY HOTEL, *38 Hang Hom Street. Tel. (84 4) 8243944, Fax (84 4) 8285355. Singles $20/ doubles $25.*

Belly up to the bar to get a room: the reception desk has a fully-stocked bar behind it. The hotel is new and in a convenient location. The furniture is nice and the overall atmosphere good. This is a solid choice for an inexpensive room.

MELODY HOTEL, *17 Hang Duong, Hanoi. Tel. (84 4) 8263029 or 8267820, Fax (84 4) 8243746. Singles/doubles $30 to $40. Credit cards accepted.*

The Melody Hotel is a decent but completely unremarkable accommodation often booked by tour groups. Rooms have all the standard conveniences including tourist office, phone, satellite TV and bathtubs.

NGOC TUNG HOTEL, *30 Hang Cot Street, Hanoi. Tel. (84 4) 259464, Fax (84 4) 282847. Singles 15 to $25/doubles $30-$45.*

The staff will tell you that the Ngoc Tung strives to make guests "feel comfortable, like home." And not only does this 15 room hotel accomplish that with its friendly, staff but it provides comfortable accommodation. The rooms have soft chairs and standard amenities of satellite television, bathtubs, and mini refrigerators with real freezers. Lower-priced rooms do not have full amenities (such as a bathtub). The rates make this hotel a good deal.

PHUNG HUNG HOTEL, *2 Duong Thanh Street, Hanoi. Tel. (84 4) 8252614 or 8244665 or 8245453, Fax (84 4) 8269279. Singles/doubles $16 to $42.*

Open air hall-ways lead to renovated but musty rooms. The 64 room Phung Hung is close to the Dong Xuan Market between the train station and Hoan Kiem Lake. Single and double rooms have telephones, modern baths, air conditioning and television.

PRINCE HOTEL, *78 Hang Ga Street, Hanoi. Tel. (84 4) 8281322, Fax (84 4) 8281636. Singles/doubles $25 to $50. Credit cards accepted.*

The friendly, small Prince Hotel is a great value. It is run by the same family that owns the Stars Hotel. Everyone that works at the Prince will go out of their way to accommodate your needs, from personal attention to business correspondence to booking budget or luxury tours. All the rooms have comfortable furnishings and bath tubs.

THANH AN HOTEL, *46 Hang Ga, Hanoi. Tel. (84 4) 84 4) 8267191, Fax (84 4) 8269720. Singles $25/doubles $ 30.*

Large, sunken rooms which are remolded but feel older characterize the indoor/outdoor hotel. Although it has only 11 rooms, the hotel has rambling breezeways. Each room has a window. The friendly staff is very welcoming and ready to negotiate rates for long stays and groups.

THAN HA HOTEL, *34 Hang Ga Street, Hanoi. Tel. (84 4) 8246496 or 8282812, Fax (84 4) 8282248. Singles/doubles $25 to $30. Breakfast, service charge and tax included.*

The fifteen rooms have new furniture, satellite TV, refrigerator, and telephone. Spacious bathrooms are the selling point of this hotel.

THUY LAM HOTEL, *17 B Hang Ga Street, Hanoi. Tel. (84 4) 8281788, Fax (84 4) 8250468. Singles/doubles $20 to $50.*

The Thuy Lam is a small, quiet hotel with adequate rooms. The staff arranges tours including a one day stint to Hoa Binh, the country's largest electricity plant. Bicycles ($1 per day) and cars ($5 per hour) are for rent.

VENUS HOTEL, *10 Hang Can, Hanoi. Tel. (84 4) 261212, Fax (84 4) 8246010. Singles $15/doubles $20.*

This small hotel is frequented by European tourists. The lobby has an eerie darkness, even on a sunny day at noon. The rooms are unimpressive and not so clean, but slightly cheaper than the surrounding places.

Outside the Old Quarter
Expensive

HOA BINH HOTEL, *27 Ly Thuong Kiet Street, Hanoi. Tel. (84 4) 8253315 or 8254655, Fax (84 4) 8291237. Singles $96 to $157/doubles $124 to $184. Breakfast included. Credit cards accepted.*

The Hoa Binh is a decent 102 room tourist hotel. The building dates from 1926, and still retains a bit of its original charm. The renovation does little to recreate the original atmosphere. Nonetheless the rooms are spacious and have modern amenities. The hotel has a restaurant and bar.

THE METROPOLE, *15 Ngo Quyen Street, Hanoi. Tel. (84 4) 8266919. Singles/doubles $220 to $450. Credit cards accepted.*

The Bluet family, legendary French hoteliers, opened the Metropole in 1911, during the golden days of colonial rule. Somerset Maugham and Graham Greene stayed here. In 1992, the hotel was restored to its former elegance by Pullman-Sofitel after nearly 40 years of being run as a state enterprise. Much of the interior is the original antique wood. This is the only true luxury hotel you will find in Hanoi. The Metropole is often booked-up far in advance. You should make reservations over one month ahead of your visit.

THANG LOI HOTEL, *Yen Phu Street, Hanoi. Tel. (84 4) 8268211, Fax (84 4) 8252800. Singles/doubles $120 to $200.*

The Thang Loi is close to the tranquil West Lake. It is a large tourist hotel with nice grounds, full recreational and athletic facilities and parking.

Moderate

DONG LOI, *94 Ly Thoung Kiet Street, Hanoi. Tel. (84 4) 8255721 or 8267957, Fax (84 4) 8267999. Singles/doubles $55. Credit cards accepted.*

The modern Dong Loi has been in operation since the 1930s. Its 30 rooms were recently renovated. The furnishings are nothing special, but the location is convenient if you are traveling by train since the hotel is about two blocks from the train station.

HOTEL DRAGON, *57A Quang Trung Street, Hanoi. Tel. (84 4) 8259119 or 8229138, Fax (84 4) 8227871. Singles $30/doubles $45.*

This small hotel is across the street from Thein Quang Lake. The location gives you the convenience of being near the city center without the traffic congestion and noise. The rooms all have standard amenities. The restaurant specializes in Cha Ca, the regional fried fish. You can enjoy the early evening breezes from the restaurant's balcony which overlooks the lake.

HOTEL VILLA BLEUE, *82 Ly Thuong Kiet Street, Hanoi. Tel. (84 4) 8247733 or 8247712, Fax (84 4) 8245676. Singles $50 to $120/doubles $60 to $120. Breakfast included. Credit cards accepted.*

This Villa, which is being made into a hotel, is a gem in the rough. Original floors and French touches make a stay here a trip back in time. The hotel has a good, central location on a street that is not too busy. The restaurant serves good Vietnamese food.

MILITARY GUEST HOUSE, *2 Le Thach Street, Hanoi. Tel. (84 4) 8252896, Fax (84 4) 8259227. Singles/doubles $ 120 to $150.*

Once reserved for visiting dignitaries, the remodeled government guest house accepts tourists. The location is central and the service is good. You can arrange tours at the front desk.

Budget

SOFIA HOTEL, *6 Hang Bai Street, Hanoi. Tel. (84 4) 8266848. Singles/doubles $20 to $25.*

Although the Sofia appears decent from the outside, the inside tells a different story. The rooms are dirty and full of bugs. You will have better budget choices in the Old quarter.

WHERE TO EAT

Expensive

INDOCHINE, *Vietnamese, 16 Nam Ngu Street, Hanoi. Tel. (84 4) 8246097. Credit cards accepted.*

Indochine serves the best neo-Vietnamese cuisine in the city. The elegant restaurant is located on a small street in an unassuming building. On cool nights, the patio tables are a perfect setting. Reservations are recommended.

GIO MOI, *Chinese, 63 Le Duan Street, Hanoi. Tel. (84 4) 8229839. Credit cards accepted.*

Locals will tell you that Gio Moi is the most authentic Chinese food in the city. The lengthy menu reads like a book, but the waitpeople are happy to explain the specialties to you. Seafood is the specialty, especially shrimp.

LE BEAULIEU, *French, 15 Ngo Quyen Street. Hanoi. Tel. (84 4) 8266919. Credit cards accepted.*

The French restaurant downstairs in the Metropole Hotel has an extensive menu. The food meets the high standard set by the hotel, and of course the service is excellent.

SEASONS OF HANOI, *Vietnamese, 95 Quan Thanh, Hanoi. Tel. (84 4) 8435444.*

The Seasons offers elegant dining and delicious food. New twists are added to traditional Vietnamese food to create flavorful cuisine.

Moderate

A LITTLE ITALIAN, *Italian, 81 Thu Nhuom Street, Hanoi. Tel. (84 4) 8258167.*

This has long been a favorite of visitors who love Italian food. The selection of pizza is extensive and sure to curb your yearning for tomato sauce and cheese.

DA TANO RISTORANTE, *Italian, 10 Hang Chao Street, Hanoi. Tel. (84 4) 8234850.*

Da Tano offers something which is difficult to find in Vietnam—good pasta. Most Italian restaurants stick to pizza, but Da Tano goes for the real meals and pulls it off beautifully. The sauces are superb. Try to save room for dessert.

OPERA CLUB, *Vietnamese and European, 59 Ly Thai To, Hanoi. Tel. (84 4) 8268802 (upstairs) or 8246950 (downstairs). Credit cards accepted.*

The Opera Club is not a club at all, but two restaurants with decor reminiscent of the turn of the century. The restaurant upstairs serves excellent Vietnamese dishes with the flavors of southern cuisine. The downstairs restaurant serves European meals which are full of French overtones. During the day, the Opera Club fills up with the power-lunch crowd.

Inexpensive

252 CAFE, *Western, 252 Hang Bong Street, Hanoi.*

This cafe serves excellent pastries and light meals. The food is rich, filling and inexpensive. The home-made yogurt is out of this world.

LA VONG, *Vietnamese, 14 Cha Ca Street, Hanoi. Tel. (84 4) 8253929.*

Other restaurants along this street serve cha ca, but this is the authentic place to get it. The Vong family reputedly made the first cha ca (fried fish) at this restaurant ages ago. Cha ca are spicy fried fish cakes served with a special sauce. The fish is so good that the street bears the name. The flavor is delicate and extraordinary. This is a simple cafe with a lot of history and tasty food.

RESTAURANT 22, *Vietnamese, 22 Hang Can Street, Hanoi. Tel. (84 4) 8267160.*

To get to this well-known Vietnamese restaurant follow the signs through a dark alley-hallway and upstairs. You know the kitchen is clean because you walk right through it to get to the dining room. The cheese soup is really a light French onion with a few chunks of cream cheese. Basic and tasty Vietnamese dishes are served for very reasonable prices.

SEEING THE SIGHTS

Hoan Kiem Area

The Old Quarter of Hanoi is an excellent place to stay. Restaurants, parks and points of interest are with walking distance. This is truly the heart of the city and the commercial center is nearby.

The labyrinth of streets that compose Hanoi's **Old Quarter** are just north of Hoan Kiem Lake. Each street is named for the products of the artisans that live and work there, such as Chicken Street, *Hang Ga*, and Bamboo Street, *Hang Tre*. Many of the workers maintain ancient shrines dedicated to their crafts. At the northern border of this area is Hanoi's main market, the rambling **Cho Dong Xuan** (cho is Vietnamese for market). Dong Xuan market is full of food, goods used in traditional Chinese medicine and cooking, as well as animals. You can spend hours in the market and on the surrounding streets enjoying the colorful marketplace.

The large Long Bien Bridge which extends from the market across the Red River was formerly known as the Doumer Bridge. **Doumer Bridge**, constructed in 1902 and named for the French governor Paul Doumer, was of strategic importance in the war against the French, since it was the main link over the river. The bridge also shows the scars of bombing raids from the Vietnam War.

Hoan Kiem Lake is the setting of an ancient myth; the name Hoan Kiem means "returned sword." During the Chinese occupation in the 15th century, Le Loi, the farmer-turned-leader, received a magic sword from a turtle in Hoan Kiem Lake. With this magnificent sword he liberated his country and assumed the throne. He gratefully returned the sword to the turtle in Hoan Kiem Lake.

Today Hoan Kiem Lake is one of the centers of city life. The lake is quite small and is surrounded by a pleasant park. In the early morning, people come out to practice tai chi, jog and walk along the willow lined path that outlines the lake. During the afternoon and on weekends the lake is a favorite place for reading and strolling. The cafes around the lake are frequented at all times of the day. Hang Gai, a major thoroughfare running east-west from the northern tip of Hoan Kiem Lake is where you will find the largest selection of souvenirs in the city.

The lake has two temples, the smaller one stands isolated in the southern half of the lake and cannot be visited. The larger temple stands in the lake, just off the northwestern bank. This is the **Ngoc Son (Jade) Temple,** and is dedicated to Van Suong, one of Vietnam's greatest writers. To reach the Jade Temple, cross the Huc Bridge, a beautifully carved wooden bridge built in the 19th century. There is an admission charge to enter the temple.

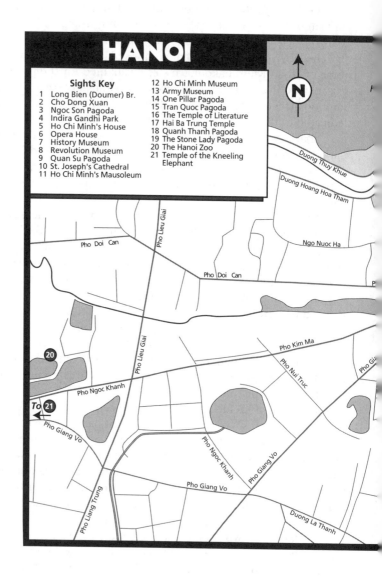

HANOI

Sights Key

1 Long Bien (Doumer) Br.
2 Cho Dong Xuan
3 Ngoc Son Pagoda
4 Indira Gandhi Park
5 Ho Chi Minh's House
6 Opera House
7 History Museum
8 Revolution Museum
9 Quan Su Pagoda
10 St. Joseph's Cathedral
11 Ho Chi Minh's Mausoleum
12 Ho Chi Minh Museum
13 Army Museum
14 One Pillar Pagoda
15 Tran Quoc Pagoda
16 The Temple of Literature
17 Hai Ba Trung Temple
18 Quanh Thanh Pagoda
19 The Stone Lady Pagoda
20 The Hanoi Zoo
21 Temple of the Kneeling Elephant

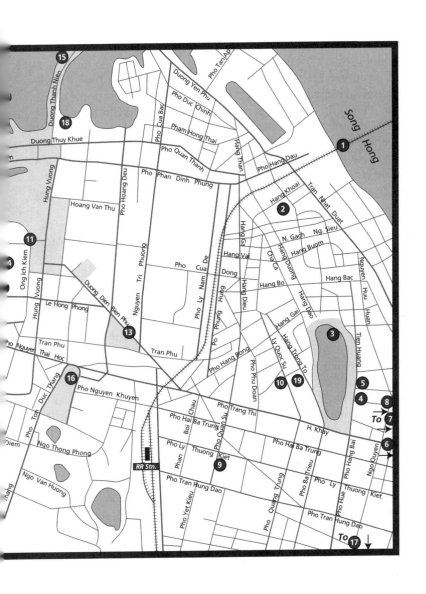

Indira Ghandi Park is located just west of the lake. If you continue west past the main post office, along Le Lai Street, you will find what was once the city center for the French.

Among the concentration of French colonial buildings is a museum dedicated to Ho Chi Minh in the building that was once the president's home. The president lived in a simple wooden house during his leadership of the country. **Ho Chi Minh's House**, *48 Hang Ngang Street, Hanoi,* is considered a national treasure and affectionately called the home of Bac Ho ("Uncle Ho"). It stands under shady trees. Here Ho Chi Minh wrote Vietnam's Declaration of Independence. You will find Ho Chi Minh's House behind the former residence of the French Governor.

Further south the French charm of the city is evident in the renovated **Metropole Hotel**, *15 Ngo Quyen Street, Hanoi*. Across the street from the Metropole is the Government Guest House, built in the 19th century as the residence for distinguished foreign guests.

Just behind the Metropole stands the city **Opera House**, built by the French in 1911, a small version of the great Paris Opera House. Most recently the Opera House was used as a theater. Currently it is undergoing extensive renovation and is completely shut down. A period-style hotel is being constructed adjacent to the Opera House.

In ancient times **Quan Su Pagoda**, *73 Quan Su Street, Hanoi*, was a residence for visiting Buddhist dignitaries. The pagoda is located just a few blocks from the train station. It was constructed in the 17th century and is also called the Ambassadors' Pagoda. Since 1934 the Vietnam Buddhism Association has officially used Quan Su Pagoda as its headquarters.

Just a few blocks north of Quan Su Pagoda stands a center of Catholicism, **Saint Joseph's Cathedral**, *40 Nha Chung Street, Hanoi*. The church has been active for over 100 years and is still in use, with regular Sunday services. Although it is supposed to be open to the public, the main gate is often locked during the day. The church was built by the French in 1886, in European style, complete with stained glass and buttresses. It looks as though it could be standing in a small European town instead of central Hanoi. The church is a few blocks east of Hoan Kiem Lake.

According to legend, during the 15th century, while breaking ground for a citadel, workers discovered a stone statue of a woman. **The Stone Lady (Ba Da) Pagoda**, was constructed to house the statue. The Stone Lady Pagoda, *Nha Chung Street*, is between Saint Joseph's Cathedral and Hoan Kiem Lake.

Museums in the Hoan Kiem District

The state archaeological collection is in Hanoi's **History Museum**, *1 Pham Ngu Lao Street, Hanoi, Tel. (84 4) 8252853 or 253518*. During French rule, the museum was built (1926) to hold the relics of the French archaeological school's excavations, Ecole d'Extreme Orient. Originally named Musée Louis Finot, the museum was renamed in 1958. The collections represent artifacts from the entire country. The most comprehensive historical picture of pre-communist Vietnam is brought together in the displays here.

The **Revolution Museum**, *25 Tong Dan Street, Hanoi, Tel. (84 4) 8253766 or 254151 or 254323*, pays tribute to the country's turbulent past. The collection is more of a history book come to life than a museum. The exhibitions trace the communists rise to power through the struggles of the Vietnamese people. The timeline begins with the Chinese Han Dynasty and moves forward with an emphasis on modern wars.

In the center of the city you will find the **Women's Museum**, *36 Ly Thuong Kiet Street, Hanoi, Tel. (84 4) 8259129*. The museum houses a collection dedicated to women and their roles in Vietnamese history. The exhibits show the sociological aspects of women's life at various points in history.

Ba Dinh Area

The northern part of the city center (just west of the Old Quarter) holds most of the sights you will want to visit in Hanoi. The large **West Lake**, *Ho Tay*, is the focal point of the area. West Lake is a recreational area that is especially popular on weekends. Bordering the southeastern tip of West Lake is the much smaller Truc Bach Lake.

Probably the most imposing monument in the entire country is the building dedicated to holding the remains of the founder of modern Vietnam. **Ho Chi Minh's Mausoleum**, *Ba Dinh Square* , is the final resting place of Vietnam's most beloved leader, who is on display in a glass case "a la Lenin" for the world to see. The building should resemble a lotus blossom from a distance, however it actually looks like a giant block of stone.

Travelers you meet will probably have stories about their visit to the mausoleum, since it leaves an indelible impression. The level of decorum expected of visitors is so high and the atmosphere is so regimented that many find the mausoleum nearly comical. The building is ironic because Ho Chi Minh himself intended to have his remains cremated. However, no Vietnamese person (especially the guards) would venture to read amusement or irony into the mausoleum, so take it seriously while inside. The mausoleum is closed on Mondays. Hours: 7:30 am to 11 am, Tuesday to Sunday.

The National Assembly Hall stands directly opposite the Ho Chi Minh's Mausoleum. This also serves as the national Communist Party headquarters. The building is not open to the public.

Temples and Pagodas in the Ba Dinh Area

Within walking distance of Ho Chi Minh's Mausoleum you will find some of the country's most interesting pagodas. One of the most unusual religious monuments is the **One Pillar Pagoda**, *Chau Mot Cot*, on *Ong Ich Kiem Street, Hanoi*. The original pagoda on this site was built in 1049 by order of King Ly Thai Tong as a tribute for the blessing of the birth of a son. The pillar measures 1.25 meters in diameter, and was originally made of a single tree trunk. The French razed the Pagoda when they left Hanoi; it was rebuilt in 1954. The pillar was reconstructed in cement. **Dien Huu Pagoda** is a smaller sanctuary adjacent to the One Pillar Pagoda.

Tran Quoc Pagoda stands on a peninsula off the southwestern shore of West Lake. This ancient temple was first built on the Red River. Centuries later it was moved, and it has undergone numerous renovations. The temple is famous for its ancient bronze statues. Tran Quoc Pagoda is on Thanh Nien Street, which divides West Lake and Truc Bach Lake.

Just south of Ho Truc Lake, on the corner of Than Nien and Quan Thanh Streets stands the **Quan Thanh Temple**. This temple is dedicated to Tran Vu, a figure important in both Chinese and Vietnamese myths. The original structure, built in 1028, received a full renovation in 1893. The central bronze statue of Tran Vu was constructed in 1677; a smaller bronze of the artist, Trong, was made by his students.

In the western part of Ba Dinh on the grounds of the Thu Le Park stands the **Temple of the Kneeling Elephant** , first built in the eleventh century and rebuilt since, was dedicated to a Vietnamese prince who dispelled invading Chinese forces with an elephant brigade. The **Hanoi Zoo** is also part of Thu Le Park. It is a small, well-run zoo which proudly features native elephants in its collection.

Museums in the Ba Dinh Area

The country's long history of armed conflict, from ancient to modern times is chronicled in the **Military Museum,** *28A Dien Bien Phu Street, Hanoi, Tel. (84 4) 8234264, Tuesday through Sunday 8 to 11:30 am and 1:30 to 4 pm.* Exhibits trace the long, difficult military campaigns of the last three thousand years through paintings, relics and memorabilia. The museum sits on land that is part of the city's great citadel. The Citadel is currently used by the military. One of the Citadel towers dating from the early 19th century stands outside the building.

The museum's exhibits continue outside, with ruins of armament from the Vietnam War on display.

The **Fine Arts Museum**, *66 Nguyen Thai Hoc Street, Hanoi, Tel. (84 4) 8265801 or 8233084,* opened in June 1966. This worthwhile collection documents centuries of Vietnamese art. The famous Vietnamese large bronze drums from the first millennium BC are on display, as well as folk art and modern art. Works by modern Vietnamese artists including To Ngoc Van, Nguyen Pahn Chanh, Tran Van Can are shown.

Ho Chi Minh Museum, *3 Ngoc Ha Street, Hanoi, Tel. (84 4) 8263752 or 8255435,* presents a history of Uncle Ho's life and his struggle to rise to the leadership of the unified nation he did not live to see. The collection opened in May 1990. This is the country's main tribute to the history surrounding Ho Chi Minh. You will find the museum adjacent to Ho Chi Minh's Mausoleum.

The Dong Da Area

The Temple of Literature is one of the most impressive monuments in Vietnam. It is found in the Dong Da area, just south of Nguyen Thai Hoc Street, close to the points of interest in Ba Dinh. The Temple of Literature is on Van Mieu Street, a directly west of the train station.

Temple of Literature, *Van Mieu*, is a Confucian temple built during the Ly Dynasty in 1070 and was the first part of *Quoc Tu Giam*, Vietnam's first university. The university was open from the 10th to the 18th centuries; only men were allowed to attend. In 1482, King Le Thanh Tong ordered the placement of stelae with the names of all graduates in the previous forty years. The tradition continued until 1787, with a total of 82 stelae erected. The stelae remain a testament to the Confucian value of education. The large, tranquil grounds of the temple are worthy of a long, relaxed visit.

Hai Ba Trung District

The **Hai Ba Trung District** is primarily a residential area just south of the city center. Here you will find the **Hai Ba Trung** Temple. The Trung Sisters are national heroes because they led a nearly successful uprising against the Chinese in the 12th century. The tribute to the women revolutionaries was first built in 1142 AD. The clay statues of the sisters are surrounded by 12 female generals. The main part of the temple is closed.

Lenin Park is a large, tranquil park located on Le Duan Street, south of Tran Nhan Tong Street. You will find Bay Mau Lake here. In the mornings the park comes alive with people practicing tai chi and in the evenings the State Circus performs. Prior to 1960 the area was wasteland and the park is said to have been built by volunteers. Spooky Soviet armament stands under large trees, which makes for an ironic accompaniment to the lovely trees and peaceful lake. The gauge railway runs through a neighborhood near this park.

The **Friendship Cultural Palace**, which is across from Lenin Park, was built by the Soviet Union and opened in 1985. The complex has areas for performance, study and recreation.

Outside the City

Co Loa Citadel, *Dong An District, Hanoi,* a once great fortification of the third century BC, now stands in ruins. Nine spiral towers covered five square kilometers. Today remnants of only three remain, as wells as some statues dedicated to King An Duong, who lived in the citadel.

NIGHTLIFE & ENTERTAINMENT

Cheo, folk opera, is a village tradition which is a central element of Vietnamese culture. It is an ancient form of slap-stick entertainment. You can see performances at the Vietnam Cheo Popular Theater, *1 Giang Van Minh Street, Hanoi. Tel. (84 4) 8266193 or 8257403.* Other theaters include: Cheo Theater, Kim Ma Street, Ba Dinh District and Cheo Club, Nguyen Dinh Chiey Street, Hai Ba Trung District.

Water puppetry is a Vietnamese art form in which water is used as a stage for brightly colored puppets. Adults often seem to enjoy the shows more than the kids in the audience. The main theater for water puppetry performances is the Central Water Puppet Theater, *32 Truong Trinh Road, Hanoi. Tel. (84 4) 8244545.*

The **Opera House**, a reproduction in miniature of the Paris Opera House, is currently being renovated and is closed.

Hanoi is a reserved city as far as nightlife goes. The city's few bars are trendy, in general. Tourists wanting to drink a few casual beers hang out at the Darling or Queen's Cafe in the Old Quarter. Among the bars where expatriates frequent are the following:

BLUE BAR, *57 Ly Thai To Street, Hanoi. Tel. (84 8) 8249247.* This slick bar, close to the Opera House, draws a trendy crowd. The large karaoke room can handle big groups.

EMERALD BAR, *53 Hang Luoc, Hanoi. Tel. (84 4) 8259285.* This is genuine pub in the middle of the old quarter. The atmosphere is laid back, but prices are high for the area.

SPORTS & RECREATION
Golf

The **Dong Mo Golf Course**, set amid mountains and forest, is about 50 kilometers (31 miles) from Hanoi. The course has 18 holes For more information, contact **Son Tay Tourist Company**, *Dong Mo Tourist Center, Ha Tay Province. Tel. (84 34) 8332279.*

Tennis
You will find tennis courts for public use at the following places:
- **Worker's Cultural Palace**, *Tran Hung Dao Street, Hanoi.*
- **The Youth Club**, *5 Tang Bat Ho Street, Hanoi. Tel. (84 4) 8255533.*
- **Ba Dinh Club**, *Hoang Van Thu Street, Hanoi. Tel. (84 4) 8253024.*

Swimming
- **Thang Loi Hotel**, *78 Yen Phu Street, Hanoi. Tel. (84 4) 8268211.*
- **International Club**, *35 Hung Vuong Street, Hanoi. Tel. (84 4) 8252310.*

SHOPPING
Commercial and Tourist Service Center, *1 Ba Trieu Street, Hanoi. Tel. (84 4) 8265244 or 265245, Fax (84 4) 8256418.* Located across the street from Hoan Kiem Lake, this mini-mall has a good selection of shops offering art and better souvenirs. The travel office here arranges private and group tours.

Khai Silk, *121 Nguyen Thai Hoc Street or 96 Hang Gai Street, Hanoi. Tel. (84 4) 8233508 or 8436251.* A wide assortment of high-quality clothes is offered here. Special orders and tailor-made outfits can be arranged.

Le Minh Silk, *79-111 Hang Gai Street, Hanoi. Tel. (84 4) 8288723 or 8285840.* This shop specializes in tailor-made silk clothes.

HANOI'S ART GALLERIES
These galleries display and sell modern paintings form some of the country's leading artists:
Center for Artistic Exchange, 43 Trang Tein Street, Hanoi. Tel. (84 4) 8240038.
Gallery 44, 44b Ham Long Street. Hanoi. Tel. (84 4) 8253063.
Van Yen Art Gallery, 2 Quang Trung Street, Hanoi. Tel. (84 4) 8250684.
Red River Gallery, 71A Nguyen Du Street, Hanoi. Tel. (84 4) 8229064.

My A Wood Carving, *66 Nguyen Thai Hoc Street, Hanoi. Tel. (84 4) 8233953.* Sells artistic wood carvings with Oriental designs.

Tien Dung, *88 Hang Gai Street, Hanoi. Tel. (84 4) 8248004.* A good variety of souvenirs and crafts are sold.

Tuong Duong Shop, *82 Hang Gai Street, Hanoi. Tel. (84 4) 8260220.* You will find some of the lowest prices on lacquerware and souvenirs at the Tung Duong Shop.

The **Dong Xuan Market** (Hoan Kiem district) is the city's largest marketplace. The indoor/outdoor complex sprawls on for blocks in every direction. Other markets include: **Hang Da Market** (Hoan Kiem District), **Mo Market** (Hai Ba Trung District), **Cau Moi Market** (Dong Da District) and **Ngoc Ha Market** (Ba Dinh District).

DAY TRIPS & EXCURSIONS

One of the most popular day trips is to an artisan's community of potters. **Bat Trang** is an amazing village of about 2,000 people. The families have made pottery for generations. Eight-hundred ceramic kilns have produced ceramics for over 500 years. Bat Trang is about 30 kilometers south of Hanoi.

The **Blessing (Thien Phuc) Pagoda**, is a major center of worship. Three Buddhist sects pay homage at this temple, which sits atop Sai Son Hill, 40 kilometers (25 miles) from Hanoi.

Ha Tay Province is a beautiful area of rolling hills and lakes. Most site in Ha Tay Province can be visited during a day trip from Hanoi. The cafes run daily tours to the Perfume Pagoda.

The Perfume (Huong) Pagoda is situated on the Huong Mountain, 65 kilometers (40 miles) south of Hanoi. The pagoda may be reached by boat or by a 3 kilometer (1.5 mile) trek. The Perfume Pagoda is actually three religious sanctuaries. The outermost pagoda is the Path to Heaven (Thien Chu) Pagoda; followed by the Purgatory (Huong Tich Chu) Pagoda. The innermost shrine is the Perfume Pagoda. Pilgrims travel to the Perfume Pagoda for the religious holidays celebrated according to the lunar calendar, which fall in March and April.

West Pagoda, *Tay Phuong*, sits on a hill in Tay Phuong town, about 40 kilometers (25 miles) from Hanoi. The pagoda holds 75 wooden statues of monks. First built in the eighth century, reconstruction took place in the seventeenth and eighteenth centuries.

PRACTICAL INFORMATION
Banks
• **Vietcom bank**, *49 Ly Thai To Street, Hanoi. Tel. (84 4) 8257563 or 8226456 or 78 Nguyen Du Street, Hanoi. Tel. (84 4) 8262065 or 8268032.*
• **State Bank of Vietnam**, *49 Ly Thai To Street, Hanoi. Tel. (84 4) 8258388 or 8258380.*
• **Industry and Commerce Bank**, *16 Phan Dinh Phung Street, Hanoi. Tel. (84 4) 8232008 or 8232009.*

Post Offices
• **Main Post Office**, *75 Dinh Tien Hoang Street, Hanoi. Tel. (84 4) 8262919 or 8266627, Fax (84 4) 8261111 or 8250000.* This is a full-service post

office by Hoan Kiem Lake. The desk in the foyer on the left provides information in English.

The following are branch post offices:

- **Hoan Kiem Post Office**, *66 Trang Tien Street, Hanoi. Tel. (84 4) 8254420.*
- **Dong Da Post Office**, *Tay Son Street, Hanoi. Tel. (84 4) 8254105 or 245230.*
- **Ba Dinh Post Office**, *22 Nguyen Thai Hoc Street, Hanoi. Tel. (84 4) 8257819*
- **Hai Ba Trung Post Office**, *Mo Market, Hanoi. Tel. (84 4) 8254269 or 265447.*

Hospitals

- **AEA**, *4 Tran Hung Dao, 4th Floor, Hanoi. Tel. (84 4) 8213 555, Fax (84 4) 8213523.* Medical care can be provided to foreigners.
- **International Department of Bach Mai Hospital**, *Giai Phong Street. Tel. (84 4) 522 083 or 522 089.* This hospital is for foreigners.
- **Viet Duc Hospital**, 48 Trang Thi Street, Hanoi. Tel. (84 4) 253 531. This hospital operates a twenty-four hour emergency surgery facility and has English speakers on staff.
- **Friendship Hospital**, *1 Tran Khanh Du, Hanoi. Tel. (84 8) 252 231.* This hospital maintains rooms for foreigners.
- **The Institute of Acupuncture**, *Thai Thinh Road, Hanoi. Tel. 84 4 534253 or 534275*, and **Institute of Traditional Herbal Medicine**, *29 Nguyen Binh Khiem Street, Hanoi. Tel. (84 4) 8262850.* Should you seek traditional oriental medicine, these places may be of service, but you should bring a translator.

Government Offices

- **Entry-Exit Procedure Office**, *89 Tran Hung Dao Street, Hanoi. Tel. (84 4) 8266472.* Should you want to attempt to get a visa extension, or need an exit visa, you must go to the Entry-Exit Procedure Office.

International Relief Organizations

- **UNDP**, United Nations Development Program, *25-29 Pahn Boi Chau Street, Hanoi. Tel. (84 4) 8254254.*
- **UNESCO**, United Nations Educational, Scientific and Cultural Organization, *8 Khuc Hao Street, Hanoi. Tel. (84 4) 8225440.*
- **UNFA,** United Nations Population Fund, *Block 3 Giang Vo Quarter, Hanoi. Tel. (84 4) 8254763.*
- **UNHCR**, United Nations High Commissioner for Refugees, *60 Nguyen Thai Hoc Street, Hanoi. Tel. (84 4) 8256785.*
- **UNICEF**, United Nations Children Fund, *72 Ly Thuong Kiet Street, Hanoi. Tel. (84 4) 8261172.*

•**WHO**, World Health Organization, *2A Van Phuc Street, Hanoi. Tel. (84 4) 8252148.*

Mini Marts

A number of new mini-marts sell incidentals and necessities you may need: **Hanoi Mini Mart**, *Hon-Duc Vien Market;* **Hanoi Star Mart**, *60 Ngo Thi Nham Street;* **Mini Mart**, *14 Ly Nam Street.*

Tourist Offices

•**Commercial and Tourist Service Center**, *1 Ba Trieu Street, Hanoi. Tel. (84 4) 8242330 or 8265244, Fax (84 4) 8256418.*

•**East Asia Company**, *23 Hoa Ma Street, Hanoi. Tel. (84 4) 8268492, Fax (84 4) 8265302.*

•**Ecco Vietnam**, *50A Be Trieu, Hanoi. Tel. (84 4) 8254615, Fax (84 4) 8266519.* Ecco tours can get you back to nature, and even arrange buffalo-hunting trips.

•**ESPECEN Tours**, *79 Hang Trong, Hanoi. Tel. (84 4) 8266856 or 8261071, Fax (84 4) 8269612.* This company operates 11 offices in Hanoi. Their prices are high and they cater to French-speakers.

•**Esperanto Tour**, *1 Ba Trieu Street, Hanoi. Tel. (84 4) 8265244 or 8265232.*

•**Hanoi Tourist**, *18 Ly Thuong Kiet Street, Hanoi. Tel. (84 4) 8254209 or 8257866, Fax (84 4) 8254209.*

•**Queen's Cafe**, *65 Hang Bac Street, Hanoi. Tel. (84 4) 8260860. Fax (84 4) 8250000.* The Queen's cafe operates the most reputable budget tours of the north.

•**TOSERCO**, *To Hien Thanh Street, Hanoi. Tel. (84 4) 8252937 or 8263541, Fax (84 4) 8226055.* This is the government tourist office.

•**Vietnam Tourism**, *30 Ly Thuong Kiet Street, Hanoi. Tel. (84 4) 8264154 or 826089, Fax (84 4) 8257583.*

•**Vietnam Veterans Tourism Service Company**, *21 Phan Dinh Phung Street, Hanoi. Tel. (84 4) 8230245, Fax (84 4) 8237467.*

•**Viet Y**, *57 Hang Chuoi Street, Hanoi. Tel. (84 4) 48213264, Fax (84 4) 8213256.* This company arranges luxury excursions in Vietnam.

•**VINATOUR**, *54 Nguyen Du Street, Hanoi. Tel. (84 4) 8255952 or 8257245, Fax (84 4) 8252707.*

•**Youth Tourism Company**, *14A Phan Chu Trinh Street, Hanoi. Tel. (84 4) 8254628 or 263073.*

US & Canadian Diplomatic Offices

•**Embassy of the United States**, *7 Lang Ha, Hanoi. Tel. (84 4) 8431500.*

•**Embassy of Canada**, *39 Nguyen Dinh Chieu Street, Hanoi. Tel. (84 4) 8265840;* **Consulate**, *203 Dong Khoi, Suite 303, District 1, Ho Chi Minh City. Tel. (84 8) 8242000.*

NORTHERN VIETNAM

Haiphong

Haiphong, population 1.6 million, is Vietnam's third largest city. The port lies on the Gulf of Tonkin, and is surrounded by the beautiful Voi Mountains on the west. Sixteen local rivers feed into the city. The largest river, the Bach Dang, is famous in military history. This was the site of significant battles in 938 AD and 1288 AD.

Historically, the port received both European and Asian traders. Today, it is a fully modern port with industrial complexes. Many tourists visit nearby Do Son Beach Resort and Halong Bay. The mild climate keeps average temperatures between 15°C (59°F) and 31°C (88°F) year round.

Although this is one of Vietnam's major cities, most tourists come here only as a point of transfer in their journey to Halong Bay. If you are making the trip, take the morning train from Hanoi to Haiphong, then catch an afternoon boat to Bai Chai. Unfortunately, few budget travelers choose this route because the boat drivers are reputed to overcharge small groups. So, travelers usually take a scheduled group trip, or hire a car to go to Bai Chai overland.

ARRIVALS & DEPARTURES

Cat Bi Airport, *Tel. (84 31) 848309*, was built in 1950, during the French administration. **Vietnam Airlines**, *Tel. (84 31) 849242,* has daily non-stop flights between Haiphong and Ho Chi Minh City, with international connections from Ho Chi Minh City.

A 102 kilometer (63 mile) stretch of Highway 5 links Haiphong to Hanoi. Buses run to Haiphong.

Trains leave Hanoi every morning for Haiphong; the ride takes about 4 hours.

ORIENTATION

There is not much reason to be a tourist in Haiphong. The town is dingy and full of industry. Most visitors only pass through or use Haiphong as a stop-over to Halong Bay. The Do Son Beach is 20 kilometers (12 miles) out of the city.

GETTING AROUND TOWN

You can rent motor-bikes or cars with drivers at local hotels. The ferry dock is on Ben Binh Street.

WHERE TO STAY

BEN BINH (UNITOUR), *6 Ben Binh Street, Haiphong. Tel. (84 31) 857208 or 857222 or 857224. Singles $35/doubles $40.*

This 15 room hotel is part of the tour agency, UNITOUR. The facilities appear over-used and include a restaurant and swimming pool. The pier where ferries dock is located across the street.

DUYEN HAI HOTEL, *5 Nguyen Tri Phuong Street, Tel. (84 31) 842134 or 842157 or 842134, Fax (84 31) 841140. Singles $28 to $34/doubles $34 to $38.*

The Duyen Hai has a nice staff and is a reasonable hotel. The hotel has a restaurant and bar.

HOA BINH HOTEL, *4 Luong Khanh Thien Street, Haiphong. Tel. (84 31) 846907 or 846909. Singles $16/doubles $35.*

This 44 room tourist accommodation is popular in part because of its location near the train station, and in part because it offers budget rooms for under $10 per night. These are the unrenovated rooms without air-conditioning which you must request.

HOTEL DE COMMERCE, *62 Dien Bien Phu Street, Haiphong. Tel. (84 31) 847206, Fax (84 31) 842674. Singles/doubles $25 to $35.*

This French colonial building is a hotel located in the center of the town. The rooms are new and comfortable. This is the choice of many business travelers. Overall this hotel gives guests a good deal; it offers full amenities with comfortable surroundings at a reasonable price. Facilities include a business center. The hotel restaurant is highly recommended.

WHERE TO EAT

The recommended places to eat in Haiphong are **hotel restaurants**. The food at hotels, especially those in Do Son, is the best in the area. A word of caution: some tourists report becoming ill from local restaurants. Many travelers make a rule to eat only at the hotels in Haiphong.

SEEING THE SIGHTS

Du Hang Pagoda lies about 2 kilometers (1.25 miles) from the city center in Le Chan District. First built by a Ly Dynasty ruler at the turn of the first millennium AD, the pagoda has undergone frequent and extensive renovation. In the mid-thirteenth century King Tran Nhan Tong taught Buddhist doctrine here.

Hundreds of woodcarvings adorn the large **Hang Kenh Communal House** which was built in 1856. Folk songs and traditional ceremonies are performed here during a three day ceremony beginning on the sixteenth day of the second lunar month.

DAY TRIPS & EXCURSIONS

Many villages in the area have specialized artisans. For example, nearby **Bao Ha Village** is home to artists that make wood carvings. You can hire a car and driver from your hotel to visit one of these villages.

Spectacular limestone formations and evergreen forests draw visitors to **Cat Ba Island**, which lies about 30 nautical miles from Haiphong, in Halong Bay. The national park on Cat Ba Island remains, for the most part, untouched by development, although increasing numbers of tourists visit every season. Over 350 small islands divide Halong Bay from Bai Tu Long Bay. (See the next section on Bai Chai and Halong Bay for more information.)

DO SON RESORT

Do Son town is surrounded by two rivers, Lach Tray and Van Uc. The French settled the area as a resort. Do Son Beach, about 20 kilometers (12 miles) from Haiphong, attracts vacationers from Hanoi. Don Son Resort Road is full of new hotels. Annual buffalo fights are held in Do Son. The following are a few of the hotels in Do Son.

DO SON HOTEL, Do Son Resort Road, Haiphong. Tel. (84 31) 861331. Singles/doubles $30 to $50.

HAI AU HOTEL, Do Son Resort Road, Haiphong. Tel. (84 31) 861176. Singles/doubles $30 to $35.

HAI YEN HOTEL, Do Son Resort Road, Haiphong. Tel. (84 31) 861302. Singles $30 to $40/doubles $35 to $45.

VILLA 1/6, Do Son Resort Road, Haiphong. Tel. (84 31) 861408. Singles/doubles $30 to $40.

PRACTICAL INFORMATION

- **Foreign Trade Bank**, *Nguyen Tri Phuong Street, Haiphong. Tel. (84 31) 842658 or 842187.*
- **Foreign Trade Bank**, *11 Hoang Dieu Street, Haiphong. Tel. (84 31) 842187.*
- **Viet Tiep Hospital**, *Cat Ba Street, Haiphong. Tel. (84 31) 846227 or 846266.*
- **Post Office**, *5 Nguyen Tri Phuong Street, Haiphong. Tel. (84 31) 842371 or 842372.*
- **Haiphong Toserco**, *40 Tran Quang Khai Street, Haiphong. Tel. (84 31) 842288 or 842269 or 842517, Fax (84 31) 842977.* This office operates four hotels in Haiphong.
- **Haiphong Tourism**, *15 Le Dai Hanh Street, Haiphong. Tel. (84 31) 842432 or 842959 or 842957, Fax (84 31) 842674.*

•**Haiphong Tourist Service Company**, *40 Tran Quang Khai, Haiphong. Tel. (84 31) 842977.*

•**Vietnam Airlines Office**, *Cat Bi Airport, Haiphong. Tel. (84 31) 848309 or 845217.*

Halong Bay

Halong Bay is one of the highlights of northern Vietnam. Legends tell of a dragon who gorged out the 3,000 islands. The rocky caves and limestone cliffs amid vivid blue water and crisp air provide a spectacular backdrop for an invigorating trip. UNESCO proclaimed Halong Bay part of the world heritage.

Halong Bay can be reached by boat from Haiphong or overland from Hanoi. From Hanoi, the roads are in terrible condition and reconstruction and repair may cause delays, but the countryside is beautiful. You can see farmers irrigating rice fields with buckets tied between two lengths of rope; the buckets raise the water into the field when the ropes are pulled taught. As you approach the coast, mountains rise against the skyline.

At the mouth of the bay sits Halong City, which is divided into two halves and connected by a bridge. These two halves, Bai Chai and Halong City, provide tourists with accommodations and food. Most visitors choose to stay on the Bai Chai side of the city. The bars and restaurants along the beach can become lively when the town is full of tourists. Both towns have good restaurants and are excellent bases to explore the natural scenery in the area.

Quang Ninh Province is an industrial center. Heavy rains fall from June through August, when the temperature often exceeds 30°C. Winters are cool and the high humidity keeps a bite in the air.

ARRIVALS & DEPARTURES

Boats cross the bay from Haiphong to Bai Chai. The trip takes about three hours. If you choose to hire a boat to make the trip, keep in mind that tourists are often overcharged for the trip.

Regularly scheduled buses run from Haiphong to Halong City. Cafe tours operate mini-buses that make the rough ride, usually as part of a package tour.

Every Saturday Heli-Jet Vietnam, *15 Ngo Quyen Street (in the Hotel Sofitel), Hanoi, Tel. (84 4) 8266919, extension 8015, Fax (84 4) 8250168,* offers helicopter flights between Hanoi and Halong. Flights from Hanoi leave and 8:00 am and the flight leaves Halong at 3:30 pm and arrives at Hanoi's Gia Lan Airport at 4:15 pm.

ORIENTATION

Hotels literally line the street of Bai Chai, the western of the twin cities. Along the waterfront you will find plenty of restaurants and cafes that serve good, inexpensive food.

At the base of the city, the waterfront is full of tourist boats that make tours of the bay.

WHERE TO STAY

There are many inexpensive mini-hotels along the main street. You can find an adequate room for about $10 double occupancy. These hotels may be a bit run-down, but they offer an alternative to the more expensive tourist-style accommodations.

BACH LONG HOTEL, *Bai Chai Street, Halong City. Tel. (84 33) 846274. Singles/doubles $20 to $25.*

The Bach Long is on the waterfront. The hotel offers standard amenities and is thoroughly a tourist hotel, right down to the sprawling souvenir shop downstairs. Many rooms have good views of the bay. The hotel is a short walk from the area where boats dock.

HA LONG HOTEL, *Bai Chai Street, Halong City. Tel. (84 33) 846320 or 46321 or 46357, Fax (84 33) 846226. Singles $50/doubles $80.*

The 100 room Ha Long Hotel sits high over the bay. This is the closest to a luxury accommodation that you will find in the area. All the rooms have full amenities, such as air-conditioning and television. You will probably need a car to get around if you stay here.

HOANG LONG HOTEL, *Bai Chai Street, Halong City. Tel. (84 33) 846311 or 46318. Singles $32/doubles $35.*

This 56 beach-front hotel offers decent rooms at reasonable rates.

HERITAGE HOTEL, *88 Halong Road, Halong City. Tel. (84 33) 846888, Fax (84 33) 846718. Singles/doubles $80 to $100. Credit cards accepted.*

This large hotel claims a four star rating and offers the area's most comfortable accommodations. Amenities include tennis courts, a swimming pool, two restaurants and a business center - all this and views of the bay.

WHERE TO EAT

The Bay Chai side is full of cafes that serve good food and stay open late. Near the waterfront, waitpersons will run across the street to show you menus.

Two good choices in this area are **THUY TIEN RESTAURANT** and **PHUONG OANH RESTAURANT**.

SEEING THE SIGHTS

To enjoy the thousands of small, varied and beautiful islands, hire a boat to take you around Halong Bay. At Bai Chai and Hon Gai quay you can hire a boat to go explore the islands of Halong Bay. Or you can make arrangements through your hotel. Among the thousands of beautiful miniature islands you can visit by boat are the Wooden Stakes Grotto and the Poem Mountain.

Hang Dau Go Grotto (Wooden Stakes) has historical importance as well as beauty. This enormous, brilliantly colored grotto is in the middle of an island, 8 kilometers in Halong Bay. You must make a climb of nearly 100 steps, but it is well worth it to see the marvelous stalactites and stalagmites. During the 13th century, when the Mongols were pushing into the nation's borders, General Tran Hung Dao hid wooden stakes here which skewered the enemy as they advanced. The stakes were later moved to the Bach Dang River to cut off the enemy's advance there as well. The grotto was also used as a hide out for Vietnamese troops. Smaller grottoes such as Bo Nau (Pigeon) Grotto, Trinh Nu (Virgin) Grotto abound in the area.

Bao Tho Mountain (Poem Mountain) is a monumental tribute to Vietnam's literary history. The fifteenth century poet king, Le Thanh Tong, inspired by the beauty of Halong Bay, wrote the poem and ordered it carved into the mountain. The poem is 105 meters in length. You can see the poem if you approach the mountain by boat. Trails on the mountain lead to the top of the carving.

DAY TRIPS & EXCURSIONS

Mount Yen Tu was a sacred Buddhist retreat in the 13th century. It reaches a height of 1,068 meters. You reach Mount Yen Tu on Highway 18 thorough Uong Bi Town.

Cat Ba archipelago is a group of over 350 islands, the largest of which is a national park. Cat Ba Island has long, deserted beaches, limestone formations and is surrounded by coral reefs. Generally tourists make a day trip of Cat Ba Island by hiring a boat in Bai Chai for the day. However, tourists have had problems at Cat Ba Island. Reportedly unauthorized individuals have constructed gates and attempt to charge admission to the park.

PRACTICAL INFORMATION

- **Provincial Bank**, *Bach Dang Street, Bay Chai. Tel. (84 33) 825770.*
- **Quang Ninh Bank**, *Ben Doan Street, Quang Ninh Province. Tel. (84 33) 825434.*
- **Post Office**, *Bai Chai Street, Quang Ninh Province. Tel. (84 33) 846205.*

• **Halong Tourism**, *Bai Chai Street, Quang Ninh Province. Tel. (84 33) 846405 or 846272, Fax (84 33) 846287 or 846284.*
• **Quang Ninh Tourism**, *Bai Chai Street, Quang Ninh Province. Tel. (84 33) 846351 or 846318 or 846274, Fax (84 33) 846318.*

Lao Cai

Lao Cai, the provincial capital of Lao Cai Province, is a bustling town on the Chinese border. Steep mountains, wet weather, and diverse foliage characterize this province. Dao, H'mong, Tay and Thai populations reside in the mountains.

Few travelers stay in Lao Cai; most continue directly on to Sapa and highland villages or cross the border into China by train.

Direct train service only recently made it possible to travel directly to China without staying in Lao Cai. You can purchase tickets to China at the Hanoi train station. If you plan to return, be certain you cross at a border that permits re-entry.

WHERE TO STAY

SONG HONG GUEST HOUSE, *Pahn Boi Chiu Street. Tel. (84 20) 30004. Singles/doubles $5.*

This large white house with French doors is just a few steps from the bridge where you cross into China

PRACTICAL INFORMATION

• **Lao Cai Bank**, *Lao Cai Town. Tel. (84 20) 820167.*
• **Lao Cai Post Office**, *Tel. (84 20) 822335 or 822334.*

Sapa Town

Sapa sits high in the mountains of Lao Cai province, near the Chinese border. The small town is rapidly becoming a more frequented tourist destination, especially for those fond of trekking and curious about the minority people. Sapa's business community are ethnic Vietnamese. Travelers come here attend the weekend market and enjoy the beautiful natural surroundings.

At an elevation of 1650 meters above sea level, Sapa enjoys a cool climate, prone to fog and rain, with year-round high humidity. During the winter frost is common and the temperature may dip below freezing.

Jesuits first visited the site of Sapa in 1918. The French later settled Sapa in 1932, to build a mountain resort. Many of the chateaux from this period are hotels today.

Sapa is in one of the most spectacular areas in the county. The superb natural beauty is matched only by the kind indigenous people. Until recently, tourist were unknown to the area. Rapid development is spurring transformation in the region. This is one area that tourists should see before further changes take place.

Concerns are growing about the effects of foreign influence on the indigenous highlanders. Their traditions and ways of life that have existed for centuries now are open to foreign cultural influences.

ARRIVALS & DEPARTURES

By Bus

Buses run regularly from Hanoi.

By Cafe Tour

Private mini-vans run by the cafe tourist agencies in Hanoi make the trip on a regular basis. The trip takes about ten hours by car or mini-van, and at least fifteen hours by bus.

By Car

Highway 2 connects to Highway 70, running from Hanoi to Lao Cai. The trip takes about 10 hours. Many tourists prefer to hire a four-wheel drive vehicle and driver to venture into the highlands.

By Train

The train only goes as far as Lao Cai.

A tourist bus to Sapa meets the train at the station platform in Lao Cai. Move fast from the train to the bus, since the bus often fills to capacity. Local buses leave from the city center; they cost less but take longer and the vehicles are older.

Although the journey is only 38 kilometers (23 miles) from Lao Cai to Sapa, it can take from one to three hours on the winding mountain roads. You can hire a motor scooter to go all the way to Sapa, but since the roads are steep and curvy, this is inadvisable if you have any amount of baggage.

The post office on the main street in Sapa is the only place to buy return train tickets to Hanoi. For some reason the train station in Hanoi will not sell you a roundtrip ticket so when you purchase your return train ticket to Hanoi, the lady at the post office requires that you purchase a bus ticket to Lao Cai. She also tacks a commission on the train ticket.

The ticket lady is used to disgruntled customers, and since she has a monopoly, she does not attempt to please her clientele. The train ticket costs about $20, and the bus ticket $3.

The train ticket can be purchased upon arrival at the Lao Cai station; however if you do this you will probably miss the tourist bus to Sapa.

ORIENTATION

Sapa is so small that the hotels do not use street addresses. You will find guest houses and restaurants along the main street. The market runs along the narrow street behind the church. There are no taxis, cyclos or bicycles for hire, but the town is small enough to cover on foot.

WHERE TO STAY

Inexpensive

REST BANK'S HOUSE, *Dien Thoai Street, Sapa. Tel. (84 20) 871210. Singles/doubles $15.*

The hotel is new and the large, white building does appear to be in operation because the reception area is but an empty counter, and plastic still covers the furniture. Nevertheless, you can get a room with phone, TV and a balcony. Plenty of parking. The staff will go out of their way to let guests know they are welcome, although little English is spoken here.

HAM ROUNG GUEST HOUSE, *Sapa Town, Lao Cai Province. Tel. (84 20) 871305, 871304, 871251, 871312, Fax (84 20) 871303. Single/doubles $15.*

This group of yellow houses sits at the top of the steps which lead past the market. Satellite television is the only amenity which sets this hotel apart from others in Sapa. The rooms are clean and comfortable, but without heating. The showers do not offer a reliable hot water supply. Live snakes kept in a cage outside by the parking area are prepared as the specialty of the house. The restaurant is large enough to handle groups. To reach Ham Roung Guest House by car turn left on the alley which leads through the market just before the church. The stands make this a tight fit for mini-vans.

PLANNING COMMISSION GUEST HOUSE, *Khach San Ke Hoach, Sapa. Tel. (84 20) 871289. Singles/doubles $10.*

This yellow villa is lies half-way to the top of the steps leading past the market. The large comfortable rooms have private baths, and some have pleasant views of the town. The grounds lie on a hill and have park benches.

POST OFFICE HOTEL, *Sapa. Singles/doubles $15.*

The hotel sits on the street leading out of town. The large, yellow hotel has the city's post office in what appears to be the lobby. Actually the hotel lobby is in the restaurant. The rooms are simple; many have balconies that overlook the city. The Post Office Hotel hosted the Canadian ambassador during her 1996 visit.

Inexpensive
AUBERGE DANG-TRUNG, *Sapa, Lao Cai Province. Tel. (84 20) 871243. Singles (with shared bath) $3/doubles $10/triples $12.*

Both the hotel and restaurant are known simply as "Auberge." The small guest house has decent rooms with fireplaces. The restaurant has an outdoor terrace and serves vegetarian dishes, including spring rolls, noodle soup and French fries. Guests can have food brought to the rooms. The young staff strives to provide full tourist services including cars for hire, film and Sapa Guidebooks at reasonable prices, and currency exchange which takes travelers checks.

EASTERN GUEST HOUSE, *Sapa, Lao Cai Province. Tel. (84 20) 871246. Singles/doubles $6.*

Across from the school, about .5 km outside the town center on the road leading into town from Lao Cai.

THE GREEN BAMBOO CAFE, *Sapa, Lao Cai Province.*

This is a villa-style guest house on the far end of main street, but had not opened at the time of publication.

PHUONG NAM GUEST HOUSE AND CAFE, *Sapa, Lao Cai Province. Tel. (84 20) 871286. Singles/doubles $6.*

The claim to fame of the Phuong Nam is that it hosted the New York Times reporters who visited Sapa in 1995. The location is quiet and a terrace overlooks the houses built on the lower part of the hill of Sapa Town. The family that runs the guest house is very welcoming.

ORCHID HOTEL, *27 Thien Hung, Sapa. Tel. (84 20) 871239. Singles/ doubles $5.*

Budget travelers often wind up at this hotel, possibly because it stands on the main street which one walks past from the point that the local bus stops. The Orchid has been around for awhile and does not seem concerned by newer establishments charging similar rates. The rooms have hot water, but little upkeep

ROSE GUEST HOUSE, *Sapa, Lao Cai Province. Tel. (84 20) 871263. Singles/doubles $5.*

The proprietor offers 10 rooms with private baths and hot water which often fill-up on Friday and Saturday evenings. The Rose lies in the middle of what is becoming Sapa's "hotel row." Buses going to Lao Cai depart from here. Tasty small cakes and pastries (2,500 dong each) are sold by the reception desk.

STUDENT GUEST HOUSE, *Sapa, Lao Cai Province. Shared rooms for $4 for 1 bed/$2 per person for 2 beds.*

This dorm-style accommodation has the lowest prices in town. The showers are hot and the surroundings reasonably clean.

SON HA CHAMBRES A LOUER (Rooms for Rent), *Sapa, Lao Cai Province. Singles $5/doubles $6.*

Follow the street downhill past the soccer field New, reasonably comfortable accommodation run by a kind family.

SUNRISE HOTEL BINH MINH HOTEL, *Sapa, Lao Cai Province. Tel. (84 20) 871331.*

The six rooms with private baths are clean and very reasonably priced at $4 single, $6 double, and $8 triple. The friendly family that runs this mini-hotel makes it a pleasant place to stay. The sign in front advertises "frozen beer," but don't believe it—the beer in the cafe/reception area is just very cold.

VU KIEU TRINH, *Sapa, Lao Cai Province. Singles $5/doubles $6.*

It is easy to miss the Vu Kieu Trinh Hotel. The villa-style guest house is off the main road leading into town, across from the Post Office Hotel. Rooms are dark but new and clean. This is a good bet for budget travelers.

WHERE TO EAT

AUBERGE DANG-TRUNG, *Sapa, Lao Cai Province. Tel. (84 20) 871243.*

There are a few restaurants on Sapa's main street. The Auberge serves the best food in town. The soups are fresh and the portions are very large. The restaurant fills to capacity often in the winter.

SEEING THE SIGHTS

Trek up the country's highest mountain, **Fanxipan** and sleep under the stars. The journey takes 3-4 days, weather permitting. It is recommended that hikers bring their own sleeping bags and tents, as none are currently available, although some make the trip with only the small canopy shelter provided by the guide.

The trails are non-existent in some places so you must hire a guide ($20/day) who will bring food. In many cases, your guide will be a local who wants to make some money, but has no special qualification.

STAY WITH A VILLAGE FAMILY

For a taste of real life in the Northern Highlands, tours will take guests to minority villages where you spend the night with a family in one of the traditional long-houses. The villagers are very welcoming and enjoy bringing foreign guests into their houses. Families are known to have their children warm up the beds for foreign guests, although some houses have only mats on the floor. Auberge Dang Trung, Tel. (84 20) 871243, is the most reliable place to arrange tours and to rent cars or motorbikes.

SHOPPING

Shopping comes to you in Sapa. Although only a short while ago the highlanders were not used to foreigners, today they are overly enthusiastic about selling their wares to tourists. You will probably be approached by women selling embroidered shirts, hats and bags. And this will not let up until you're out of the city limits. The highland women carry their shops in the baskets on their backs; they hang around outside restaurants at all hours of the day and night in the hope of making just one more sale.

On Saturday, highlanders from all over the region gather for market day. In front of the church you will be able to buy a variety of handicrafts.

DAY TRIPS & EXCURSIONS

The **Silver Water Fall**, *Thac Bac*, is about 2 kilometers from Sapa. A long, suspended bridge made of bamboo is near the falls.

Just walking along the mountain roads and trails on foot is the best recreation. You can buy a small (but good) map of the area at the Post Office in the Post Office Hotel. Also, a guide book called Sapa is sold in town and will give you details on where to go for good hikes. The book costs $2 and is available at Auberge Dang-Trung and other guest houses.

The town of **Bac Ha** is about 70 kilometers from Sapa. On Sundays, the town comes alive with a regional market. The Hmong and Dao people crowd into the streets and onto a mound where horses and house wares are sold. Very few tourists currently visit this market. The best way to reach Bac Ha is by car from Sapa.

The **Auberge Dang-Trung** hotel in Sapa, *Tel. (84 20) 871243*, has vehicles for rent. They can arrange an old army jeep which carries four passengers to take you to Bac Ha to see the Sunday market. Also, you can rent a motor bike with a driver here or arrange for a guide to take you trekking.

BAC HA SAO MAI GUEST HOUSE, *Bac Ha. Tel. (84 20) 880288.*

This is the only guest house in Bac Ha. It is a house with clean and comfortable rooms and modern baths.

PRACTICAL INFORMATION

· **Post Office** *is in the Post Office Hotel, up the hill along the city's main street.*
· **Bus tickets** to Lao Cai can be purchased at the post office on the main street.

16. CAMBODIA

In the beautiful culture of the **Khmer** people, you find the roots of the better-known Thai style. Traditional architecture features graceful stacked roofs with flared ornaments streaming skyward like wisps of smoke from each corner. The Cambodian people are welcoming, and always offer visitors warm smiles.

The Khmer, which constitute over 90 percent of Cambodia's population, are originally from the Mekong Delta. Sometime around the year 800 AD, the Khmer empire established their capital in the area of Angkor Wat, near present-day Siem Reap. In the 15th century, after an attack by the Thai army, the holy city was abandoned. The capital of the Khmer empire moved to Phnom Penh. The city has remained the Khmer capital since that time.

In 1970, as the Nixon administration began to pull American troops out of Vietnam, the American involvement in Cambodia began. American forces carried out intense bombing raids on Cambodia through 1973. Phnom Penh fell to the Chinese-backed Khmer Rouge in 1975.

In the years that followed, over one million Cambodians were massacred under the regime of Pol Pot. Vietnamese forces invaded Cambodia and installed a government in 1979. This forced the Khmer Rouge into hiding and the fighting continued.

In 1989, the Vietnamese army withdrew from Cambodian land. This was followed by a tenuous cease-fire between the Khmer Rouge and the government. Free elections were held under United Nations supervision in 1993. The resulting coalition government consists of co-Prime Ministers Hun Sen, a former member of the Khmer Rouge who fled to Vietnam in 1977 and the Foreign Minister during the reign of the Vietnamese installed government, and Prince Ranariddh, son of King Norodom Sihanouk.

There are other past officials of the Vietnamese-backed government and former Khmer Rouge officers in the coalition government. The agreement also allowed the Kingdom of Cambodia's mercurial Prince

Norodom Sihanouk to take the title of King after agreeing not to run for political office.

Cambodia is in the midst of a struggle for stability and peace. The Khmer Rouge exists as an anti-government military faction that has control of much of northwestern Cambodia (near the Thai border). Recently, the factional divide and subsequent weakening of the Khmer Rouge, including the defection of senior Khmer Rouge officials such as Ieng Sary (the number 2 leader of the Khmer Rouge after Pol Pot), has offered hope that peace may be in the near future.

BASIC INFORMATION FOR CAMBODIA

Conditions in Cambodia are slightly more rugged than in Vietnam. You should bring a flashlight, since blackouts are commonplace. Although no vaccinations are required for entry, it is advisable to take precautions against malaria. Drink only bottled water and eat only cooked food.

Always carry an umbrella, sporadic and intense downpours are common throughout the year. The best season for a visit to Cambodia is during the winter, from November through March, when temperatures are mild.

*The **Cambodian Riel**, which trades at 2,500 to $1 US dollar, is the national currency. You may not need to exchange money, since dollars are accepted universally. Most banks and hotels will accept travelers checks. Credit cards are accepted in a select few establishments.*

ARRIVALS & DEPARTURES

Vietnam Airlines and the Cambodian national airline, **Royal Air Cambodge**, have daily flights from Ho Chi Minh City to Phnom Penh.

You can purchase your visa for Cambodia upon arrival. Simply fill out the forms at the counters just inside the airport terminal and pay the $20 fee. Or you may arrange the visa in Vietnam, at the Cambodian Embassy in Ho Chi Minh City or Hanoi. The fee is $26, however you have the option of securing a re-entry permit for Vietnam, which you cannot do at the Phnom Penh airport.

Pochentoung Airport in Phnom Penh is a modern, comfortable facility. You must pay an airport tax of $15 on international flights and $5 on domestic flights.

At the main doors a throng of taxi drivers will crowd around insistently offering rides. The safest way to get to the city is to go to the taxi desk in the departures terminal and hire an official airport taxi. The cost is higher than what you may negotiate with the independent drivers, but you will receive a safe ride with a non-threatening driver. The independent drivers are a risk. They may deliver you to the wrong address or lie to you in order to get you to stay at a hotel of their choosing.

GETTING AROUND CAMBODIA
By Land
It is inadvisable to travel through rural Cambodia, and on highways and trains, especially around Battambang. The Khmer Rouge guerrilla army still poses a threat in many areas of the country, and the thoroughfares are often the scene of sporadic violence.

Bicycling enthusiasts have been known to cross the Vietnam/Cambodia border by bicycle. This is risky at best and therefore highly inadvisable.

By River
Boats travel from Phnom Penh to Angkor Wat. While some adventure seekers may consider this method of transportation, the boat trips are imprudent. The main danger of these boats is that they are often seriously overloaded, sometimes holding a few times their capacity. The trip takes 15 hours, and is not a bargain-hunters dream since it costs $25 one-way. The boat dock is on Sisowath Quay.

TAKE CARE IN CAMBODIA
As you plan your trip to Cambodia, you should keep in mind that a small number of foreign travelers have been kidnapped and killed. While you are not likely to run into any trouble, particularly if you are in Phnom Penh and Angkor Wat, you should keep this in mind, especially if you intend to ride the trains or hit the highways.

You must also be aware of the land mine situation. Cambodians are sadly the victims of land mines on a daily basis. If you are in Phnom Penh and Angkor Wat and stay on the beaten path, you should not have a problem. Don't, however, attempt to cross an unknown field, for example, without being 100% sure that there are no mines.

Phnom Penh
Tranquil **Phnom Penh** has 1.2 million inhabitants. It sits at the meeting point of three major rivers: the Mekong, Sap and Bassac. During the French colonial period, many considered Phnom Penh the most beautiful city in Indochina. However, this city has been at the heart of some of the most horrible turmoil of the modern era.

Phnom Penh is a modern city that strives to overcome economic difficulty, and poverty is a serious problem. Prices, even for simple items such as food, are not low. Fruit and vegetables found in markets are significantly more expensive than in Vietnam.

International aid workers make up a large portion of the expatriate community in Phnom Penh. Cars are a common site, and motorbikes are uncommon.

ORIENTATION

Phnom Penh sits on the peaceful Mekong, Sap and Bassac Rivers. Street names were replaced with numbers some years ago, making a rather confusing grid that has streets from 100 to 500. Norodom Boulevard is the city's main thoroughfare. Sisowath Quay a major street which runs along the river where you will find most bars and restaurants that cater to foreigners.

GETTING AROUND TOWN

During the day you can easily get around by cyclo and a ride anywhere in the city should cost less than $.50. Motorbikes will pull up to you to offer a ride. Be sure to negotiate the cost of your ride before you depart. You can hire a motorbike with a driver for about $6 per day. And a car with a driver will cost about $30 per day and can be arranged through a tourist office.

After nightfall foreigners always should get around by taxi or private car. Crime against foreigners is on the rise, and it is advisable not to walk on the streets after dark.

WHERE TO STAY

BERT'S BOOKS AND GUESTHOUSE, *79 Sisowath Quay, Phnom Penh. Tel. (855 23) 360806. Singles $6.*

Bert advertises that his guest house is "the only truly cerebral hostelry in the kingdom," which is no doubt accurate. Upstairs from Bert's cafe and used bookstore, rooms are offered to travelers. The laid-back atmosphere and rugged clientele make Bert's a great place to stay if you can put up with the discomfort of no air conditioning and slightly grungy surroundings. Bert himself is a wealth of information about getting around the city and country.

HOTEL PASTEUR, *109 Pasteur Street, Phnom Penh, Cambodia. Tel. (855 15) 919234 or (855 17) 202655. Singles/doubles $15.*

Hotel Pasteur is located in center of the city, just a short walk from Sisowath Quay, the National Museum and Royal Palace. This mini-hotel is run by a man from France. The simple rooms offer air conditioning and private bathrooms. The staff is friendly and helpful, and seems to truly enjoy having foreign guests. The restaurant downstairs serves some of the best Cambodian food in town and is inexpensive.

LA PAILLOTE HOTEL, *234 Street 130, Phnom Penh, Cambodia. Tel. (855 23) 22151, Fax (855 23) 26153. Singles/doubles $20.*

Centrally located, this is a safe and decent accommodation. Rooms have air conditioning and private baths. La Paillote is a popular restaurants with tourists. The hotel is located on the corner of Street 130 and Street 53, close to the central market.

ROYAL PALACE HOTEL, *93 Monrieth Road, Phsar Damkor, Khan Toulkok, Phnom Penh. Tel. (855 23) 729992, Fax (855 23) 720008. Singles $60 to $150/doubles $65 to $200. Credit cards accepted.*

The Royal Palace is a modern tourist-class hotel with 123 rooms. The hotel has two restaurants, one Chinese and the other a rooftop bar-be-que and beer garden, and two lounges. Rooms feature satellite television, air conditioning and modern bathrooms. The hotel offers full services including room service, convention facilities and a health club and swimming pool.

SOFITEL CAMBODIANA HOTEL, *313 Sisowath Quay, Phnom Penh, Cambodia. Tel. (855 23) 26288, Fax (855 23) 26392. Vietnam office: (84 8) 293664. Singles $170/doubles $200. Credit cards accepted.*

When you step into the Cambodiana, you enter a world of luxury. The 214 rooms are of the highest international standard. The hotel is built with traditional Khmer style on the exterior; the interior offers fully modern rooms with the comfort of a Sofitel. On the premises you will find six restaurants, recreation areas, business center and a casino on a mini-cruise ship. The crystal-blue pool overlooks the river. Often the Sofitel offers weekend specials for double occupancy rooms, so call in advance to check.

WHERE TO EAT

Moderate

CACTUS, *French, 94 Sihanouk Street, Phnom Penh.*

The Cactus is a casual French restaurant with good, inexpensive food. During the day the Cactus becomes a sidewalk cafe with outdoor tables shaded by umbrellas.

ETTAMOGAH PUB, *Western, 154 Sihanouk Boulevard, Phnom Penh. Tel. (855 23) 62461.*

This informal sports bar is a popular hang-out for expatriates. The menu is basically pub food, like hamburgers and french fries. The satellite television shows the latest sporting events from around the world.

FOREIGN CORRESPONDENTS CLUB, *Western, 363 Sisowath Quay, Phnom Penh. Tel. (855 23) 427757, Fax (855 23) 427758.*

The FCC overlooks the river and is central to the foreign community. On the downstairs bulletin board you will find notices about local events. A small bookstore sells guidebooks, t-shirts and souvenirs. Upstairs, the restaurant overlooks the river. You can sit in the cool indoor dining room or on the breezy deck. The comfortable rattan interior, causal atmosphere and good food make the FCC a good place to dine and socialize. A wide array of English language periodicals are available to read.

IRISH ROVER, *Western, 87 Sihanouk Street at 51 Street, Phnom Penh.*

Irish-style bar with a pleasant outdoor area. A variety of imported beer is available as well as the Cambodian standard, Angkor beer. The pub food is good; give the fish and chips a try. The Irish Rover draws a good crowd on weekend nights.

SEEING THE SIGHTS

The **Independence Monument**, built in 1958, is a large replica of a Khmer temple. The clean lines and rhythmic beauty of the monument reflect the grandeur of Khmer architectural style. Most people just drive by the monument, which is located south of the Royal Palace at the intersection of Norodom and Sihanouk Boulevards. A walking visit allows you to take in the details, which hint at the beauty and magnificence of ancient Angkor Wat.

The Royal Palace is no longer open to the public. You can stroll by and appreciate the architecture. The spectacular array of buildings are designed to reflect the Bayon Temple at Angkor Wat.

The **Silver Pagoda** is located just south of the Royal Palace on Okhna Street. It is an ostentatious tribute to the Khmer government and religion. The pagoda's floor is composed of 5,000 silver blocks, yet the spectacular floor is overshadowed by the centerpiece: a gold Buddha decorated with over 9,000 diamonds.

The first temple of **Wat Phnom**, located at the northern end of Norodom Boulevard, dated from the late 14th century. Its name means "temple on the hill," and it is said that the city is named for Wat Phnom. Unfortunately, none of the ancient temple remains. The present structure dates from 1926. The main temple is surrounded by smaller temples, all of which are still in use.

Buddhism is practiced by the Khmer people, and you are likely to see saffron-robed monks strolling on the grounds of Wat Phnom and throughout the city.

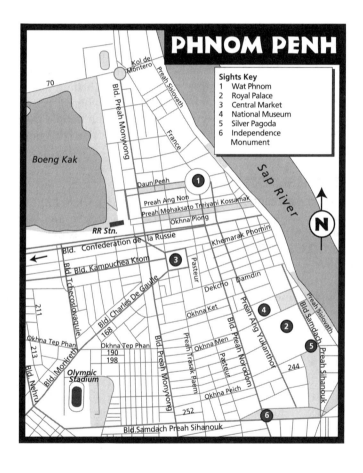

PHNOM PENH

Sights Key
1 Wat Phnom
2 Royal Palace
3 Central Market
4 National Museum
5 Silver Pagoda
6 Independence
   Monument

Museums

The beautiful **National Museum**, built in 1920, holds the nation's most exquisite ancient statues and carvings. Admission is $2. When you enter the outer courtyard, start your tour from the left. As you walk around the courtyard you will see statues that span the eras of ancient Khmer civilization, from its artistic beginnings to the modern era. Royal Palace woodcarvings made during the era of French colonial rule are the most modern artifacts in the musuem collection.

The **Tuol Sleng Museum** is housed in a jail which was first built as a school. Under Pol Pot the school was transformed into a prison which housed political prisoners, thousand of whom were brutally tortured and killed. The museum allows visitors to walk through the rooms where torture took place and see the inhumane conditions where prisoners were kept. The Khmer Rouge photographed many of the people they killed and photographs of the victims are on display. A visit to this museum is an extremely moving and powerful experience.

NIGHTLIFE & ENTERTAINMENT

Foreigners are cautioned against walking after dark in Phnom Penh. A few bars do stay open and enjoy a clientele of foreign residents, tourists and locals. All of the restaurants listed above are bars as well.

NAGA FLOATING CASINO, *behind the Sofitel Hotel on Sisowath Quay, Phnom Penh.*

Roulette, black jack, poker, baccarat cater to the elite of the area who have enough money to gamble. The campy atmosphere is accented by obnoxiously bright carpeting and an indulgent use of mirrors. The upper floors are reserved for VIP customers.

SPORTS & RECREATION

Mekong Island, *13 Eo Street, 240, Phnom Penh, Tel. (855 23) 427225,* offers daily tours of the Mekong River and villages close to Phnom Penh. The boat tour includes visits to villages on Mekong Island, lunch and a traditional dance show. The Mekong Island boat departs at 9:30 am and returns by 3 pm to the dock at the Hotel Sofitel. The tour costs $30 per person. Cruises along the Mekong at sunset are available for $7 per person.

You will find recreational facilities to suit most interests at the **International Youth Club**, *Duan Penh Street (west of Wat Phnom), Phnom Penh. Tel. (855 23) 427228, Fax (855 23) 427238.* The large outdoor pool is popular with locals and foreign residents alike. The gym has a variety of weights for workouts. Volleyball, tennis, squash and badminton courts are available. Hours for the pool, volleyball courts and gym: daily, 7 am to 8:30 pm; racquet courts: daily, 6 am to 8:30 pm. Visitors are welcome; a nominal fee is requested.

Seeing Hands Massage, *Maryknoll RBC Center, Wat Sarawan Pagoda, Street 178, Phnom Penh*, offers Japanese-style shiatsu massage. The masseurs are trained as part of rehabilitation program for blind Cambodians. The massage costs $2 per hour and is very popular with the expatriates living in Phnom Penh. You should stop by the pagoda to make an appointment at least one day in advance. Wat Sarawan Pagoda is located on Street 178, about one-half block east of Norodom Boulevard. Massage is given from 9 am to 7 pm, Monday through Saturday.

SHOPPING

Bert's Books, *Number 79 Sisowath Quay, Phnom Penh*, is more than a used bookstore, its an experience. Bert, a long-time expatriate, runs a guest house and cafe amid shelves of well-read paperbacks. This is a great place to hang out and meet the backpackers passing through Cambodia.

The centrally-located **Toto Bookstore**, *75 Norodom Boulevard, Phnom Penh, Tel. (855 23) 60625*, offers a good selection of English-language newspapers, as well as books about Cambodian history and politics.

You can purchase lovely handicrafts made by victims of the war at the **Giftshop of the National Center for Disabled Persons**, *3 Norodom Boulevard, Phnom Penh, Hours: 8 am to 5 pm*. Beautiful embroidery, purses, clothes and other gift items available. Not only do you take home a souvenir of high quality, but you assist the rehabilitation program by shopping here.

PRACTICAL INFORMATION

Banking
• **Indosuez Bank**, *70 Norodom Boulevard, Phnom Penh. Tel (855 23) 427233, Fax (855 23) 427235.*

English Language Newspapers in Cambodia
The **Bayon Pearnik**, *PO Box 54, Phnom Penh. Tel. (855 23) 917146*, is a free monthly which presents the more cavalier slant of the expatriate community,

Cambodia Today, *179 BEO Road 63, Boeng Keng Kong 1, Phnom Penh, Cambodia, Tel. (855 23) 360566, Fax (855 23) 360566*, is a full-color daily which offers articles of general interest.

The weekly **Cambodia Times**, *252 Monivong Boulevard, Phnom Penh, Tel. (855 23) 724297, Fax (855 23) 724497*, offers the most comprehensive scope of national events of English-language papers.

The essential visitors guide and map is found in the pull-out section of the **Phnom Penh Post**, *PO. Box 12-1074, Soi Suan Phlu Post Office, Bangkok, Thailand 10121, Tel. (855 23) 426568, Fax (855 23) 426568.*

Foreign Embassies

This is a partial list of foreign embassies in Phnom Penh:
- **Embassy of The United States**, *Number 27, Street 240, Phnom Penh. Tel. (855 23) 426436, Fax (855 23) 426437.*
- **Embassy of Australia**, *Number 27, Street 240, Phnom Penh. Tel. (855 23) 426000, Fax (855 23) 426003.*
- **Embassy of Canada**, *Number 11, Street 254, Phnom Penh. Tel. (855 23) 426001, Fax (855 23) 426003.*
- **Embassy of Great Britain**, *Number 27, Street 75, Phnom Penh. Tel. (855 23) 427124, Fax (855 23) 427125.*

Medical Assistance

- **Access Medical Services**, *Number 4, Street 432, Phnom Penh. Tel. (855 23) 364877.* This office has an English-speaking staff and expatriate doctor.
- **SOS International Medical Center**, *83 Mao Tse Tung Boulevard, Phnom Penh. Tel. (855 15) 912765 or 912964; Fax (855 23) 364127.* This facility offers 24-hour emergency care.

Travel Offices

- **Angkor Tourism**, *Number 178C, Street 63, Phnom Penh. Tel./Fax (855 23) 362169.*
- **Diethelm Travel**, *8 Sothearos Boulevard, Phnom Penh. Tel. (855 23) 426648, Fax (855 23) 426676.*
- **Royal Air Cambodge**, *24 Kramuon Sar Avenue, Phnom Penh. Tel. (855 23) 428830, Fax (855 23) 428806.* Royal Air Cambodge flies to Siem Reap, Battambang, Stung Treng, Rattanakiri, Koh Kong, Sihanoukville, Mondolkiri. The office is at the corner of Kramuon Sar Avenue and Monivong Boulevard. Flights to and from Vietnam are conducted in partnership with Vietnam Airlines.

To make travel arrangements in Vietnam, contact:
- **Diethelm Travel**, *1a Me Linh Square, District 1, Ho Chi Minh City. Tel. (84 8) 8294932.*
- **OSC Travel**, *143 Nguyen Van Troi Street, Phu Nhuan District. Tel. (84 8) 8441584.*

Tours from the United States

The US company **Classical Cruises & Tours**, *Tel. (800) 252 7745*, offers luxury tour packages which include Phnom Penh and Angkor Wat.

Siem Reap & Angkor Wat

Siem Reap in a small town just outside the ancient temple complexes of **Angkor Wat**. Although the area is commonly called Angkor, the 232 square kilometers are actually home to many temples built over a roughly five hundred year period, from the 9th to the 13th centuries.

Despite recurring problems with the Khmer Rouge guerrillas in rural Cambodia, Siem Reap is a relatively secure area. A military base and soldiers who act a guards at some areas of the temples help keep the area safe.

ARRIVALS & DEPARTURES

Royal Air Cambodge has seven direct flights from Phnom Penh to Siem Reap everyday. The flight from Phnom Penh takes about 45 minutes and the fare is $55 each way.

You may not be able to purchase your ticket from Phnom Penh to Siem Reap in advance, but this should pose no problem. When you arrive at the airport, simply proceed to the departures terminal. You can buy an open ticket at the counter, and you must pay in cash. U. S. Dollars are accepted. Most tourists choose not to fly thorough Battambang, since the sporadic fighting between the Khmer Rouge and government forces in the countryside presents a constant danger.

Once you arrive at the airport in Siem Reap, you will find a number of tourist information booths by the exit. You can get a taxi to town here, arrange transportation to the temple sites, and make hotel bookings. The ride from the airport to Siem Reap costs $2.

ORIENTATION

In order to see the many temples surrounding **Angkor Wat**, you must spend at least two days in Siem Reap. You can hire a car or motor bike and driver to take you to the sites. The main entrance to Angkor Wat is 8 kilometers from Siem Reap.

Siem Reap and the major ruins of Angkor Wat, Angkor Thom, Bayon, Ta Prohm and Banteay Srey are secured by the military, and are considered safe. A paved road connects these areas, and visitors report no problems. Do not be surprised if you see armed military personnel guarding some of the less visited temple sites.

There are many temples and ruins outside the secure area. Although the mysteries of the temples are tempting, it is dangerous to venture to any of these. Do not go through the western gate (to the Western Baray), even if your guide believes the area is safe—it is not.

Moreover, be certain to stay on the marked paths. Certain parts of the temples have unstable architecture. Throughout the area you will see renovation crews working on restoration projects. It is just a matter of time until all the structures are reconstructed. Land mines still pose a threat, so do not stray into the surrounding jungle.

GETTING AROUND TOWN

You should rent a car or motor bike with a driver to visit the temples. Usually your driver will pick you up in the morning, bring you back to Siem Reap for lunch and a rest, than take you back to the temples in the late afternoon, after the heat of the day has passed. Your hotel or guest house can arrange a motor bike with a driver. Some drivers speak English and can tell you quite a bit about the temples.

The road around the temples is about 25 kilometers (11 miles) long. Transportation by motorbike costs about $8 per day, and by car costs about $25 per day.

WHERE TO STAY

ANGKOR VILLAGE, *Wat Bo Road, Sangkat 4, Siem Reap. Tel. (855 63) 963503. Singles/doubles $40 to $50.*

This is the recommended place to stay in Siem Reap. Angkor Village is a lovely bungalow-hotel located in a quiet area of Siem Reap. The twenty modern wooden bungalows are comfortably furnished and have modern baths. The central lounge is a covered garden where drinks are served. Some rooms have only fans ($40 per night); most have air conditioning ($50 per night). The hotel restaurant serves breakfast, lunch and dinner; the food is excellent. Credit cards are not accepted.

DIAMOND HOTEL, *Vithei Achasva Road, Muang District, Siem Reap. Tel. (855 63) 963995. Singles $55/doubles $65.*

The Diamond is a large, tourist hotel. The air conditioned, modern facilities offer comfortable rooms. The front desk can arrange a car or motorbike with a driver for touring the temples. Credit cards are not accepted, but travelers checks are welcome.

Guest Houses

On Road Number 6 and along Sivutha Road you will find a number of inexpensive guest houses. Each house rents out rooms to tourists. Most rooms have a window air conditioning unit and a bathroom. Rooms cost about $10 per night. These guest houses seldom are booked-up, and are the most popular accommodation for budget travelers. A favorite of many travelers is listed below.

THE GREEN GARDEN HOME, *51 Sivutha Road, Siem Reap. Singles/ doubles $12 per night.*

The Green Garden is a small guest house run by a kind couple. The rooms are quite comfortable. Each has two double beds, air conditioning and a private bath, but no hot water. After a long day at the temples, you can relax in the beautiful back yard or on the patio.

WHERE TO EAT

There are a few cafes in the center of the city, near the market. However, they charge tourists extremely high prices. For less than a sub-adequate meal at one of these cafes, you can enjoy the city's best restaurant, the Green House.

THE GREEN HOUSE RESTAURANT, *Cambodian, moderate, 58 Mondol Street, Siem Reap. Tel. (855 15) 920467.*

The Green House is the nicest restaurant in town. The open-air dining room provides a refined yet casual setting for you to enjoy a meal. The menu features traditional Cambodian food. Thai, Chinese and French dishes are also available. The Green House is a good place to relax and socialize in the evening.

SEEING THE SIGHTS

Angkor Wat is the largest religious building in the world. At the turn of the first millennium AD, when London was a town of thirty-five thousand inhabitants, the city of Angkor held nearly one million. About seven hundred years ago the city of Angkor was at its peak.

In the 15th century, the inhabitants of the area deserted Angkor Wat and the Khmer capital moved to Phnom Penh. The reasons for the city's abandonment remain a mystery. An invasion by the Thai army played a central part to forcing the Khmer out, but speculation cites the possibility of epidemics or economic decline as important factors.

The city was unknown to the West until 1860, when the French scientist and explorer, Henry Mouhot, came across Angkor Wat. Mouhot died from illness less than a year later, but word of the fabulous city covered in jungle spread quickly. Travelers began to visit the area.

The Main Temples

Angkor Wat, strongly influenced by Hinduism, is the largest temple in the world. The building is immense, covering an area of 1 kilometer (nearly one-half mile) in width and .8 kilometer (nearly one-third mile) in length. To enter Angkor Wat you walk over two large bridges, past the 200 meter (one-eighth mile) wide moat.

Angkor Wat was built in the 12th century by King Suryavarman II. The temple is meant to resemble the image of sacred mountains of Hindi mythology. There are further mysteries of Angkor Wat. The temple is aligned with the cycles of the sun and moon. On the summer solstice the sun rises directly over the main tower. The reason for this is unknown.

Angkor Thom

The second large temple complex is **Angkor Thom**. A wall surrounds the seven square mile (18.2 kilometer) complex. Angkor Thom was built in the 11th century by King Jayavarman. The road through Angkor Thom passes through the ancient city gates, which have magnificent carvings.

Like Angkor Wat, the buildings are constructed of stone, and no mortar was used. A significant difference between the two is that Angkor Thom is dedicated to Buddhism.

The central temple in Angkor Thom is Bayon. Here 50 temple towers, each carved with four faces, create an awe inspiring atmosphere. Visitors often come to watch the sunrise slowly illuminate the giant stone faces. These faces look in all directions to protect the temple. Some scholars believe the faces are the image of the king himself, others believe them to be the Buddha.

Angkor Thom contains 2 older temples, both of which are undergoing reconstruction. Phimeanakas was built over the span of a century by no less than three rulers: Kings Rajendravarman, Jayavarman and Suryavarman I. The temple was completed during the 11th century. Baphoun dates from the reign of King Udayadityavaraman II in the early 11th century. Both of these temples are influenced by Hinduism.

Ta Prohm

Ta Prohm is also a monument from the reign of King Jayavarman VII, and was constructed at the beginning of the 13th century. This temple was built by the king after the completion of Angkor Thom, and is the latest of the great monumental construction period. The complex is intended to pay tribute to the mother of King Jayavarman VII. Giant trees growing out of the Ta Prohm temple structures create a story-book atmosphere.

One of the most important things to remember while visiting Angkor is to stay on the paths and trails at the sites. The temples are secure, and you should expect to see armed soldiers in the town and at the remote areas of Angkor. However, you could put yourself in danger by leaving the trafficked area. Also, within the temples some areas are dangerous because of the instability of the ancient architecture.

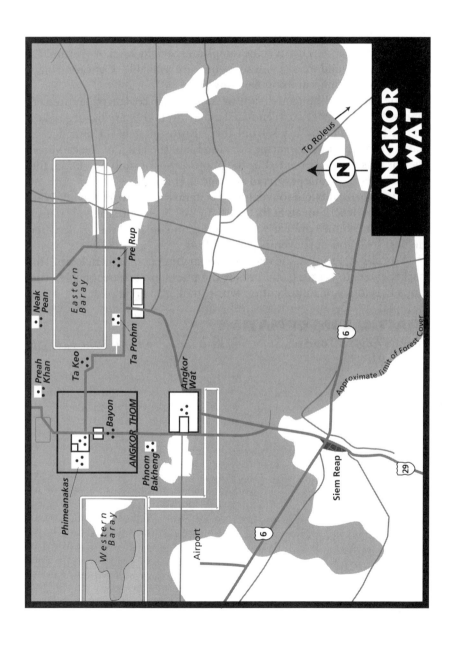

SHOPPING

You should purchase one of the English-language guidebooks which are available throughout the town and at the temples. These provide in-depth analysis of the history and art of the temples.

You will find merchants at the temples, especially Angkor Wat and Ta Prohm, where cold drinks and souvenirs are available. Cotton sarongs and temple rubbings are popular souvenirs.

The temple rubbings are made by rubbing charcoal on paper pressed against the carvings. (You will noticed that many of the carvings at Angkor are buffed to a shiny black from this.) Unfortunately the practice of making the rubbings is wearing down some of the relief of the carvings. For this reason, it is better to buy the photocopies of rubbings. Often the photocopies have sharper detail and better contrast.

A group of cafes and souvenir kiosks stands across from Angkor Wat. You can get decent meals at these restaurants, which are the only places to eat if you venture out early to catch the sunrise. And the kiosks offer the best selection of souvenirs you will find.

You also can shop at the main market in the center of Siem Reap. The market caters to tourists, and usually the prices are not negotiable. The shops here offer beautiful cotton fabric, baskets, and jewelry.

PRACTICAL INFORMATION

• **Bopha Angkor Tourism**, *Street Number 6, Tel. (855 15) 913839, Fax (855 15) 913839.*

INDEX

Airlines, 51, 62-63, 55; domestic, 55
Airport Tax, 45
American Chamber of Commerce, 81
An Giang Province, 131, 133-134
Angkor Wat (Cambodia), 29, 33, 49, 55, 263-268 map 267
Angkor Thom (Cambodia), 263, 266
Animal life, 26, 33
Antiques, 45
Ao dais, 14, 27, 204
Area codes for cities, 75
Assembly Halls (Chinese), 185, 189

Ba Ho Falls, 179
Ba Hoa Mountain, 180
Ba Na, 29
Bac Bo, 24
Bac Ha, 18, 221, 252
Bac Lieu, 19, 139-140
Bac Mo Resort, 218
Bach Dang, 241
Baggage, 45
Bai Chai, 17, 241, 244, 245-246
Bani, 165
Banking, 71
Bao Ha Village, 243
Bargaining, 46
Bat Trang, 238
Bayon (Cambodia), 263, 266
Beaches, 24
  Ca Na, 151
  Cua Dai, 191
  China Beach 194, 201
  Lang Co, 202, 218
  Mui Ne (Coco Beach), 24, 91, 146, 147
  Nam O, 194
  Non Nuoc, 202
  Thuy Dong Beach, 24, 146, 152

Truong Khoe, 139
Vung Tau, 145
Bicycling, 60, 98, 164, 174, 222; trips, 78
Bien Ho Lake, 169
Binh Chau Hot Springs, 145
Bird sanctuaries, 19, 130
Black Lady Mountain, 127
Botanical gardens 116, 154, 160
Bronze drums, 37
Buddhism, 29, 31, 33, 34, 87, 120, 242
Budget traveling, 46, 98
Buon Don, 29
Buon Ma Thout, 20, 29, 165-168
Bus travel, 56-57
Bush, George, 41
Business hours, 63

Calendar, 63
Cam Pho Communal House, 189
Cam Ly Falls, 160
Cambodia, 29,33, 40, 41, 130, 133, 253-268; Arrivals and Departures, 254; Getting Around, 255; Precautions, 255; Visa, 254
Cantho 18, 19, 26, 134-137
Cantho University (see Universities)
Cao Dai Temples, 18, 199
Cao Daism, 31
Cape Saint Jacques (see Vung Tau)
Cat Ba Island, 16, 243, 246
Car Travel 51, 54, 57, 64, 99
Catholicism, 31
Central Highlands, 14, 20-21, 26, 29, 33, 43, 57, 84, 165-172, 179
Central (coastal) Lowlands, 26
Cham, 12, 29, 31, 33-36, 37, 130, 173, 180, 183, 191, 194; architecture,

33-36; museum, 200;
Cham temples, 20, 21
  Ba Toc (Hoa Lai), 35, 150
  Bahn It, 36, 183
  My Son, 21, 35, 191-193, map 192, 202
  Po Hai, 35, 148
  Po Klun Gari, 35, 150
  Po Nagar, 34, 36, 177
  Po Rome, 36, 150
  Thap Doi, 36, 182
Champa, 29
Chau Doc, 133
Cheo (see opera)
Chicken Village, 163
Children (tourists), 46
China 15, 24, 26, 29, 38, 40, 165, 184; border with Vietnam, 59, 247; travel, 59, 247
China Beach, 194, 201
Chinese language, 30
Cholera, 48
Cholon (Chinatown), 30
Christianity, 26, 31, 120
Citadels, (Hanoi) 231, 236, (Hue), 212-213
Climate, 42-43
Clothes, 66 what to pack, 43-44
Coco Beach (see beaches)
Coconut Monk, p. 132
Committee for Cooperation and Investment, 50
Communism, 39
Con Dao Islands, 94, 146, 152
Consulates in Vietnam, 65
Confucianism, 26, 37, 189
Cost of living and travel, 64
Crime, 60
Cruises, 51-52
Cu Chi Tunnels, 127
Cu Mong Lake, 183
Customs, 45; Canada, 44; US, 44
Currency: see money
Cyclo, 60, 99, 173, 222

Dak Lak Province, 20, 29
Dakto battlefield, 171

Dalat 14, 20, 60, 79, 90, 92, 154-164
  Entertainment, 162
  Map, 161
  Seeing the sights, 159-160
  Shopping, 162
  Travel offices, 164
  Where to eat, 158-159
  Where to stay, 155-158
Dam Bri Waterfalls, 163
Dan Kia Lake, 164
Danang, 39, 49, 194-203
  Banks, 203
  Entertainment, 200
  Seeing the sights, 199-200
  Travel offices, 203
  Where to eat, 199
  Where to stay, 195-199
Dao, 29, 247
Dao Tan Opera Company, 180, 183
Dehydration, 69
Demilitarized Zone (DMZ), 21, 39, 56, 200, 201
Dengue fever, 48
Diarrhea, 69
Diem, Ngo Dinh, 40, 116
Dien Tho Palace, 213
Do Son Resort, 241, 243
Doi Moi, 41
Dong Da, 219, 220
Dong Duong, 194
Dong Khanh (Emperor), 215
Dong Noi Cave, 33
Door-eyes, 189
Doumer Bridge, 229
Dragon boats, 206, 217
Drink, 88-89
Duong Dong, 138
Dutch, influence of, 38

Ede, 29, 165
Electricity, 64-65
Embassies in Vietnam, 65-66, 240
Embassy of Canada in Hanoi, 65, 240
Embassy, of US in Hanoi, 41, 50, 66, 74, 240
Embassy, of Vietnam in US, 41, 49
English language, 30

Ethnic groups, 27
Etiquette, 66, 73

Faifo: see Hoi An
Fall of Saigon, 40
Fanxipan 18, 22, 251
Farming, 22, 24
Fax, 74
Festivals (see holidays)
Fish sauce (nuoc mam), 139
Fishing, 26, fishing villages, 139
Floating houses, 130
Floating markets, 136
Food, 64, 86-89, 189, 204, 223
French, influence of, 12, 14-15, 24,
    27, 38, 88, 113, 154, 165, 144, 152,
    184, 194, 210, 219, 220, 247;
    language, 30
Friendship Cultural Palace, 236
Fruit, 87

Gia Long, 38, 39, 182, 203; tomb, 213
Golf, 15, 79, 122, 148, 236
Greene, Graham, 90, 100, 226
Guest houses, 210
Guides, 57

Hai Van Pass, 29, 194, 202
Haiphong, 16, 26, 241-244
Halong Bay, 16, 22, 24, 241, 244
Halong City, 244, 245
Han Dynasty, 33, 37
Hang Dau Grotto, 246
Hang Kenh Communal House, 242
Hanoi, 15, 16, 21, 26, 37, 42, 55. 59,
    79, 91, 204, 219-240
    Art Galleries, 237
    Banks, 238
    Entertainment, 236
    Hanoi Hilton (POW jail) 15, 220
    Lakes, 219, 221, 222, 229, 233
    Old Quarter, 222-225, 229-234
    Map, 230-231
    Seeing the sights, 229-236
    Shopping, 229, 237-238
    Sports and recreation, 236-237
    Temples and pagodas, 229, 234

Travel offices, 240
Transportation, 220-221
Where to eat, 227-228
Where to stay, 222-227
Zoo, 234
Hash House Harriers, 80, 123
Hau Giang Province, 131, 134
Hau Sanh, 150
Hay Tay Province, 238
Health concerns, 68
Health insurance, 69
Hepatitis, 48
Hien Lam Pavilion, 213
Hien Long Bridge, 201
Highways, 58, 78, 200
Hinduism, 31-32, 33, 120, 119, 133
History, 33-41
HIV, 68, 69
H'mong, 28-29, 72, 247
Hoa, 194
Hoa Hoa, 31
Hoan Kiem Lake (see Hanoi, lakes)
Hoang Lien Mountains, 24
Ho Chi Minh, 39, 204
Ho Chi Minh City (Saigon), 12, 18,
    20, 21, 26, 30, 42, 55, 59, 61, 78,
    79, 90, 96-130, 141
    Art Galleries, 124
    Banks 128
    Entertainment, 120-122
    Districts 97-98,
    Map, 114-115
    Religious services, 120
    Seeing the sights, 113-117
    Shopping, 124-127
    Sports and recreation, 122-124
    Temples and pagodas, 118-119
    Travel offices 128
    Useful phone numbers 129
    Transportation 97, 98-99
    Where to stay, 100-107
    Where to eat, 107-112
Ho Chi Minh Trail, 22, 23, 200
Ho Chi Minh Mausoleum (Hanoi) 16,
    233
Hoi An, 184-194, 194, 203
    Seeing the sights, 188-190

Shopping, 191
Where to eat, 187-188
Where to stay, 186-187
Hoi An Tourist Service and
    Monument Management Author-
    ity, 185
Holidays: festivals, 67-68, 150, 242;
    public, 64
Hon Chang Rock, 178
Hong Kong Vietnam Yacht Race, 80
Horse racing, 82
Hospitals, 70, 239
Hotels, 45-47; best recommendations,
    90, colonial, 92-93
Hoi An 13, 38
Hue, 14, 21, 42, 93, 200, 201, 219
    Banks, 218
    Citadel, 212-213
    Entertainment, 217
    Map, 205
    Seeing the sights, 212-217
    Shopping, 217-218
    Tombs of the kings, 203
    Transportation, 206-207
    Where to stay, 207-211
    Where to eat, 211-212
Hung Dynasty, 37

Immunizations, 47-49, recom-
    mended, 47, Cambodia, 254
Independence monument,
    (Cambodia), 258
Imperial Tombs, 21, 213-215, map,
    214
India, influence of, 29, 33. 34
Indira Ghandi Park (Hanoi), 232
Indochina Peninsula, 22
International Relief Organizations,
    239
Islam, 32, 33, 120, 133
Islands, 94, 132

Japanese Covered Bridge, 189
Japanese Encephalitis, 47-48
Jayavarman, King (Cambodia), 266
Jesuits, 30

Khai Dinh (Emperor), 215
Khanh Hoa Province, 173
Khmer, 11, 12, 26, 29, 34-35, 73, 130,
    136, 138, 253, 258
Khmer Rouge, 41, 253-254, 263
Kim Phung Hill, 214
Kien Giang Province, 137-139
Kontum, 20, 170

Lak, 165
Lak Lake, 165
Lake of the Sighs, 163
Lam Dong Province, 154
Land area, 22
Lang Co, 202, 218
Langbiang (Lady) Mountain, 164
Language classes, 52
Language groups, 27-28, 30
Lao Cai 16, 18, 221, 247, province,
    247
Laos, 22, 165
Laquerware, 73
Lat, 164
Le Loi, 38
Le Loi Street (Ho Chi Minh City),
    113
Le Son Square (Ho Chi Minh City),
    113
Legal issues, 73
Lenin park, 235
Long Hai, 24
Long Xuyen, 134
Love Markets, 18, 28, 252
Ly Dynasty, 37, 38

Magazines, 70-71, 77
Malaria, 47-48
Marble Mountain, 194, 202
Marathons, 80
Marriage, 68
Maughm, Somerset, 90, 100, 226
Medicine, availability of, 44
Mekong Delta 12-13, 18-20, 23, 26.
    29, 78, 130-140, 253
Mekong River (see Rivers)
Meat, 87

M.I.A's, 41
Minh Hai Province, 139
Ming Mang (Emperor), 213-214, 219
Ming Dynasty, 38
Mnong, 165, 194
Money, 44, 45, and banking, 71
Monkey Island, 177
Mongol Khans, 34-35, 37
Mosques: Central (Ho Chi Minh
    City), 119
Motorbikes, 58
Motorcycle tours, 54
Mountain ranges, 22, 24, 29
Mui Ne Beach (see beaches)
Muong, 29
Museums
    Art (Hanoi), 234, (Ho Chi Minh
        City), 116
    Ceramics (Hoi An), 188
    Cham (Danang), 200
    Ethnic Minority (Buon Ma Thout),
        167
    History, (Hanoi) 233
    History (Ho Chi Minh City), 117
    Ho Chi Minh, Hanoi) 235, (Hue),
        217
    Hoi An Museum (Hoi An), 188
    Hue, 213
    Lac Giao Communal House
        (Buon Ma Thout), 167
    Military (Hanoi), 234
    My Lai Massacre (My Lai), 183
    Rach Gia (Rach Gia), 138
    Revolution (Ho Chi Minh City),
        117
    Tong Duc Thang (Long Xuyen),
        134
    War Crimes (Ho Chi Minh City),
        117
    Women's (Hanoi), 233
    Women's Traditional House (Ho
        Chi Minh City), 117
Museums (Cambodia), 258
My Lai Massacre, 183
My Son, 21, 35, 191-193, map 192,
    202
Mytho 18, 131-132

Nam Giao Arena, 215
Names, 72
National Theater (Ho Chi Minh City),
    113
Newspapers, 72
Nguyen Dynasty, 14, 203, 219
Nguyen Hue (see Gia Long)
Nghe An Province, 27
Ngu Binh Hill, 218
Nha Trang, 14, 20, 36, 43, 49, 81, 92,
    92, 93, 154, 173-179
    Seeing the sights, 177
    Shopping, 179
    Sports and recreation, 178-179
    Where to eat, 176
    Where to stay, 174-176
Northern Highlands 15, 24, 28-29, 43,
    84, 247-252
Notre Dame Cathedral, 113

Oc-Eo, 19
O-du, 27
Oceanographic Institute, 178
Open ticket buses, 56-57, 174, 185
Opera (Cheo), 236, (Tuong), 180
Opera House (Hanoi), 232
Orchids, 132
Overseas Chinese, 30
Overseas Vietnamese, 30

Pagodas: see Temples and pagodas
Paris Agreement, 40
Passport, 50, if stolen 74, 239
Pasteur, Louis, 154
Palace of Harmony, 213
Paulo Condor Prison, 152
Perfume Pagoda, 56, 238
Perfume River, 20-204
Phan Rang, 20, 35, 149-151
Phan Thiet, 35, 43, 78, 91, 146-148
Pharmacies, 69
Phnom Penh, 55, 253-262
    Banking, 261
    Map, 259
    Seeing the sights, 258
    Shopping, 261
    Sports and recreation, 260-261

Travel offices, 262
Where to eat, 257
Where to stay, 256-257
Pho Binh Cave, 33
Phu Quoc Island, 19, 94, 138-139
Phu Quy Island, 95, 153
Pleiku, 20, 168
Po Co River, 170
Po Nagar (see Cham temples)
Population, 22
Post Office, 72
Pot, Pol, 40, 253-254, 260
Prenn Waterfalls, 163
Provinces, 26, 131, 194, 195, 238, 244, map 25, of the Central Highlands, 154, of the Mekong Delta, 131-140
Public transportation, 60

Quang Nam Province, 194, 195
Quang Ninh Province, 244
Quang Trung, Emperor, 180, 182
Qui Nhon, 20, 36, 180-184
Quoc Hoc School, 204

Rach Gia, 137-138
Radio, 72
Restaurants, 63
Reunification Express, 59
Reunification Hall (Ho Chi Minh City), 116
Rivers, 23, 135
    Duong River, 23
    Mekong River, 13, 19, 23, 130, 256
    Red River, 23, 219
d'Rhodes, Alexander, 30, 184
Royal Palace (Cambodia), 258
Running, 80, 122

Sa Huynh, 184
Saigon: see Ho Chi Minh City
Sailboarding, 179
Sailing 80-81, 122, 148, tours, 54
Saint Joseph's Cathedral, 232
Sam Mountain, 19, 133
Sapa 16-18, 83, 93, 221, 247-252

Scuba diving, 81, 173, 178
Seafood, 87
Seeing Hands Foundation (Cambodia), 261
Sen, Hun, 253
Siem Reap (Cambodia), 253, 263-268
Skin Diving, 11, 81
Sihanouk, King (Cambodia) 253
Silk, 73, 125, 163, 190, 194, 200, 237
Silver Pagoda (Cambodia), 258
Silver Waterfall, 252
Soc Trang, 19
Song Huong (see Perfume River)
South China Sea, 11, 26, 29, 173, 194
Snorkeling, 81, 173, 177, 178
Spectator sports, 82, 122
Sports, 78-85
Statue of the Martyr of Vietnam, 200
Staying out of trouble, 73
Study Tours, 52
Suryavarman, King (Cambodia), 266
Swimming pools, 82, 122

Ta Prohm (Cambodia), 263, 266
Tai, 27, 28
Tan Son Nhat Airport (Ho Chi Minh City), 96
Tang Dynasty, 34
Tang Tho Library, 213
Tang Phong Island, 132
Tay, 247
Tay Son, 38, 182, rebellion, 182, 185
Taxis 61, 97, 99, 222
Tay Ninh, 18
Tea, 47
Telegrams, 74
Telephones, 47, 75
Television, 76
Temples and pagodas
    Cao Dai (Danang) 199, (Tay Ninh), 127
    Chau Ba Bhau (Ho Chi Minh City), 118
    Chau Phap Hoa (Vung Tau) 146
    Chuc Thanh, 191
    Dieu De (Hue), 216
    Dien Huu (Hanoi), 234

Du Hang (Haiphong), 242
Citadel (Hue), 213
Giac Lam (Ho Chi Minh City), 119
Guangong (Hoi An), 190
Hai Ba Trung (Hanoi), 235
Hai Tang (Hoi An), 190
Jade (Hanoi), 229
Kneeling Elephant (Hanoi), 234
Lady Chau Xe (Chau Doc), 19, 133
Linh Phouc (Dalat), 163
Linh Son (Dalat), 160
Linh Ung, 202
Literature (Hue) 216
Long Son (Nha Trang), 177
Mariamman (Ho Chi Minh City), 119
Munirangsyaram (Cantho), 136
Ngoc Hoang (Ho Chi Minh City), 118
One Pillar (Hanoi), 234
Ong Bac, (Cantho), 138
Perfume, (Hanoi), 56, 238
Phat Lon (Cantho) 138
Phuoc An Hoi Quan, (Ho Chi Minh City), 119
Phung Son Tu, (Ho Chi Minh City), 118
Quan Thanh, (Hanoi), 234
Quang An, (Ming Huong) (Hoi An), 190
Quang Minh Nith, 202
Quan Su, 232
Stone Lady, 232
Thap Thap, 183
Thich Ca Phat Dai, (Vung Tau) 144
Thien Hau Pagoda, (Ho Chi Minh City), 119
Thien Mu (Hue), 215, 216, 217
Thien Phuc, (Hanoi), 238
Thien Vien Chuoy Chiey, (Vung Tau), 146
Thien Vuong Co Sat, (Dalat), 160
Tran Family, (Hoi An), 190
Tran Hung Dao (Ho Chi Minh City), 118
Tran Quoc, (Hanoi), 234

Vien Giac, (Hoi An), 190
Vinh Nghiem (Ho Chi Minh City), 118
West (Hanoi), 238
Xa Loi, (Ho Chi Minh City), 118
Tennis, 83, 122, 237
Tet, 14, 63, 154
Tet Offensive, 40
Thai (minority), 247
Than Long, 219
Thanh Toan Bridge, 216
Thieu Tri (Emperor), 214
Thuong Hai Village, 215
Thuy Dong Beach (see beaches)
Thuy Toan, 216
Tiger Arena, 215, 216
Time zone, 76
Tipping, 76
Tombs of the Kings (See Imperial Tombs), 21, 213-215, map, 214
Tours, 52-55, 179; cafe tours 55, 56, 64, 98, 136, 248
Train, 21, 52, 58, 247; classes of seats, 59
Tra Kieu, 193, 194
Tran Dynasty, 37
Tran Nhan Tong, King, 242
Travel agents, 52
Travel offices (in Vietnam), 54
Travel Permits, 50
Trekking, 83, 169, 251
Truc Bach Lake, 222
Trung Family House, 188
Trung Sisters, 37
Truong Song Mountains, 22
Tu Duc (Emperor), 214, 215
Tuong (see opera)
Typhoid, 48

United Nations, 40, 41
Universities: Cantho, 136; Hanoi, 41, 52
US Government travel publications, 49-51

Valley of Love, 164
Vegetarian food, 87
Viet Cong, 39

Viet Kieu, 30, 49
Viet Minh, 39
Vietnamese constitution, 27
Vietnamese language, 27, 30
Vietnam War, 15, 39-41, 116, 194,
    201, 219
Villages, 26
Visas
    Business, 50
    Exit, 239
    Extension of, 50, 239
    Tourist, 49
Voice of Vietnam, 72
Vung Tau, 26, 140-145
    Seeing the sights, 144-145
    Where to eat, 143-144
    Where to stay, 142-143

Wat Phnom (Cambodia), 258
Water, drinking, 44, 64, 76, 89

Water puppetry, 236
Waterfalls, 154, 163, 179
Wedding Market (see love markets)
Weights and measures, 77
West Lake (see Hanoi, lakes)
Wetlands 12-13
White Palace (Vung Tau), 145
Wine, 89
Working out, 84-85, 122
World War II, 27, 194

Yachting, 80
Yali Waterfall, 171
Yersin, Dr. Alexander, 154, 173;
    tomb, 179

Zoos
    Ho Chi Minh City, 116
    Hanoi, 234

FROM THE PUBLISHER

Our goal is to provide you with a guide book that is second to none. Please remember, however, that things do change: phone numbers, prices, addresses, quality of food served, value, etc. Should you come across any new information, we'd appreciate hearing from you. No item is too small, so if you have any recommendations or suggested changes, please write to us at the address below.

Have a great trip!

Vietnam Guide
Open Road Publishing
P.O. Box 20226
Columbus Circle Station
New York, NY 10023

TRAVEL NOTES

TRAVEL NOTES

TRAVEL NOTES

TRAVEL NOTES

TRAVEL NOTES

TRAVEL NOTES

TRAVEL NOTES

TRAVEL NOTES

TRAVEL NOTES

OPEN ROAD PUBLISHING
Your Passport to Great Travel!

*Going abroad? Our books have been praised by **Travel & Leisure, Booklist, US News & World Report, Endless Vacation, American Bookseller,** and many other magazines and newspapers!*

Don't leave home without an Open Road travel guide to one of these great destinations:

Austria Guide, $15.95	**Bahamas Guide**, $13.95
Czech & Slovak Republics Guide, $16.95	**Belize Guide**, $14.95
France Guide, $16.95	**Bermuda Guide**, $14.95
Holland Guide, $15.95	**Central America Guide**, $17.95
Ireland Guide, $16.95	**Costa Rica Guide**, $16.95
Italy Guide, $17.95	**Guatemala Guide**, $17.95
London Guide, $13.95	**Honduras & Bay Islands Guide**, $15.95
Paris Guide, $12.95	**Southern Mexico & Yucatan Guide**, $14.95
Portugal Guide, $16.95	**China Guide**, $18.95
Rome Guide, $13.95	**Hong Kong & Macau Guide**, $13.95
Spain Guide, $17.95	**Vietnam Guide**, $14.95
Israel Guide, $16.95	

Forthcoming foreign guides in 1997: Greek Islands, Turkey, Moscow, Japan, Philippines, Thailand, Mexico, Kenya, and more!

Open Road's American Vacationland travel series includes:
America's Most Charming Towns & Villages, $16.95
California Wine Country Guide, $11.95
Disney World & Orlando Theme Parks, $13.95
Florida Golf Guide, $19.95
Las Vegas Guide, $12.95
San Francisco Guide, $14.95

Forthcoming US guides in 1996 and 1997: Hawaii, Colorado, Arizona, New Mexico, Boston, and more – plus a unique Open Road publication on safe, healthy trips abroad: *CDC's Complete Guide to Healthy Travel,* the authoritative Centers for Disease Control's recommendations for international travel.

PLEASE USE ORDER FORM ON THE NEXT PAGE

ORDER FORM

Name and Address: _____

_____

_____

_____ Zip Code: _____

Quantity	Title	Price

Total Before Shipping _____

Shipping/Handling _____

TOTAL _____

Orders must include price of book <u>plus</u> shipping and handling. For shipping and handling, please add $3.00 for the first book, and $1.00 for each book thereafter.

Ask about our discounts for special order bulk purchases.

ORDER FROM: **OPEN ROAD PUBLISHING**
**P.O. Box 20226, Columbus Circle Station,
New York, NY 10023**